CW00525851

THE LONG WEEK-END
1897-1919

THE LONG WEEK-END
1897-1919

Part of a Life

WILFRED R. BION

EDITED
BY
FRANCESCA BION

'an association in which the free development of each
is the condition of the free development of all'

Free Association Books / London / 1986

Published in Great Britain in 1986 by
Free Association Books
26 Freegrove Road
London N7 9RQ

© The Estate of W. R. Bion 1982

First published in 1982
by Fleetwood Press

British Library Cataloguing in Publication Data

Bion, Wilfred R.
  The long week-end 1897-1919 : part of a
  life.
  1. Bion, Wilfred R. 2. Psychoanalysis—
  Great Britain—Biography
  I. Title II. Bion, F.
  942.082'092'4 RC339.52.B4/

  ISBN 0 946960 43 7

Printed in Great Britain by A. Wheaton & Co. Ltd., Exeter

Bion family crest
'Nisi dominus frustra'

'Except the Lord build the house, they labour in vain
that build it: except the Lord keep the city, the
watchman waketh but in vain.'

Psalm 127. i

FOREWORD

Wilfred Bion was born in Muttra, in the United Provinces of India, in 1897. Many generations of his family (of Huguenot descent) had served in India—as missionaries, in the Indian Police, and in the Department of Public Works. At the age of eight he was sent to England to attend preparatory school, never again to return to India. All his life he retained a strong affection for the country of his birth; he died in November 1979 two months before a planned visit to Bombay.

His autobiography was left unfinished, but the years covered by this book form a distinct period which ended with demobilization just before he went up to Oxford to read History. He felt then that he had to start life again, building on unsure foundations. He regarded himself as uneducated, out of touch with the world outside school and the army, and demoralized by his experience of war. Nevertheless his outstanding athletic ability in rugger and swimming saved the day—just as it had done during his schooldays.

Although he felt that the war had left him unable to take advantage of the opportunities offered at the university, he always recalled with gratitude the talks he had with H. J. Paton, the philosopher. By 1924 it was clear to him where his interests lay—in psycho-analysis. He started medical training at University College Hospital, London, won the Gold Medal for Surgery, qualified in 1930, and then went on to psycho-analytic training. At University College Hospital he had contact with another outstanding man, Wilfred Trotter, the surgeon and author of *Instincts of the Herd in Peace and War*. Both Paton and Trotter played a very great part in his intellectual development.

After the Second World War, during which he served as the Senior Psychiatrist on the War Office Selection Board, he devoted the rest of his life to the practice of psycho-analysis. He became one of the foremost original thinkers in this field, and also in that of group behaviour, lecturing widely and writing prolifically—many papers and some fourteen books, most of which are now required reading in training institutes.

He was Chairman of the Executive Committee of the Tavistock Clinic, London, in 1945; Director of the London Clinic of Psycho-analysis from 1956-62; and President of the British Psycho-analytical Society from 1962-65.

In 1968 a request that he work in Los Angeles provided the opportunity to escape from what he called 'the cosy domesticity' of England. The vast open spaces of the western United States awoke in him memories of his childhood in India: the culture, however, was altogether new to him. It released him from the confines of traditionalism and enabled him to entertain his 'wild thoughts'; his mind was as wide open to new impressions during the last decade of his life as it had ever been in youth. So it was that in the alien, vital, dangerous but superficially idyllic environment of California he was stimulated to write the trilogy, *A Memoir of the Future*, a psycho-analytically orientated autobiographical fantasy—the most controversial and least understood of his works.

The qualities of courage and leadership, already evident by the time he was twenty years old, stood him in good stead as a psycho-analyst. He made plenty of enemies, as original thinkers always do, but no amount of hostility ever deflected him from his determination to be true to himself and to his beliefs.

Although he originally intended to stay only three or four years in California, he did not return to England until 1979. He died two months later in Oxford, with the 'dreaming' spires' visible from his hospital bed.

Those who were fortunate enough to be touched by his wisdom and affectionate concern were never quite the same again. We who knew him well will carry something of him with us for the rest of our lives.

Francesca Bion
Abingdon, Oxfordshire.
1982

PREFACE

In this book my intention has been to be truthful. It is an exalted ambition; after many years of experience I know that the most I can claim is to be 'relatively' truthful. Without attempting any definition of terms I leave it to be understood that by 'truth' I mean 'aesthetic' truth and 'psycho-analytic' truth; this last I consider to be a 'grade' of scientific truth. In other terms, I hope to achieve, in part and as a whole, the formulation of phenomena as close as possible to noumena.

Many names are mentioned; experience shows that it is impossible to prevent conjecture from replacing gaps with 'facts'. The 'facts' are not of my choosing; they can be so fashioned to serve any aim that the speculator might have. Anyone can 'know' which school, regiment, colleagues, friends I write about. In all but the most superficial sense they would be wrong. I write about 'me'. I do so deliberately because I am aware that that is what I should do anyhow. I am also more likely to approximate to my ambition if I write about the person I know better than anyone else—myself.

The book, therefore, is about the relationships of one man and *not* about the people, communities, groups whose names are mentioned. If I could have resorted to abstractions I would have done so. Such a procedure, without any preparation, would leave the reader grappling with meaningless manipulations of jargon.

INDIA

1

OUR ayah was a wizened little woman who, in so far as I connected age with her at all, was assumed by my sister and me to be very old, much older than our father and mother. We were very fond of her, perhaps more fond than of our parents. On second thoughts, perhaps not. My mother was a little frightening. For one thing she might die because she was so old. She was not so old as our ayah; my sister and I agreed that *she* was not less than, say, two or maybe three hundred years old, and though this was a ripe age she did not seem likely to die. Our mother, on the other hand, was peculiar; it felt queer if she picked me up and put me on her lap, warm and safe and comfortable. Then suddenly cold and frightening, as it was many years later at the end of school service when the doors were opened and a cold draught of night air seemed to sigh gently through the sermonically heated chapel. Sermons, the Headmaster, God, The Father Almighty, Arf Arfer Oo Arf in Mphm, please make me a good boy. I would slip off her lap quickly and hunt for my sister.

In the evening we would stand together by the travelling harmonium while my mother, in the light of an oil lamp, carefully picked out tunes which my sister and I joined her in singing, about the green hill—so green compared with parched burning India of the daylight that had just finished—and its tiny jewelled city wall. Poor little green hill; why hadn't it got a city wall? It took me a long time to realize that the wretched poet meant it had *no* city wall, and longer still to realize he meant—incredible though it seemed—that it was *outside* the city wall.

I went into this question thoroughly—and others like "Is golden syrup really gold?"—with my mother, and later with my father, but without being satisfied by either. I concluded that my mother didn't really know; though she tried very hard she seemed as puzzled as I was. It was more complicated with my father; he would start but seemed to tire when I did not understand the explanation. The climax came when I asked my question about golden syrup for the 'hundredth time'. He was very angry. "Wow!" said my sister appreciatively.

Later, when I wanted to know what 'persona non grata' meant, I kept it and similar problems to myself. I developed a sixth sense about the 'hundredth time' long before I learnt enough mathematics to count up to one hundred. Even then I seemed to have established such a gulf between applied and pure mathematics that I could not satisfy myself—then or now—of the connection between one hundred and 'the hundredth time'.

I went away snivelling. My sister, after having said, "Wow!", wasn't much use and by the time I had reached my mother I had forgotten what I had come for. Anyhow, she was 'busy'. This was another word like 'hundredth time' which it was as well to regard as precautionary. My mother was proved by my sister also to be, like so many grown-ups, 'peculiar'. She went one day and stood firmly 'at ease' in front of her. Then enunciating her words very clearly and precisely, she said, "Lavatory, lavatory, lavatory". The effect was gratifying to me though, thinking over the matter, disappointing. She did not get her ears boxed. My mother said, "I've a good mind to...", but she did not achieve fulfilment.

When it was all over I took my sister into a corner and worked the thing out properly. "You're a *very, very* naughty little girl" I said, keeping as closely as I could to my mother's intonation. Then I, very carefully, boxed her ears.

The result was cataclysmic. "Whatever is the matter?", I said in amazement at the incredible volume of sound she could command. My mother appeared with a frightened ayah close behind, then the kitmegar who was soon kicked out by the ayah. My sister by now had recovered what I can only call her composure to the point at which her screams were not inhibited, as mine were, by curiosity; she devoted herself whole-heartedly to bawling. She was sitting up pointing with an imperious figure straight at me.

"You wretched boy!" said my mother extremely angrily, "What have you done?"

Deafened and now thoroughly frightened, I said, "Nothing!"

"Nothing?" said my mother furiously, "Why, look at her!"

I did. I had to admit to myself as I looked at (I would almost say 'down', as one could of a pointing revolver) the furious child and her accusing finger, that my disavowal was extremely implausible.

Arf Arfer—as I knew him from now on—had turned up. Someone else had been 'busy' and was therefore also in an explosively unstable condition. My mother was shaking me.

"I don't know *what* to do with the boy" she said.

"Let me have him", said my father sternly.

"Oh God, not that!", I felt wordlessly, mindlessly.

"These children!", said my mother. Then, in an unguarded moment, she addressed my sister as well as me. "You're both as bad as each other!"

Up to that point I had fancied that her screams were abating. "Renew a right spirit within me", but if that was my unspoken prayer it had been wrongly addressed. Her screams were renewed. We were separated.

My father sat me kindly and patiently on his lap. Encouraged, my screams—or were they hers?—dinned less intensely in my ears. I began to collect myself. After much patient questioning I was able to remember why I hit her.

"She was being naughty", I said with a sudden dawning of memory. "She...and...so..." I faltered. I could not remember what she had been naughty about, or how.

"Yes? Go on", said my father patiently.

I could not. I had no idea.

The storm burst; he turned me bottom up and gave me 'a good beating'. But this I did not know about; I only heard of it as I heard him telling my mother later. He was still angry and his eyes were turned fiercely on me.

From that day on I hated them both "with all my heart and all my soul for ever and ever. Amen". A few minutes? Seconds? Years? Later I had forgotten all about it; so had they. But as no doubt they suspected I had learned my lesson and so had my sister. So had my parents for they too seemed uneasy, especially when I shrank from them and kept as far away from my sister as possible. "Why don't you two play together?", my mother would ask in a puzzled way.

2

THE great advantage of the ayah was that although grown up she could be dealt with. When my sister was furiously angry she would try to distract her. From what? I do not know—for reasons which I have forgotten I was extremely circumspect in dealing with my sister.

The long call of a Sarus crane gave the ayah an opening. "Oh, listen" she said in synthetic rapture "to the pretty Dickie Bird". My sister stopped screaming at once, magically, then exploded in rapturous laughter. "*Dicky* bird, *dicky* bird!", she said with adequate scorn as soon as she could speak again. Sycophantically I joined her, being careful not to become too involved. I had no idea what it was all about, but at least the hateful child had got her socks on.

In a sunny room I showed my father a vase of some yellow flowers for him to admire the skill with which I had arranged them.

"Yes", he said, "very good".

"But do look Daddy."

"I am; it's lovely." Still I was not satisfied. "It's very pretty isn't it?"

"Yes", he said, "it is."

"I'm not lying Daddy. I did it all myself."

That stopped him in his tracks. He was upset. "Why did you say that?"

"What Daddy?"

"I never expected you to be lying."

"Well, I wasn't", I replied becoming afraid that Arf Arfer would appear. Arf Arfer was very frightening. Sometimes when I heard grown-ups talking they would indulge in bursts of meaningless laughter. "Arf! arf! arf!" they would go. This would happen especially when my sister or I spoke. We would watch them seriously, wide eyed. Then we would go into another room and practise. "Arf, arf, arf!", I would say. More shrilly she would join in, "Arf, arf, arf!", and in the end it would make us laugh because it sounded so silly.

Sometimes it would be puzzling to know why the grown-ups

were so big and why they spoke as if we were 'silly'. Then my sister would clasp her hands behind her back and, straddling her legs in front of one of them, peer into his face and say, "Arf, arf!" very loud and clear. A man with a large reddish face, like my balloon when the air was leaking out of it, looked down at her. He looked angry and I was afraid he was going to turn into Arf Arfer. I dragged her away. "Don't do that—it's naughty". For a terrible moment I was afraid she was going to scream. She changed her mind. "Arf Arfer in Heb'n", and she began to laugh. That was a great relief and I began to laugh too—till I suddenly remembered. I turned serious and got out of it; or tried to. But she wanted me to stay. "Arf arfer!". I was alarmed; I did not want her to go on; I did not want to think it was funny. Arf Arfer was not to be trifled with.

Sometimes in my dreams I thought I heard Arf Arfer arfing. It was a terrible frightening noise. Once I saw jackals sitting in a circle while one gave the 'fiaow' call. It was bloodcurdling. "That's Arf Arfer" I thought.

Arf Arfer was related, though distantly, to Jesus who was also mixed up with our evening hymns.

'Geesus loves me this I know, For the Bible tells me so'.
I could not be bothered with the Bible at this time in the evening because it was dark and frightening and the animals had started howling. They started all at once, together, when the sun went down. I felt Gee-sus had the right idea, but I had no faith in his power to deal with Arf Arfer. Nor did I feel sure of God whose attribute seemed to be that he gave his 'only forgotten' son to redeem our sins. By this time I had become wary of probing too deeply into the doings of these night-time things; secretly I felt the green hill city and Geesus were ill-treated.

I came across them as I nightly said my prayers kneeling in front of my father, my eyes fixed on his watch chain swaying on his waistcoat. "Pity my Simply City". After a long time I ventured to ask my mother what had happened to my Simply City. She seemed puzzled, and as I was too scared to say how I had come by it she was not able to enlighten me. Once I thought I had found the trail when my father told me that if I was good I should have a railway engine worked by 'electric city'. This excited me so much that I asked him a mass of questions about 'electric city'. He was delighted at such an astonishing emergence of intelligence where he had long given up expecting to find any. He believed I was excited by the thought of the engine and was amazed that I was actually enthralled by electricity—so much so that after a time he began to wonder why I could *not* pronounce it correctly.

"Does the railway go over it?"

"No, it goes through the engine."

"Is it green like the other one?"

"No; well, it hasn't really a colour. But you could call it green—a very bright bluish green. Yes, I think you could call it a green", said my father hoping against hope, but beginning to fear that his son's gleam of intelligence was only by way of some extraordinary accident.

For my part I began to fear that the train was going to turn out to be some ghastly misunderstanding.

"Will it go fast? Really fast I mean—faster than any trains in the world?"

"Well yes, they are very fast of course. But this is not a real train you know. It's only a little one."

Depression began to close in on me. I was not at all sure about a blue city even... "Is it *very* bright? As bright as bright?" I asked.

He was getting tired. He decided to close the discussion. "Wait and see", he said with a hard, bright jocularity. I ended up with a wish to drop the subject for ever.

"You do want the train don't you?", my father asked anxiously. Electric trains for children in those days must have cost a small fortune and my parents were not wealthy.

"Yes", I said listlessly, "can I go and play now?"

I suppose I could hardly have chosen six more devastating words. My father was a sensitive man and I could feel that something had gone terribly wrong. He was upset, though I could not imagine why. He patted me on the head with a gentle sign of dismissal. "Perhaps it is too old for him", I heard him say to my mother later. I did not want to hear about it again. Simply City; Electric City; Green hill far away where our dear Lord was 'crucerfied' and died to save us all.

Perhaps some things were too old even for the grown-ups. It did not occur to me till many years later that any of those in a position of authority could be called on to solve problems that were too old for them.

One day a dignified, authoritative Indian appeared at our camp and asked for me. I understood that I was to be polite. I was in fact used to being polite to strangers; what was unusual on this occasion was that this strange Indian wanted to be polite to me. He salaamed. As I stood there he produced a silver cup, about four inches high as I remember it. This he presented to me with a decorous bow. Then he withdrew, leaving me to understand that I was to keep it. My father said he would look after it for me—and that was all.

When the Indian had gone my questions started. "Why did he want me?" "What is the cup for?" "Who was he?" "Where...?" But my parents were uncommunicative.

"Must I give it back to him?" This because I was used to the never-to-be-broken rule that neither my father, nor mother, nor sister, nor I, nor any servant of the household was ever to accept a gift of any kind—huge trays of sweetmeats, fruit and flowers were the gifts most often offered and invariably ceremoniously returned. This time, I was told, was different; the man would be deeply shocked and offended if his gifts were not accepted. The incident must have made a deep impression for I often asked about the cup and as often was met by an evasive response. To this day I have not seen it again.

I suspect that my father and mother were afraid I would 'get ideas' if I were allowed to have contact with any kind of 'pagan superstition' at variance with the pure, unsullied belief of our puritan and their missionary forbears. These were indeed made in a formidably robust and uncompromising mould. My Uncle Harry and my mother, as I discovered later, were not on speaking terms because he had denounced her as an "abandoned woman". This sounded interesting and exciting; my curiosity finally produced an explanation. The quarrel had started because one Sunday my mother had worn a hat which had aroused Uncle Harry's wrath by being too lush for the austerity proper to his church. I was on my mother's side as I was most fond of this hat which was of wide diameter and decorated with bunches of bananas and pears and other luscious fruits rather like the trays which Indians had striven to present to my father. But the glory was a bunch of black grapes of some transparent material which made them incredibly realistic and horticultural. I longed for my mother to leave them to me in her will. Alas! Fashions change and that hat was discarded long years before I was old enough to be given those grapes.

3

ONE day there was a Big Game shoot to which my father had been invited as he was well known as a fine shot. Preparations had been going on for some time, but my sister and I knew nothing of the great day which came and went without our small world within the camp being disturbed. As we travelled about the country with my father on his tours, the camps—expertly erected and struck by a staff of Indians paid and employed by the government—were considerable affairs and housed some fifty engineers and others who like us were members of the families of the higher paid technicians. Being of the 'Chief's' entourage, my mother, sister and self were like local insignificant royalty. There were no other children so one or other of the temporarily unemployed Indians was usually told to keep an eye on us so we did not stray.

The hunt was on my birthday, the day for which my electric train was designed. It was unwrapped by me and after much fumbling it stood revealed. It was a beauty—a model of one of the latest London trains, perhaps even of the first London electric train. In a fever of excitement not, I was pleased to note, shared by my sister, it was set up, the battery fixed and the motor set off with a slight push from my father's finger.

That initial jolt was the highest speed it ever achieved. As I watched the miserable crawl I tried to see it devouring the miles in its headlong rush through space; I might even have succeeded if it had not, like my tank many years later, stopped. It just stopped.

"It's stopped?" I said inquiringly. My father was as upset as I was. He picked it up and examined it. I watched his face, and as I watched I could see from his expression that it had indeed stopped. My sister, who was being taught to read by Mother, came to life. "Full top?"

Full top indeed. "Never mind," said my father brightly, "we'll soon get it going after I've seen to the mails", and he went to the office tent.

I told the bearer who was a good friend of mine but no engineer. He reassured me and, mobilizing his religious beliefs, carried the train off to the kitchen supply tent. There he smeared it plentifully with ghee. "It was", said the March Hare, "the best butter." Then he set it down in the hot sun telling me that after an hour or so it would rush off cured.

"Will it go fast—really and truly very fast? As fast as...?" I could not think of anything fast enough, but so it would assuredly be.

An hour or so later my father found me sitting watching it. "Now", he said, "let me have it and we shall soon get it... but, whatever is this?" He put it down suddenly to wipe the greasy mess off his fingers.

"Did you do this?"

Thank God, no. Arf Arfer with his great black wings beating had already obscured the sun. I cowered away. I feared. I wanted to tell my friend the bearer to run, run for his life before Arf Arfer got him.

"I didn't do anything", I said starting to weep.

My sister, who always seemed to appear at the wrong time, had already started to scream. For a wild moment I had an impulse, immediately stifled, to point at her and say *she* had done it.

To have two yelling brats on his hands was too much. This time my father turned and fled. I was afraid *he* was going to cry and indeed he must have been bitterly disappointed.

I did not care. The sky was clear; the sun shone; Arf Arfer had gone.

Ultimately even the bearer was miraculously saved because although he could not claim it was the best butter he could cite, as his authority for the treatment, the ayah. *She* it was who had told him about electric 'terains'. Her head trembled as the storm beat about her, but like a reed shaken by the wind she bowed to its fury and it passed her by.

That night Arf Arfer came in terror 'like the King of Kings'. The hunt had killed a tiger and the body had been brought to our camp. His mate came to claim him and for the next two nights the camp was circled by fires and torches burning bright to keep her out. With her great head and mouth directed to the ground so as to disguise her whereabouts she roared her requiem. Even my fear was swallowed up in awe as almost from inside our tent there seemed to come a great cough and then the full-throated roar of the tigress's mourning. All that night and the next it continued while even our brave dogs shivered and snarled and cowered. No sooner had the sun set to release the orchestra of the tropical night than we were aware of the added diapason.

"She won't eat us Daddy? You are sure she won't?"

We slept safe in their tents for those nights. On the third night her vigil was short. She went away before midnight and came no more.

I asked my mother a few nights later if she thought Jesus loved the tigress. She seemed surprised at first, but after a little thought she said she was sure he did. I was glad because I did not want the tigress to be lonely.

"Where is she now?"

"Oh I don't know child—far, far away I expect. Why do you ask?"

'Remember also the humble beasts', says the Edinburgh War Memorial.

Far, far away; where 'Saints in Glory stand, Bright as day'. How was the tiger going to get on there? We had a beautiful picture of an assortment of animals, including a lion and a lamb; a little boy, or it may have been a little girl, wearing a nightgown stood with his arm round the lion's neck. They stood about doing nothing in particular, like the people in Picasso's 'Saltimbanques'. Doing nothing in particular. Nobody ever believed I was doing nothing.

"What is he doing now?"

"Who?" asked my mother having lost track of the conversation. "Jesus—i mean the tiger", I felt suddenly embarrassed, thinking I ought to have asked after the lamb. If the tiger, as seemed reasonable, was in heaven, it ought to be having a fine time chasing the animals as our dog Bootles did; only Bootles was so slow he couldn't chase anything. Once he even let a mouse hide under the hair of one paw while he just stood there smiling because everyone was laughing so much.

"Come child," said my mother giving me a kiss, "I can't stay here all day talking—I'm busy".

Through the tent flap the sun beat down on the floor draining the colour out of the grass and making everything beyond the circle of light an intense black.

Intense light; intense black; nothing between; no twilight. Harsh sun and silence; black night and violent noise. Frogs croaking, birds hammering tin boxes, striking bells, shrieking, yelling, roaring, coughing, bawling, mocking. *That* night, *that* is the real world and real noise. When the super clever monkeys with their super clever tools have blown themselves into a fit and proper state to provide delicate feeding for the coming lords and ladies of creation, super microbe sapiens, then the humans who cumber the earth will achieve their crowning glory, the gorgeous colours of putrescent flesh to rot and stink and cradle the new aristocracy.

4

TIME I went to school to knock this nonsense out of my head—I hadn't a mind then, only a 'head'. This stage did have a twilight. No doubt it should have been a dawn—the dawn of intelligence. It came to me this way: I was taken along a long road by my ayah together with a little box for my lunch. In this box was some guava cheese of which I was inordinately fond. So far, so good; 'school' was making a good start.

Woodstock turned out to be a vast barrack-like building unlike any house I was familiar with. There was a group of three children with whom my ayah left me. The largest one, who wore glasses, appeared to be unhappy; to defend herself against the other two she was repeating in a ritualistic monotone,

"Sticks and stones may break my bones,
But words—they cannot hurt me."

She seemed peculiarly miserable but staunchly repeated the rhyme while the other two—boys I think—butted her, pushed her and mocked her. They did not tire and only stopped when a bell was rung, whereupon they, dragging me with them—"Come on!"—rushed into a large room of shrieking boys and girls.

"Here, you!" said the nearest one to me, "Do you want a box on the ears?" A box of any sort, thinking of my little lunch box with its guava cheese nestling inside, was attractive.

"Yes", I said. Whereupon he clouted my head. Shocked, I let out a yell of dismay.

By this time a grown man was trying to restore order by hitting about freely with a ruler at any brat within ruler reach.

"You!" he said, seeing me, "What are you crying about?"

"He hit me!" I wailed.

"Well we don't want any cry-babies here! And don't tell tales."

"Sneak! Sneak!" loudly whispered one or two near to me. The master's attention, distracted by his attempts to get within ruler's reach of another yelling ruffian, went back to restoring order. I sobbed quietly, hoping no one would notice me in the prevailing tempest. Nor did they. My little box had gone. I didn't care because the room was becoming relatively quiet and I had no wish to ruffle the surface.

I cannot say how I came out of the room nor how I came to be walking back the same road with my ayah. My attention was distracted by two girls presumably also on their way back from Woodstock. They were putting their faces close together and sticking out their tongues, not in derision but excited and pleased. They would lick each other's tongues, burst out in excited laughter and then repeat the game. I was fascinated—Woodstock forgotten—and would have been pleased to watch, had I been allowed. But my ayah was shocked; she clearly did not think it right for ruling-class white children to behave like that. So I was dragged off unable to see how the game ended—it must have ended though I could not imagine how.

This time I didn't ask my father and mother questions. The Master Race *did not* behave like that.

"He is only four." said my mother. "Perhaps it will be different when he goes to school in England; a lot can happen in four years."

So now there was another problem—becoming eight and 'England' which was not Woodstock. I am now becoming eighty which is nicer, though I have had a long time to wait, and as my mother said, "a lot can happen in four years".

The previous Christmas I had been asked what present I would like. I had set my heart on a Union Jack. When it came I did not know what to do with it. It seemed silly only to wave it. It was so much more exciting *before* christmas—like being at the siege of Lucknow where there was a brave girl who put her ear to the ground and heard the bagpipes and knew the 'Campbells were coming'. Only no one believed her. Then they came and a wicked man called Tippa Sahib—well, perhaps it wasn't, but he was very wicked anyhow—ran, or perhaps marched away. It did not solve my problem with the Union Jack; you can't stand there waving it like that silly old woman, saying "Welcome home boys! Welcome home!" That was later—much later; it hadn't happened yet. That was history. I had to learn history before I was eight; and mathematics, and Paul of Tarsus. That wasn't history; that was Scripture. Scripture and Jesus-loves-me-this-I-know-for-the-Bible-tells-me-so. I didn't like Scripture. Or England—that was Geography; my mother showed me how like a bear it was with a baby on its back. And another small one called the Isle of Wight coming out of its... but I knew *that* wasn't Geography. It made me sad like everything else after Woodstock; growing up, being a big boy now, England...

5

A LONG two years of 'Shadows of the evening steal across the sky'; my mother felt it; I felt it.

"What?"

"Nothing."

My mother would caress my head with what seemed a new tenderness. Even my little sister seemed to become less of a bitch and more like a wide-eyed inhuman robot. Nobody knew why. Only I understood. It was like being in front of an inscrutable, patient schoolmaster. "Well", he seemed to say, as if waiting for me to repeat my homework. "Well, what next?" Pause. And then as if recollecting something very difficult and painful and future, "In England..." "Yes, well, and then?" No good. "I don't know." "Surely you haven't forgotten?" I had. "Think!"

My mother just stroked my cheeks and dreamt without fear but with sadness. I couldn't stand it.

"Moth-er! You aren't sad are you?"

"Sad?" She would laugh. "Of course not! Why should I be sad?"

Well, why should she be sad? I couldn't think. It was ridiculous. Sad? Of course not!

But she was.

Nicholson: Hodson of Hodson's Horse. Nickel Sehn—the Indians had such queer names! It made you laugh—like my mother. The Indians would laugh too if they knew that one of those cowardly little white brats was frightened. An Indian came into Nicholson's tent and he was so frightened he died of fright. Wasn't that splendid? No; it only made *me* die of fright, at night time when I could hear Nickel Sehn roaring in the forest, imperatively, with authority. And Arf Arfer. And then the bird with a cruel beak and saucer-like eyes would ring a bell, for fun, because it scared the wits out of bloody little English brats. Mummy! Christ! Whoever was that screaming?

Soon I would be in England which was full of little boys, brave boys like Havelock and Outram—not like me. "Shsh...", my mother was saying. "It's only a dream. Go to sleep dear."

21

I knew I was not brave. About a year before I had a gun, an air gun which you loaded like this—it's quite simple really—you bend it across your knee and it breaks like this—not really breaks you know, but it looks as if it breaks in halves, only the two halves remain hinged together. Then you get a pellet and... suddenly before I could find a pellet the two halves snapped together and there it was hanging from my thumb. Christ! Whoever is that screaming? Screaming, screaming, screaming. Oh God, my throbbing hand! My mother came in. "Whatever...", and then she saw. Over seventy years later I can guess she is releasing my thumb. My father is there; they won't let me see, but there is blood everywhere. There! It doesn't hurt much does it? And a real bandage, just like a real soldier!

But it throbs; bang, bang, bang it goes. Why does my heart beat like that in my thumb? "Shsh", my mother is saying, "it's only a dream. Go to sleep my darling." The scar on my thumb is clear now, seventy years later. I don't suppose it made much scar on my mind because I do not remember a time when I wasn't a sissy. Even Outram and Havelock, and the girl who heard the bagpipes in Lucknow, and Nicholson with his beard and stern eyes scared me stiff. *Your King and Country Need You*, thundered Kitchener from the hoardings—but that was years and years later.

6

I WAS now very conscious of my self, but the self of which I was conscious—timid, morose—was not worthy of myself. I cherished a photo in which I was running fast, laughing rapturously, probably being chased by my father or mother. *That*, I liked to think, was what I looked like—not the glum depressing object that I saw for so many years. I never again saw anything else. Yet there was that snapshot; I must have looked like it only for those one or two moments of my life. My character, when I glimpsed it, was horrible—in contrast with my wishes.

My sister and I played to, but not with, each other. Each was an obstruction to the other, a sentient piece of furniture. Even when I discovered the pleasure of masturbation by lying on my stomach on the floor and wriggling, she could make nothing of it. She tried, but had to report failure. I think I attempted to persuade my mother of the importance of my discovery; she must have sneaked to my father, for to my acute embarrassment, and theirs, they came silently into the room and found me at it. They thus actually *discovered* me doing what I had tried to share with my sister. Indeed, they not so much discovered me doing it as *caught me at it*. I felt horribly guilty. I had an impulse to look at what they had found but I could not find it quickly enough, for the guilty sense of imminent danger was overwhelmed by the fear that they were looking at me. Yet I knew that this could not be true. I was picked up and kissed, so clearly it was not me they had seen when... well, when what? Their expressions had frozen into a form I had never before seen; nor horror or dismay, but silent, undramatic.

The experience had a peculiar, adhesive quality like fluff on clothes. There were bits of the Bible—the last place where you would expect it—where there were 'things' which had this same quality. 'Giggling' too; *that* was mixed up with it. The grown-ups didn't giggle; they laughed in a peculiar way. My parents didn't giggle; they were solemn.

One day we were all together, singing a hymn, 'Sometimes a light surprises the Christian when he prays'. My mother said to my

23

father, laying aside her hymn book, "I don't think I have ever heard of anyone who had that experience, have you Fred?" She seemed sad. After thinking for a moment my father replied, ill at ease, "Yes I think so, but *I* have not had it."

I was watching, listening intently. Why were they so sad? I put my hand on my mother's to comfort her. They had not till that moment noticed my presence. The spell was broken; my mother stroked my hair and the subject was not resumed. Queer. I often wondered what it was about.

"Why are you sad Mummy?" I asked her later; she laughed the suggestion aside. "Yes," I insisted, "you know—the light surprises", I reminded her.

"Some day you will understand—when you're grown up", she said.

"But", I persisted, "you are grown up and you didn't say you understood." She coloured slightly and laughed. That uneasy laugh! Not arf, arf, arf, like the men in the club when I asked one of them for an ice-cream. That *had* made my father angry. People got angry very quickly and suddenly especially about nice things like ice-cream and lying on your tummy and 'wiggling'. I thought I had better keep clear of 'light surprises' too.

But I *did* like asking questions. This made people go arf, arf, arf. Once they thought it so funny it made me frightened and angry. I felt hot all over and made up my mind to keep my questions to myself.

"You must learn to keep your mouth shut", said my father harshly.

I was astonished. "But, Daddy, I *always* keep my mouth shut! Why must I keep it shut?"

"There you go again! Just when I have told you not to!"

This defeated me. I was about to ask him another question when I found myself crying instead. I thought it time to run away; he did not like it when I was a silly little cry-baby.

Very soon after my father and mother caught me wiggling on my tummy another dreadful thing happened; they got out my bath tub—which was peculiar because it was not bed time. Remembering about keeping my mouth shut—just in time—I nearly burst with curiosity. Why were they mixing hot and cold water? What was that queer thing they put in the water? Why did they feel it with their fingers? It was fascinating—like the time I was playing trains in church during the sermon, forgot I wasn't to make a noise and let out a terrific scream because my railway engine was going to bump into another railway engine and had to whistle at once, as *loud* as possible, to save all the passengers. *This* time I remembered not to be such a fool. To my growing surprise I was seized, stripped by my mother and dumped in the tub! I tried to scrambled out. "Mm...", I yelled, carefully keeping my mouth shut. They subdued me and I had to sit there for three minutes by my father's watch. Then my mother lifted me out and dried me.

What had she wet me for, since I was dry to start with? This was repeated on two subsequent days—but I was forewarned by previous experience. I kept my mouth shut but otherwise put all into resisting this queer and somehow repulsive battle. They too began to feel it was idiotic; it never happened again. I, they, we, was, were cured. Sometimes a bath surprises a Christian while he plays.

7

On the whole my experience of being read to by my parents was not a success. *Alice in Wonderland* was spoiled by my habit of asking questions and my intolerance of frustration. The mouse's tail made *me* feel, well, like the animals. Why was it dry? Who was Fury? Why? What was he furious about? Why did the tail get smaller? Yes, but why do mice's tails...? My father was torn between the desire to be patient and the wish to get on with the book. "It gets better later", he said, but it did not. I didn't like the Dodo. I wished those animals would sit still and not go scurrying off whenever Dinah was mentioned. Why was Alice so daft as to keep on mentioning—well, you know who. Why couldn't *she* keep her mouth shut?

Then, when the story cheered up and it looked as if it was getting exciting, my father would shut the book because it was bed-time. Even when Alice did get into the garden it was terribly boring, made worse by my father who kept on seeing some joke which he said was funny.

But awful as it was to hear about Alice's Adventures in Wonderland it was not half as bad as a book about a girl called Little Meg. At the start her mummy and daddy died. Then she had to look after her little brothers and sisters. Of all the stupid things—she tried to sell a box of matches 'at a street corner'. The street corner was not like being in the jungle; there seemed to be lots of houses. So you would think there would be lots of people about. But there weren't so she couldn't sell any matches. Then a very rich man came and... my sister, for reasons best known to herself, began to bawl the house down. I was not so foolish as to try comforting *her*; it seemed best to keep clear of her. As I didn't want to have to sit in a tub again I just stared at her as she had taken to staring at me. After a bit I began to bawl too because Little Meg seemed unlikely to get anywhere especially as my sister was trying to fight her way off my father's lap and had settled into a scream which fetched my mother into the room. As my father rightly remarked, it was "bed-time anyhow".

The next night was worse still. The rich man, or a policeman whom he summoned, wanted to take Little Meg and her children to gaol! For once my sister and I were unanimous; we started to wail together. The more she yelled the more frightened I became. A terrible Arf Arfish feeling rose in my throat. "Whatever is the...?" my mother began as she came into the room to find out what on earth I had been up to. Mercifully she realized I was innocent this time.

The next night my sister and I started to yell the moment we saw my father coming with that awful book under his arm. That put a stop to *that*. I have sometimes wondered about Little Meg. Did she marry Eric or Little by Little? That book I did not come to till I was at school; sufficient for the day were little Meg's children—and my mother and father's two 'beauties'.

Two beauties we were. My sister had a wooden parrot of which she must have been very fond. It was a brightly painted grotesque with large goggle-eyes. In the heat and intense boredom of Indian mid-day I was inspired to introduce some leavening into the siesta during which we were supposed to retreat to our bedroom and sleep. "Goggle-eyes", I said. There was no response. Had I the resources of religion at my disposal I might have described the experience as "the devil entering into me". "Goggle-eyes", I said, pointing to the parrot. "Goggle, goggle, goggle, goggle-eyes". My sister looked at me; she looked at the parrot; she got the idea. She was a woman of few words, but swift action. In a twinkling the adorable child of three had turned into a raging ball of fury.

My father once explained to me why the bear was such a dangerous animal despite its cuddly appearance. "He doesn't bother about stealthy movement; he will lumber around a hill-side forest with about as much discretion as a lorry-load of tin cans. You have to stay *up*hill of him because without any warning he will roll into a ball and launch himself at you—and heaven help you if you cannot get out of the path of that cannon ball of furry fury." I saw what he meant; I saw what my sister meant. But I was not wise. "Goggle, goggle—", I was about to remark into that raging inferno of screams, which a moment before had been my sister, when I became aware of a spectator; my father had been watching at the door.

There was not time to say "Nothing!" for my father did not even bother to ask me what I was doing. He proceeded to 'faire la sagesse entrer par le cul'. My reactions had been slow, but not so slow that I was unable to end up with a guilt transformed into a sense of hardened grievance, resentment and impenetrable innocence. 'Put on the whole armour of righteousness', said Saint Paul; it was a text which brought me much comfort—until I felt the inadequacy of moral armour. It is wonderful what can be done with 'nothing', but it takes a deal of doffing once put on.

After much painful experience I learned how to curl myself into a tight ball of snowy innocence and launch myself, with a small sharp piece of ice in the middle, at my foe. 'O the great days in the distance enchanted', days of hot air in the stifling Indian sun.

We quarrelled; the gleam of joy, even co-operation, which had flashed out when I discovered the pleasures of wiggling on my tummy had been extinguished. I learned to keep away; she in turn learned to demand imperiously that I should play with her. In this she discovered a valuable ally in my father's ambition to have two children, brother and sister, who loved each other with a tender, loyal and lasting affection. My mother's attitude was certainly more loving—genuinely loving—than my father's; hers was not an 'attitude' at all; his was. She loved us; he loved his image of us. She knew she had two nasty brats and could tolerate that fact; my father bitterly resented the menace of any reality which imperilled his fiction. To strangers (in so far as we met any who allowed themselves to be aware of our existence) a short and superficial contact would reveal nothing to disturb an agreeable impression. We were aided by being a good-looking pair; retrospectively I can see that we had grown in experience to become an accomplished and unpleasant pair of liars, smooth and quick to see what our betters expected of us and to provide accordingly. The awareness of something better was responsible for an unspoken and unspeakable misery which added its quota to our general nastiness. To this day I retain a certain confidence that no matter how dangerous or how unpleasant my contemporaries may be, I myself am even nastier. I cannot feel confident that I am more *dangerous* because my malice is tempered by cowardice. The resultant cunning is not without its value; I probably owe more to this quality than I have ever admitted.

8

THE approach of night and its sense of the foreboding presence of Arf Arfer penetrated my whole but fragile armour of daylight. Very rarely my parents were near a city and friends would come to dine. The men would sooner or later laugh—arf, arf, arf—and I would wake in terror. Arf Arfer had come! With his great goggle eyes and painted visage, bright, bright as... "'and, 'and", I would wail. My father would clasp my hand in his great strong one and I could sleep. Not when there was company though; on those occasions even my mother was different. If she came she was dressed in strange clothes, cold, like the place where saints in glory stand, bright, bright as day. That was no happy land for me, but more, had I known it, like the Ypres Salient, glistening, cold, cold. 'Quo fas et gloria ducunt'.

"Hush dear, shsh, what's the matter?"

Nickel Sehn was the matter, Hodson's Horse was the matter; the whole damned lot were the matter. "Go away!" I would say through my sobs. "Go away!"

None the less I loved India. The blazing, intolerable sun—how wonderful it was! The mid-day silence, the great trees with leaves hanging motionless in the breathless air, the brain-fever bird with its rising reiterated call, "Brain-fever, brain-fever, brain-fever...", then silence again.

I discovered it was a marvellous place to play trains. The intense heat conspired to produce masses of fine white dust. Nonchalantly I kicked it up and was rewarded by a great cloud that rose into the air. I did it again. Before I had time to think I was racing around, kicking up huge clouds of... steam... in front of me like a huge 'Ee Ay Ah' locomotive. The Devil entered into me: The Devil, unlike Arf Arfer, was a great friend of mine. "Go on! Do it again", he said. "Lead us not into temptation", I learned to pray, but only rather half-heartedly. Temptation, unlike heaven, was such fun. The immense speed at which I was travelling, the intoxicating sulphurous fumes of smoke which belched out from the pistons in front of me—glorious! And much superior to electric city with its old slug of buttered locomotive.

"What *have* you been doing?" my mother asked. "Just look at you! White... from top to toe!"

I couldn't 'look at me' but I saw what she meant. I was a bit dusty. She, poor woman, thought I had come in for a drink, but in fact it was the great E.I.R. express locomotive come to have its tank filled in its record-making run across India and there was not a moment to lose. I tried to make her understand that I had to go at once. It took her some time to make *me* understand—even now I can hardly believe it—that I was never to do it again. Never!

"The idea! And you have been racing around in that hot sun."

"What sun?" I was impelled to ask dully. I hadn't noticed any sun.

I did do it again. The Devil got into me, but I suspect that Arf Arfer had got in too. I was just cornering at speed, leaning over to counter the drag of centrifugal force and the lack of camber, when I was impelled to 'look at me'. I *was* a bit dusty already. I couldn't get it off so I went in to find my ayah before my mother could see. Like my sister, who couldn't understand about wiggling, she had her blind spots and I never succeeded in making her understand she was wrong about what *she* called "racing around like a mad thing in the hot sun". Later, when the monsoon came, I found she was curiously blind about *that.*

"What rain?" I asked, not hopefully, as I stood before her "soaked to the skin" as she called it. It made it worse that I felt she was laughing—inside.

"You're laughing", I said. "No", she said looking very stern. So she wasn't sad; and she wasn't laughing either.

9

I WAS not sad and I was not laughing either. Nor was Melvin. Who was Melvin?

Melvin and Cyril were two brothers, known to my father because they reminded him of two characters in a book for children, as Budge and Tod. Cyril was Budge, big, clumsy, with a raucous frightening laugh like a goat bleating. Melvin, or Tod, was my hero. He was mischievous and likeable—unlike Budge or their sister Beryl who was a sneak, always telling tales about the boys—any boys—to her father and mother, my Uncle Walter and Aunt Helen.

We were all very fond of pancakes; so my mother told the cook to make pancakes as a treat for our lunch—two each, she said, which made ten for the five of us children and two more to make a generous dozen. Melvin, who had a nose that did not mislead him in gastronomic affairs, had sought out the kitmagar. He was a nice man, fond of children. The nine year old Melvin had natural charm; he also had the skill to enhance his assets. Accordingly, when lunch was served, my mother found herself confronted with a pile of forty pancakes to serve. The kitmagar, asked to explain this extraordinary miscalculation, uneasily admitted that the chota sahib had amended his mistress's estimate of adequate supplies. Melvin, who was unabashed, augmented his meal by tearing off and eating a piece of pancake which I was about to put in my own mouth. My mother laughed, but I was not amused. My father told us to try to behave ourselves when we were at the table.

Melvin had made a garden, as had my sister and I; he had greatly improved on our efforts by fencing his with a piece of rabbit wire. This I greatly coveted. So when the day came for Budge, Tod and Beryl to leave for England I asked if I could have his fence to put round my garden. "You can put it round your head for all I care!" was his disconcerting reply. He did not want to go to England; as it was only two years before I myself would be going I feared and wondered about this place that upset even Melvin.

My dread was more apparent than it was when I was aware only of sadness and *not*-sad, when I was taken by my father on a visit to Gwalior, the fortress and home of an Indian ruler. I was aware, partly because my father impressed it upon me, that we were visitors to an Indian state and under the laws of that state. I was shown an image, carved in wood, of an Indian god. This, I was told, was a heathen god. As I looked upon its deeply carved features, the black more intense and forbidding because the brilliant sun made the shadows so harsh, I was afraid. Was the Indian Ruler like that? I didn't like it; I didn't want to go further into Gwalior. I had learned to keep my mouth shut so was able to keep it more tightly shut when I felt impelled to ask questions or say "'and, 'and'', or that I was afraid.

On our nearer approach to Gwalior we came upon a stoutly built wooden cage. It must have been fifteen feet long, ten feet high and four feet wide. This could be entered by treading on a platform which released a wooden, heavily built portcullis. I was not frightened by this tiger trap till our Indian guide pointed out a small flimsy crate which was outside, but attached to the main structure where it was furthest from the trap door. Why ever would the tiger go in? Because, my father said, tigers were lazy creatures. When they saw a kid in the crate—so that was what the crate was for—it would not burst its way into the kid but would walk round to the open end of the trap, enter and bang! it would be caught when the portcullis came down. See? I did. What did the poor kid do? I faltered. Well, of course, it didn't have to do anything, you see, for it wasn't in the trap *with* the tiger... This was enough for me. Couldn't I go home? I *want* to go home. But... couldn't I see? The kid was quite safe...

Not only did I think it would be awful to be the kid, I also knew I was an awful cry-baby and I would start to cry if we went any nearer to that fortress. My poor father! He was a famous big game shot who hunted with Corbett and King George V and General Ironside... and there was I, a sniveller who was frightened even by the sight of a tiger trap. How could my mother and father possibly have produced such a... such a... Well, such a what? I didn't know; must be to do with wiggling; that always led to something dreadful.

So much for Gwalior. No more talks about tigers; something to do with irrigation and dull enough not to frighten me—till I got home at least. By that time I would have forgotten. But I have not.

ENGLAND

1

DELHI, motor cars, rich people, English women with loud voices—"fancy! the Kingdom of Heaven filled with people like..." like my ayah and my friend Dhunia the sweeper? I hoped so but in fact I knew it would not be low caste, untouchables, like *that*, but 'untouchables' like that beautiful, laughing English Lady. Now I know that they were unspeakables too, but that I learned too late to be much help. Not even Miss Whybrow and Mrs Thompson could teach me that; I had another twelve years to go before I would even have a chance to learn.

But Delhi: New Delhi! Isn't it splendid? If only I hadn't got to go to school...

The train worked steadily, sometimes painfully over the stiffer gradients of the Western Ghats till it drew in to the terminus at Bombay. The railway station, like other architectural monuments of the British Raj, was a mixture of tawdry provincialism and Imperial domesticity which even in retrospect can evoke in me nostalgic feelings of great poignancy. I came in time to believe that these feelings were the substitute for what others called 'homesickness'. But I had no home for which I could feel sick—only people and things. Thus, when I found myself alone in the playground of the Preparatory School in England where I kissed my mother a dry-eyed goodbye, I could see, above the hedge which separated me from her and the road which was the boundary of the wide world itself, her hat go bobbing up and down like some curiously wrought millinery cake carried on the wave of green hedge. And then it was gone.

Numbed, stupefied, I found myself staring into a bright, alert face.

"Which are you—A or B?" it said. Other faces had gathered.

"A", I said hurriedly in response to the urgency I felt in their curiosity.

"You're *not*! You jolly well say 'B'. You know nothing about it!" This was only too true.

"B", I said obediently.

"You dirty little liar!" said the first one. Appealing passionately to the rest, "He just said he was A. Didn't he?" That I had to admit.

"You can't go back on that", said the advocate of B. "You must stay B or you'll be a beastly little turn-coat!" he cried heatedly.

"All right. I'll stay B."

A fight developed. I heard the first one shouting, "He *is* a beastly turn-coat; and a liar anyway. We don't want him. Do we chaps?" The crowd had grown to formidable proportions, say, six or seven. "No", they shouted.

"Don't mind them", said the second boy. "You stick to B." And I did—for the rest of my life—though it took a long time before I discovered, and even then did not understand, that the main school was divided into Houses. School House, being bigger than all others, was divided into School House A and School House B—rivals. That was the immediate issue which had been solved by my becoming for ever B.

The storm subsided as if it had never been of the slightest interest to anyone. B, *not* A; not A—B; *that* was what I had to remember.

At last the ghastly day ended and I was able to get under the bedclothes and sob.

"What's the matter?" asked one of the three boys who shared the dormitory with me.

"I don't know", I wailed. He seemed sympathetic. He considered the matter for a moment.

"Are you homesick?"

"Yes." At once I realized what an awful thing I had done. "No, B", I hurriedly said. He got into bed. This time the day *was* over.

I learned to treasure that blessed hour when I could get into bed, pull the bedclothes over my head and weep. As my powers of deception grew I learned to weep silently till at last I became more like my mother who was *not* laughing, and was *not* crying. It was a painful process; I failed often in my attempts to climb each step of the ladder. Sometimes the problem was familiar—as with lying. "I'm not lying!" I had said brightly, hoping for my father's approval of my floral arrangement. My mother would have known at once that such a mess could have been made by no one else; my father, though a brilliant engineer, was curiously dense when it came to Electric City and Simply City. So, in a luckless moment, my greed for reiterated admiration had led me to add "I'm not lying". In that moment the glorious morning was obscured, the sun stopped glowing, became darkened and scorching, his words a torrent flowing over, beyond and below me. Tears did not cool and refresh—they scalded. Where had I got such an idea? I did not know. I had plucked them in the garden; I thought they would be nice.

Experiences—'déja vu' phenomena—had provided me with a vocabulary thus:

Q What *have* you been doing?
A Nothing
Q Where have you been?/Where are you going?
A Out/Nowhere   (discrimination required)

In my new world, peopled with Nickell Sehns, Hodsons, Havelocks, all disguised as little boys, the questions—like the questioners—were often deceptively familiar or incomprehensible, like "Are you A or B?" Sometimes the questions could not be met by my armoury of answers, and my improvised answers led to further troubles.

"What's your sister's name?"

"Edna."

"Edna?" repeated with bleak incredulity, followed immediately by a gale of scornful and contemptuous laughter, not quite 'arf, arf' but pitched in a sharper higher key—Havelock with a touch of jackals at night-time.

"What does your father do?"

"Engineer." As I braced myself for the response I was deflated by sudden and unexpected tones of respect.

"No! Really? You lucky swine! You mean he really drives an engine?"

Fool that I was; why, oh why did I have to explain? The splendour faded from his face. Canals? Water? Obviously as wet as his job and as anyone who produced me could be.

"Never mind", he said generously as he realized we had now touched bottom and could sink no lower. "Have a sweet?" I was to discover *he* was B too—a friend for life. It was painful to discover, an hour or two later, that he had forgotten me. For some time I continued to hope he would remember he had offered me a sweet; I don't think he ever did.

2

On Wednesdays the bells of St. Michael's Church on the neighbouring hill pealed for a service or, as some said, "choir practice". They filled me with dread, a reminder of Sunday yet to come. In *Eric or Little by Little* which I had begun to read, the bell was always tolling. *Or the World of School* it said, and in that school it seemed that the boys died off like flies. Every Wednesday I remembered someone was dying; on Sundays I nearly died myself—every Sunday. I still feel ashamed that I was so utterly miserable, but so it was; I could not know that religion was being born.

On Sunday morning we went to church wearing Eton suits, mortar boards with bright blue tassels, our shoes polished before breakfast miraculously worn out by church time.

"What have you been doing to them?" the vixen who was our matron used to ask. "Your parents are poor; they cannot afford to buy you new shoes every term!"

Who had said they were poor? They hadn't told me. It was like *Eric or Little by Little*; or *Little Meg's Children*. I began to whimper.

'You crying? A great big boy like you! Playing trains were you?"

Yes, but there was no dust, only gravel.

"Don't let me catch you doing that again! The idea—just *look* at your *shoes!* Nearly worn right through and new only a week ago!"

She was smart, petite and... well, God rest her soul, I knew I was a horrible child and God would never make me a good boy however hard I prayed. I don't think He ever listened. I really don't.

The other boys stood around and watched; watched with their big, round eyes and hard, expressionless faces. 'Come not in terror as the King of Kings, But kind and good with healing in Thy wings'. Please God, make me a good boy. He never did, never, never, The inspection by the matron ended always with me tearful, horribly brushed and neat, indescribably scruffy.

Church was all right; even the sermon, never less than forty

36

minutes, was a respite from tormentors. I remember the relief when I learned that the text 'I know that my Redeemer liveth and shall stand at the latter day upon the earth' really should have been translated 'For I know that my Avenger liveth and that he shall stand at the latter day upon my grave'. When church was over—and sometimes there were lovely hymns like 'Onward Christian Soldiers' and 'Art thou weary, art thou languid, art thou' something 'sore distressed'—the trouble started. For half an hour we did 'Search the Scriptures'. These were booklets in which texts from a book in the Bible were printed with blank spaces; we were to fill in the chapter and the verse where they were to be found. I could not find them; other boys could. God was worse than useless. I used to pray. One day, in a sermon, the mystery was solved. "Sometimes we think", said the preacher, "that God has not answered our prayers but he has". I pricked up my ears at this. "It means", he went on, "that the answer is 'No'". I unpricked my ears.

After dinner of roast beef and Yorkshire pudding—very good I thought, but spoiled by what was to come—we went into the gymnasium where our tuck boxes were kept. We usually had no 'tuck' in them, but one fat boy with fishy green eyes and red hair always had. High off the ground, vertiginously high it seemed to me, was a horizontal pole that ran the length of the room; the smaller boys were made to crawl from one end of this to the other. For an age I was one of the small boys. As I gazed fearfully at the concrete far below and inched my way along, the eager faces of the boys below watched to see if we would falter and fall under the missiles showered at us. No one was injured while I was there so it cannot have been *very* bad in fact. But in my dreams—Oh God, my dreams!—the goggle-eyed parrots and pink round faces swam around me and I woke with a shriek. Whoever was that screaming?

One small boy who was crippled by polio escaped for one whole day because he had got his parents—who *were* poor—to provide him with a full tuck box for just one Sunday. For that day, as he handed out his goodies with nervous, shining eyes, he was voted "jolly decent". The tuck lasted the hour; with the ending of the hour so ended his glory.

I would like to think that I had nothing to do with the tormenting—I was so terrified that it is just possible that my pre-occupation with my coming turn saved me. Certainly it was not through any superior decency.

Another feature of our Sunday was The Walk. It was conducted by our head-master, a taciturn, frightening man called Hirst. It was always the same—about three miles. To prevent loitering he had a rule that any laggards were punished according to a scale by which those who came in at the gate more than two minutes after him had to do ten squares; five minutes after him, it became twenty squares. No one in my memory exceeded, and only rarely approached, the five minutes. The misery of starting Monday with a load of ten squares—four figures multiplied by themselves—was so awful that it overshadowed the walk—till I learned to imagine that I owned a beautiful little railway that ran along the side of our walk. Its coaches could just hold my friends. I myself was the engine driver of course. Ever after that I had no difficulty, no fatigue, no boredom, no squares to do on Monday. I don't think God had anything to do with this; I thought it up by myself. But if it *was* God who put the idea into my mind I can only say it was jolly decent of Him and a first class idea. For that three miles every week I was infallibly and unmistakably a 'good boy'.

At six o'clock we went to Chapel at the main school for an hour. I liked that. We did not have 'Art thou weary, art thou languid?'—which was a pity—but once we had 'Onward Christian Soldiers' and the music master, who played the organ, interposed the stirring strains of 'Come to the cook-house door boys, come to the cook-house door' as part of the accompaniment. The effect of this authentically military music made the occasion extremely moving. I also liked the hymn with the lines 'A noble army, men and boys, the matron and the maid'. I could have done without the Matron, and it seemed a bit mean to have only one maid; otherwise it called up splendid visions. 'Borne on angels' wings to Heaven, glad the summons to obey' was also a favourite till I became big and powerful, and the centre or ribald glances when I was singing about the angels' wings.

The day Thou gavest Lord is ended. Bed at—nearly—last. But first we had to say our prayers. Each knelt in prayer at the end of his bed. I must have thought of engines during this necessary but tiresome interlude. Unlike the dust, the glorious dust for ever gone, unlike the concrete and gravel of the playground, more safe even than the Walk which could be interrupted by some fool wanting to talk, one could emit clouds of steam and smoke without scuffing up one's heavenly boots and bringing financial ruin on Little Meg's parents. Shod with the gospel of peace, which the moth could not corrupt nor gravel wear out, I was going to sleep. I would leap into bed and there, if the bed did not creak too much, I could start wiggling. This was so delightful that a new danger crept in—I might laugh. The danger was real because no one had ever known me to laugh.

One day in class the master noticed that I was wiggling; it seems hard to believe now that I could ever have supposed he didn't, for my wiggling could hardly have been more anonymous than the Indian bear's progress through the forest. He was very gentle. "Don't do that Wilfred", he said, "or you will have to be sent away." I could hardly believe my ears. The other boys, witnesses of my rebuke, stared at me in stony innocence like the gods in the caves at Elephantine.

One evening Freddie Sexton and I were late in joining the devotional parade. At the end of every bed, except his and mine which were at one extreme, were kneeling boys. The sight of seven pairs of pink upturned cherubic feet was too much for Freddie; he, unlike me, was a lively, cheerful boy with a keen sense of the ridiculous. Suddenly he limped down the row, one foot on the floor, the other placed firmly on the upturned soles. Each time, as if he had been recalled by the accident of his clumsiness to the sacredness of the occasion, he said "Ooh—sorry! Ooh—sorry!. Ooh—sorry!" I saw his point; I laughed.

God, taking a leaf out of the Devil's book, entered into the seven little hypocrites praying in a row. But Freddie could hold his own.

"And you were laughing!" one boy said indignantly.

"No, not laughing"—but certainly not crying either.

"How do you know?" said Freddie, coming to my rescue. "You should have had your eyes shut!"

Like a well placed bullet this stopped him—for a moment—but he was a quick-witted Welsh boy of strong revivalist tendencies.

"I *heard* him!" he countered, but he was too late.

"You had your eyes open!" said Freddie, afire now, moral warmth glowing in his face and eyes. "You had your eyes open!"

Bevan collapsed. His smooth, soft, gentle, religious nature was something I had not encountered; later it led to my downfall. Freddie's bright eyes were something Bevan had not encountered either.

I was afraid of Freddie, but this incident aroused feelings of glee which were never wholly quenched even in the hours of great moral and religious superiority. Poor Freddie was quenched for ever by an undiagnosed acute appendicitis.

3

A YEAR later I was on an errand that took me through the church-
yard where Freddie was buried. A figure—it was Bevan—was
kneeling in prayer at his grave. He stopped as I came up, saw me,
and explained smoothly in his beautiful voice that he often prayed
at Freddie's grave.

"He did me a great injury once", he said meditatively, "but I have
prayed that he may be forgiven."

If unction can ease the path to the Almighty, Bevan's prayer
reached God; it may even have got through to Freddie. The angels
would like his laugh, "Ooh—sorry!"

Freddie's raid on the domain of the Almighty—which in my
theology had a mixed population of God, Gawd (Baptist in those
days), Gud (C. of E., privately educated and Cambridge University,
Civil Service), the Devil (not a bad sort with many disguises),
various demons (Nickel Sehn, Hodson or Hodson's Horse—I was
not sure whether he owned the horse or the other way round), and
the most awful Arf Arfer—was not the only rebellion that began to
erode my oppressor's power.

Once every two weeks we had a hymn-singing class taken by a
mistress who I thought was nice despite her ominous name—Miss
Good. She was *not* smart like the Matron, *not* like the maid in the
hymn and only smart on Sundays. She was clever, like Nigger our
headmaster, but curiously and very frighteningly gave me the
'wiggling' feeling when I "hadn't done a thing"—"really and
truly"— but who on earth would believe *that?*

Some hymns expanded my Pantheon; Gideon for example—the
'prowl and prowl around' one. This was a bit sinister with Gideon
prowling around and I wasn't quite sure if he was A or B—Powers
of Darkness, or the other crowd. Anyhow, it was a fine hymn;
while 'they' were prowling and prowling around we sang very
softly, ppp, gathering our breath ready for CHRISTIAN UP AND
SMITE THEM, fff; we gave it everything we had. That, I used to
think, must have scared the slats out of 'them'. At night time I
didn't like Gideon and the powers of darkness prowling around our
dormitory and under my bed.

This hymn-singing period gave me great pleasure and on one occasion a surprise. The hymn 'Art thou weary, art thou languid?' had a lovely, sad tune and brought me much comfort. I found out that five or six little boys liked it and were just as weary and languid and sore distressed as I was. Grown-ups, including I am sorry to say Miss Good, seemed to think we *couldn't* be weary and languid; we knew we were—most of the time. This hymn and another, 'Summer suns are glowing', were my favourites. I did not have to ask for 'Art thou weary' because five or six others always did so. 'Summer suns' was not so popular; that I had to support all myself or we would not have it. On this particular day the drizzle was coming down in its usual determined, anonymous way, more like a fungoid growth of the air than what I was used to calling rain. I put up my hand.

"Well?" said Miss Good in what I thought at the time was an unwelcoming way.

Stimulated by the ghastly weather, not laughing, not crying, not happy, not sad, and spurred by the fire of that wonderful sun, the great leaves drooping in the heat, the flowers blazing in colours of unimaginable splendour, "'Summer suns'", I said.

There was a stupefied pause. "Oh Wilfred!" she expostulated, "not *again!* Just look at it—pouring with rain! You can't want that!"

I had looked at it. It was *not* pouring with rain. What rain? It was just a dirty... well *not* rain. Rain! Now *that* was something like—if only it *would* rain—like when you heard it coming, roaring and hissing and moaning and sighing over the trees and the grass in the distance till suddenly—there it was! *That* was rain! *That* was sun! Still, there were buttercups. When I saw my mother on my next Sunday out I meant to pick her a big bunch of them to show her. 'Frail as summer flowers we flourish, blows the wind and it is gone'—that was a nice hymn too.

"Well?" It was Miss Good again. I felt tense, anxious, stubborn.

"'Summer suns are glowing'", said my small, almost inaudible voice. She, mercifully, did not persist. The others were looking at me; they were more than ever curious when we were all singing and they could see I was hardly singing at all. I never asked for 'Summer suns are glowing' again.

When Sunday came I did not collect the buttercups. My mother told me she could tell by the buttercups if I like butter; she held one under my chin and... yes! I liked butter because it showed yellow on my chin. She herself seemed unconvinced; so was I, but I was weary and languid; maybe even 'sore distressed' thinking about going back to school—though I had only been away about an hour. I did not think much of the riddle; I could not think about the marvellous, incredible, unimaginable buttercups which blazed unconsidered in the meadows around us.

It was time to go. We were in the parlour of the lodgings. She had a present for me—a half pound size Lyle's Golden Syrup tin, the container in Indian days for so many of our luxuries, filled with chocolates. I shook my head.

"You *are* a funny boy! Don't you want them?"

"Yes", I said dully.

"Then take them back with you."

But I persisted; I shook my head again. I wouldn't take them back to that... gymnasium... school.

Was I unhappy, she asked. No. Did I like it there? I nodded, yes. But I wouldn't take them back.

4

RELIGION was a sore trial. It was difficult to avoid the certainty that *I* would be a sore trial to God if he knew about my existence. Sometimes, as when I laughed at Freddie treading on the feet of boys saying their prayers, I thought He might suppose that my involvement was more active than in fact it had been. Dean Farrar contributed to my suspicion of God, and my suspicion of God—"I haven't done anything; really I haven't"—gave ghastly reality to Eric's school in which the mortality should have attracted the attention of authority.

The sense of brooding disaster was made real by the tragic life, unknowable by us, of our headmaster. He was a man of whom my father, like others, was very fond. How my father came to know him, since his visits to England were infrequent, I do not know, but so it was. Masters from the main school visited him regularly; one in particular played billiards with him once a week on a miniature table—the one luxury he possessed. The weekly click of the billiard balls exercised us curiously and was the signal for giggles which I did not understand.

The story circulated by one boy, that Hirst had married in his early twenties a girl of twenty-one who had to be admitted immediately to a mental hospital, I discovered years later to be true. To my contemporaries of nine and ten this story meant no more than any other fact about 'Old Nigger'—our name for him—such as that he wore carpet slippers, or a new tie, or—as I announced loudly one day as I scrambled upstairs to bed, unaware that I was helping myself by clutching the leg of his trousers—"Old Nigger says it's to be a half holiday tomorrow!" "Oh no he didn't", said the trouser leg gruffly; I let go hurriedly. "Ooh sir, sorry sir!" I said, filled with confusion but not afraid, for he was not a man one feared—though I had been afraid of him when he said I might have to be sent away if I 'wiggled'. Well, he must have known because his wife had been sent away. It could not have been for wiggling because my sister had not been able to wiggle. On the other hand Mrs Hirst may have been able to; and *that* might have caused it and

43

that might explain why Mr Hirst was so sad. He *was* sad; of that there was no doubt at all. Like the church bells that reminded me on Wednesday of the last Sunday and the one to come, his sadness reminded me of something. "Are you feeling homesick?" the boy in the dormitory had asked. He had not meant was I A or B—that was clear. But the church bells, and St Winifred's of 'The World of School', or Nigger Hirst—it was none of it quite 'homesick' but I was not sure what it was. 'Search the Scriptures' was a bit like it; so was Willy Bevan who was an orphan. Everyone said it in a hushed voice.

One day I tried saying it out loud. "You're only an orphan!" I shouted at him. For a moment I thought I had solved it; Willy flopped suddenly and became religious—but with his eyes open, unlike saying your prayers when you shut your eyes or pretended. His friend Pickett was there and he, as he proclaimed, heard me say it. I had meant him to—that is why I had shouted.

In less time than it takes to write, the whole pack were on to me— then stopped and watched. The goggle-eyed parrots, the hosts of Midean or Gideon. "Let's chase him", said Pickett. "No, not now. Wait till we get him on the Mountain", said Morgan, "We can use stumps then." It was agreed; even Bevan was recovering at the suggestion. We all cheered up—in the prevailing optimism even I began to feel better.

Bevan, who had been overcome by religion, though still mournful, became as exalted by 'stumps' as he had been hurled into religion by 'orphan'. When I tried to join the prevailing gleeful anticipation I was given a cold reception. "Look at the little swine", said Pickett, "he's not a bit sorry for what he's done." It was rather frightening—like the 'box-on-the-ears' which I had said I wanted at Woodstock. I modified my rapture.

The Mountain was our cricket field, very uneven and well described by our name for it; we were supposed to play football and cricket on it. By the time we got there the prevalent air of cheerfulness seemed to have dissipated the former mood till Pickett and Morgan said, "Come on now chaps! Let him have it!" Six of them took a stump each, and with shouts of "Run! you swine!" they started after me. I ran.

As I was still the smallest I had no choice. Physically I did not come to any harm other than a few bruises. Most had forgotten what it was all about, but Bevan had a tenacious religion; when he 'forgave' someone he did not do it in any half-hearted manner. I likewise did not easily 'forget' being 'forgiven'; it added a zest to my determination to steer clear of Arf Arfer and his trespasses.

It was disconcerting to discover, soon after this, that 'Trespassers will be prosecuted'. I did not dare to ask whether it was with stumps or without, but it was evident that orphans, church bells and God, to whom Bevan habitually prayed even when he was not going to bed, should be given a wide berth.

Not long after this an extraordinary thing happened on one of our Sunday trips to the main school for chapel. It was clearly in the next term; it must have been winter because we trooped up in darkness. This was usually a pleasant occasion because from the time we set off nothing particularly awful could happen till Monday morning, except nightmares and the usual squares which I continued to accumulate till I had perfected my scheme of playing trains on the Walk. The big boys were large and impressive, not frightening or nasty like Hodson with his horse, and Havelock who believed in God and bagpipes.

The gaslight in Hall was dim, the flames burned with a sinister blue tinge. A cold draught which used to spring up and moan through Hall as the sermon ended seemed that night to add a heavier message.

"It is quite wrong that no one said anything to me; not a word at any time."

I came to my senses suddenly. These were not the tones with which I was familiar when the Headmaster was preaching. The level monotonous phrase, the uninspired message, those I knew and dreaded as I composed myself for the weekly ordeal; nor had I on this occasion expected anything else.

"But", he continued, "surely if you knew that one of you, however esteemed for his games or work, was putting poison in the food of another boy you would go to one of the masters and tell him. Yet when a boy is poisoning the mind of another you say nothing."

The school had become silent and tense. This made the event even more exciting to all of us in the preparatory school. As soon as service was over the pent-up curiosity broke.

"Has he died?" I asked.

"Who?" said my friend.

"The chap he poisoned."

"No, you chump; he wasn't meaning that kind of poison."

"But he said poison; what kind of poison was it?" I asked.

My friend became embarrassed and confidential. "Tell you later." And he ran off. But he did not tell me later; a name was mentioned, of a boy in the main school; he had been expelled it was said. 'Expelled' sounded dreadful; for long the flaring gaslight, the gloom, the thrillingly serious voice of the Headmaster as he spoke of poison, dwelt in my mind. But I dared not speak of it after I had discovered that mention of... what? Besides, I did not wish to be called a fat-head or a chump.

'Expelled'. That was fine! Expelled! Adam and Eve were expelled from the Garden of Eden—by God or some archangel with his flaming sword. Then it came to me suddenly, in the 'twinkling of an eye' like Death. Of course! It was wiggling! It seemed absurd that I had not grasped the point earlier. But then doubts crept in. Mr Hirst had only said I would be sent away. That sounded awful but was not so awful as 'expelled'. I was sure I was on the right track. 'The wages of sin is Death'. Clearly I was done for and, like kittens, would sooner or later be 'put down'. On the other hand, it was 'the Mighty' who were put down... really it was too boring, depressing. I gave it up. But it did not and would not give me up.

5

LOOKING back on that appalling period of my life I do not feel, as
I did then, that it was my fault; nor the fault of my contemporaries,
or the local school authorities. The parents, staff, all were caught in
a web of undirected menace. Sex, 'wiggling' of whatever variety,
was the only redeeming thing in our lives. It was not the cause of
anything; it obtruded because it shone out—as anything that
brought relief in that dreadful darkness would have done. Since it
obtruded it became the target for hostile attention. It did not dawn
on me that it was 'wiggling'; it glowed into realization; first
darkness, incomprehension; then an incandescence in my
reddening cheeks—*they* knew even before *I* did. They always did.
"Nothing! Nothing!" I would say, "I haven't done anything!"

Years later I complained of a sore place in my mouth to a most
formidable, Christian old woman who asked me if it had not been
caused by smoking. Since I did not smoke—my first experience of a
cigarette had made me sick—I had no difficulty in saying "No". Then
I saw her eyes were staring fixedly at me and I knew I had done
something wrong. "No!" I said, "I haven't", becoming red. The
glow burned ever more brightly in my cheeks. "Honestly! I
haven't", feeling angry now as well as frightened. Of course she
believed me. She believed me in that quiet, forgiving, Christian
kind of way which showed in the bright smile which illuminated
her features—and would even have illuminated mine if only I had
been a good boy, a *nice* boy instead of a bad boy, a dirty little
wiggling horrid boy. Well, I had *not*, definitely *not* put poison in
any boy's food. But there it was; 'Conscience makes cowards of us
all'. No one told me that that did not prove I was guilty, but only
that we are all cowards. My mouth hurt; maybe my mind hurt.
Gradually I learnt—the realization of the horrible truth about the
poison in the food was one milestone on *that* path of learning—the
rules of the game. First, you go and ask for help. Then the adult
ripostes "What have you been doing?" Hell's fires have by this time
begun to blaze in one's cheeks. The next stage depends on the speed
of the protagonists; it depends on being able to anticipate the next

stage. For the small boy this is the firing off of moral grape-shot, like "I haven't done anything!", before there has been time for the adult to formulate a charge. The opponent, on the other hand—especially if an experienced adult—anticipates the repudiation of guilt by firing off an equally polyvalent forgiveness, a general absolution, before the small boy has had a chance to find out, and therefore defend himself against, the crime of which he is charged. I had in fact long since graduated in this war and did not need to consult further. The true armour, without Saint Paul to tell me, was to be innocent—if possible genuinely—*and* to keep one's apparatus of dissimulation and lying well oiled and working smoothly.

The general principle was clear enough; its formulation in precise terms for rapid translation into action was a more complex matter. There was the 23rd Psalm with that bit about having oil poured over your head till your cup, if you had such a thing handy, ran over. 'Unctuous' was the word; 'supreme' unction was not as simple as it seemed. Usually it was safe to bet on being 'innocent'; not so when others got into top moral or religious gear. I was scared. I resolved to keep as far from wiggling as possible, but since the time Hirst had spoken of the danger of being 'sent away' (and I now realized how closely this might resemble being 'expelled') I had no luck at all. *I* might resolve to have nothing to do with wiggling, but wiggling did not return the compliment. What was more, I felt so much better—even so much morally better—after wiggling, and far more able to withstand temptation. I almost always entered into lavish contracts with the Almighty to leave my 'widdler' alone. I sometimes wondered if Saint Paul was speaking metaphorically about his 'thorn in the flesh'; my 'widdler' was permanently stuck into *my* flesh.

'Sex' might have become the focus for equally exaggerated glorification, as I know now from experience of other times and places. Then I did not know what the menace was. The sonorous and impressive phrases of the headmaster, the mobilization of 'Christian So-ho-ho-holdiers marching on to-hoo war' was premature, immature grasping for certainty where no certainty was. Had I wanted to erect a primitive phallic, visual image to worship it would have taken a Curzon-like form with leather exo-skeletonous sheath to take the strain imposed by an inadequate spine.

The time was ripe for change. At last I, approaching twelve, could see hope of release into the free air of the Main School;

'freedom' was an emanation from the main school which penetrated into and pervaded my last year in the prep. It owed something to the quality of the main school which, even as I think back on it now, was enlightened and advanced for that time. The first symptom of this complex state of enlightenment and relief was peculiar and alarming. It came about in a surprising way.

As I have said, my prevalent impression, though unformulated then, was of undirected menace—it was implicit. The overt manifestation of this was a craze for playing trains, a game which dominated our communal play. It developed voluntarily, spontaneously, the school crystalizing out into a pattern of two groups, reminiscent of 'A' and 'B', having names of main railway lines—Great Northern, and our local line, Great Eastern. We used the same system of 'rails' which were tracks in the playground. Unobserved, but observing us, was Miss Good who, as I found out later, saw us as happily and enthusiastically playing together. From the worm's eye view—mine—I watched enviously. Impelled by some memory of glorious dust I tentatively joined in. At once it was discovered that I had outstanding gifts as a locomotive. Unwarned by unhappy experience with my shoes I was carried away by being suddenly 'wanted' by both teams. The glory, never achieved before or since, went to my head. I was picked for his railway by Morgan the head of one team, the other head being Pickett. Lost to the world I emerged from the hitherto well-preserved anonymity of the Walk game. Before I had realized it I was almost at once recognized by Pickett—who pointed it out to Morgan, who hardly needed to be prompted—to be "swanking" and "showing off". Gone was my glory. It was as bad as shouting "Orphan" at Willy Bevan. Not wanting to be chased with stumps I returned to my private world; I resumed my insignificant role of doing what I was told. But I had tasted what it was like to be wanted—almost famous *and* loved. Not so Pickett and Morgan who, both being big and powerfully built, had chosen to be famous and feared. They were stupid and nasty, but these opinions I kept strictly to myself. Consequent to their choice they retained their eminence for months. It surprised them and us when suddenly one day ten or twelve of us attacked the two. Shrieking and yelling we threw ourselves on them. I do not remember myself as in any way prominent although I had now been at the school for three years and could hardly be excused on the grounds of insignificance. Fists were used; the mass of us in an unco-ordinated, yelling horde piled ourselves on top of Morgan. I do not know where Pickett had got to. Then, as suddenly as the riot had started, it stopped. I remember feeling frightened, frightened of what Morgan would do to me—I could not imagine 'us' having anything done to us. Then it became clear to me that *we* were frightened—Morgan too. There was a sudden hush, no shouting, just dusting ourselves down. Perhaps Hirst came in, but I am sure we had stopped before then. Had I been asked what was going on I would have said, "nothing".

Once we had an English nurse in Delhi. I remember nothing of her—only a vague impression of ladylike superiority and a strong sense of my parents' inferiority. One day a row started; it had something to do with her use of paint. My mother questioned my sister and me about what she had been doing. I was frightened; my sister may also have been frightened. My mother could not get a word out of either of us. I did not even say "nothing".

The next English nurse, whom I liked, took us to see a sheep being killed. It was a black sheep and its throat was cut. My sister was not frightened—or perhaps she was too small to know and certainly too small to run. I was terrified and I could and did run. I told my mother and my story could not be shaken. The nurse said it was only a red scarf round the sheep's neck. She was immediately sacked; I did not want her to be sent away. My mother was furious and the girl—very young compared with the imposing aristocrat who, despite her superiority, my mother had dared question—was packed off.

That was the end of them and the beginning of our ayah. As far as I was concerned it was the end of Nickel Sehn and Co. who beat up people like her and Dhunia whom I loved.

It was also the end of that particular Morgan. It took me a long time to learn that there were plenty more where that one came from, the source of the Morgans of this life. He was promoted to the main school because he was judged 'too big'—that is, too big a bully—to remain in the prep. I heard no more of him though I did hear a little of his friend Pickett whose nastiness had a more durable quality than Morgan's.

What led to Morgan's investigation and promotion I do not know. Years later Miss Good told me that she, Mr Hirst and Miss Whybrow had no idea that anything was amiss till the day of the riot. It was supposed that we were having schoolboy fun—just a continuation of the train game which we so happily, spontaneously and voluntarily played together. How could she have known better? How indeed did she and poor 'Nigger', living in his private hell, come to know so much?

We used sometimes to go to the Upper Field to watch the main school play a match. The field had an iron swing gate separating it from the lane which led to the prep school. The distance was almost two miles between gate and school. Three or four of us decided to stand and swing on the bottom rail; the weight made the cast iron post snap. We looked with consternation, looked and ran wildly without stopping till we were safe in our school room.

What *had* we done? It fell to me some hours later to go to Nigger's study and confess. Perhaps he was amused; if so he did not show it. We had to pay for the damage. It cost us each half a crown and since this had to be found in my case out of my pocket money of threepence a week, for ten weeks I had no pocket money. It was a small price for such enormous relief. What, we wondered for some dreadful days, was going to happen? I have not found out yet.

No school could be as bad as the horror stories we invented for ourselves. Was that the source of the dreadful storms to which we were subject? Such cataclysmic disasters cannot be described. They haunt me still; even now I am impelled to write of them, but what I have written is, as soon as it is written, a boring triviality of the lives of over-privileged brats.

6

MISS WHYBROW used to judge our gardens and award a prize to the best. Like another and more famous Order of Merit it had no merit about it. But at that time I had not become hardened to an experience which for me had all the freshness and vitality of complete novelty.

I had two 'friends'; a hard-bitten little Yorkshire farmer's son, Heaton Rhodes, and John Dudley Hamilton. It was understood that we were friends; it was like A and B. It was so—so help me God—and there you were, for life. Rhodes had a beautiful garden, spick and span; it was unbeatable and everyone knew he had won. Conversely, John Dudley of the Red Hair had obviously lost—that is, he would have done had anyone bothered to consider a scarecrow's nest of such monumental non-horticulturality. Mrs Hamilton, with whom I had fallen in love, on being shown her son's achievement, burst into peals of the most fascinating and lovely laughter. In no way disturbed, John Dudley uprooted his geranium—I think of it as the only one—and threw it, not so much at her as out of the 'garden'.

Then came the judging. Miss Whybrow went round with acute observation, becoming more and more portentous. Finally, as one whose expertise and mastery of the arcane arts had been learned in communion with God in the Garden of Eden, she proclaimed, as if announcing the discovery of Tutankhamun's tomb, the winner. Yes! It was none other than J. D. Hamilton! J. D. looked as if he expected trouble. Mrs Hamilton flushed rather painfully at her son's triumph. B. H. Rhodes, who had a hot temper, waited. He told us afterwards that Miss Whybrow had seen Mrs Hamilton's car and was "sucking up" to get a ride. This certainly seemed a possibility. The Hamiltons were the only parents who owned a car—a Leon Bollet.

Years afterwards Mrs Hamilton told me she thought Miss Whybrow was a most unsuitable matron for small boys. Was it imagination that made me think the flush on her cheek as she spoke was a reminiscence of the garden prize?

There could hardly have been two boys more different than Heaton Rhodes and Dudley Hamilton. Heaton was a very tough little boy; I cannot imagine how he put up with me. He was acute, intelligent and hard. I remember how, when the form was being taken by a master from the main school—a man with a sharp tongue who on this occasion chose to be facetious at the eleven-year-old Heaton's expense—Heaton stood it, and the form's sycophantic approval of what should have been his discomfiture, with steadily mounting anger and a deepening flush. Then when the flow of sarcasm faltered he turned to a boy sitting a couple of yards away and said clearly and loudly, as if the form master was only a mechanical object like a gramophone, "Thinks he's funny don't he?" It was crushing in its finality and seemed to gain in force from the diminutive size of the speaker. When arguing, his voice had an edgy tremor and his phrases were punctuated with "nays" which intrigued me because everyone else I knew, including my parents, said "no".

Dudley was softer, larger, with a wider range of emotion and greater flexibility of expression. I never knew anyone who devoured books as he did; he did so literally as well as metaphorically. One of my earliest experiences of him was finding he had eaten large parts of every page of my *Captain*. He responded to my anguished wail denouncing and announcing the depredations of this human caterpillar, by blushing hotly and behaving as if I did not exist. As the rest of the boys in the school had not the slightest interest in whether I existed or not I was reduced to fighting him. As he was bigger I could make no impression on him and had to be content with watching him go on reading and eating my *Captain*.

At the time of his horticultural triumph we were on what passed for friendly terms. I do not believe boys at prep school age achieve more than a rudimentary love; we certainly did not. Rhodes's and Hamilton's 'people' used to ask me to their houses for occasional—I now think most generously frequent—holidays. As the unfortunate sons had to suffer for their parents' indiscretions so the parents compromised by accepting the convention that I was a friend of theirs.

I was a conscript ally in their warfare with their parents and brothers and sisters thus:

| *Dudley* | Get out Tuey. |
| *Stewart* | Shan't. |

Dudley (furious):	Get out! You stink!
Stewart	I don't.
Dudley	You do! Doesn't he Will?
Self	Well...
Dudley	There you are! You see? We both think you stink!

Mrs Hamilton and Mrs Rhodes, both in their different ways, helped to make my last year at the prep school one in which I began to break through what I see in retrospect to have been an intolerable exo-skeleton of misery. I did not see my parents; Hirst was inaccessible in his own misery which could not be eased by us; Miss Whybrow entertained hopes of an outlet for her ambitions through Hirst's calamitous situation and favouritized attractive boys like Freddie Sexton. I must have felt Mrs Hamilton's personality as spring to my prep school winter.

Mr Hamilton was a good business man and a good employer, judging by the respect in which he was held by his employees. His shrewdness frightened me though I admired his keen, alert manner.

I remember his once describing at table that someone had gone over Niagara Falls in a barrel on some kind of money-making wager. "And if he had got through that, then the next fool would have had to go over in a paper-bag." This so tickled me that although as a small boy, and a guest at that, I should have been seen and not heard, I laughed so undisguisedly that Mr Hamilton, Mrs Hamilton and several adult friends could not help catching the infection. "Paper bag!" I repeated, and would start off again, the others being swept in by my amusement.

That holiday was a revelation. I could not have believed I could ever be so happy. I was not pleased when the time came for me to go to Archer Hall where the Rhodes's lived. I was taken in the car—not that it was called a car. It was referred to, that glorious cream-coloured, brass-embellished confection distilled out of Heaven itself, as The Leon Bollet—the one and only in our world, a world made radiant by its presence in our midst.

Archer Hall was at the top of a hill and was approached by a long drive which led from a lane to the valley of the river Rib, then climbed to the farmhouse. The climb seemed to exhaust the Leon Bollet which, if it were not irreverent to speak of it in such terms, laboured at the latter end; when it turned and left for the return it deposited not only me but a patch of black oil. This introduced me to a different culture, one in which the Leon Bollet literally and metaphorically 'stank'. "Look!" said Heaton, pointing to the patch. His scorn was absolute. He said nothing else; there was no need. Suffused with guilt as if I were personally responsible I crushed back my sense of glory and was taken at once to see Prince, already known to me through Heaton's description.

7

PRINCE was a shire-horse of gigantic proportions and exquisite grace, nine, ten, fifteen, maybe twenty hands high, noble as his name denoted and of a beauty not to be expressed in words—except by Shakespeare. Alas! He was out working, but for some minutes we worshipped at the shrine where Prince was not.

Heaton showed that the rest was anti-climax; the introduction to Kathleen, Faith, Mercy and to five lesser brothers and sisters too numerous to be bothered with, and to Mrs Rhodes who could not be so easily dismissed even by Heaton. She was plump and motherly with great dignity and a capacity for affection which did not altogether conceal an air that she was not to be trifled with. She came, as did Mr Rhodes, from an old Yorkshire family, both sides of the family tracing their descent in a line unbroken for some three or four hundred years.

Heaton did not disguise his dislike of wasting time on these members of the family and their several occupations about the house when it could be spent on Prince, but he went through with it—visiting the larder first.

Mrs Rhodes would express a shrill, explosive, but immediately muted laugh; this she did as she gave me a welcoming kiss. She asked after my parents whom I had forgotten; thinking of them was inseparable from homesickness. To all such inquiries I used to reply that they were "very well thank you"; no more 'summer suns are glowing' for me. In fact they were in India, my mother having returned with my sister at the beginning of the year; they were a nuisance—the cause of having to write a letter once a week.

Life at Archer Hall was austere in a way that was new to me. I always picture the Hamiltons in summer time with the lawns brooded over by their magnificent cedar. With the Rhodes family, loving and comfortable though it was, life seemed easier to imagine in hard, bitter winds of winter. On the exposed hilltop the winds were keen, except in the height of summer when on occasion Heaton and I cycled over from school. We would find the farmhouse

open-doored and apparently deserted. Our first call was at the
larder where we helped ourselves liberally to cake. Thus refreshed
we would wander out over the farm to Heaton's favourite haunts.
In time our punctual appetites warned us it was time to return to
the house and pay our respects to Mrs Rhodes.

She would greet us with her little laugh. "I heard you had come",
she would say, "but I knew from the state of the larder before
anyone told me that 'someone' had arrived. Never mind—we have
made a fresh supply." In those days there was always 'plenty more'.
Kathleen would be glad to see us, though shy; Faith, the pretty one
was sulky and unwilling to hide her dislike of our intrusion.

The table was spread for tea. "I don't expect either of you would
mind" said Mrs Rhodes with an air of diffidence, "if you had an egg
to your tea?" We agreed that we did not, mentally noting that 'an
egg meant 'two' eggs; 'un oeuf', but 'deuz-er-ee'. Our hearts, heavy
at the impending departure, were lightened by our gastronomic
feats.

These were the summer occasions, delightful but untypical. When
I see Archer Hall it is as a great farmhouse lying amidst fields,
deserted, sleeping its winter sleep. Mr Rhodes, weathered, striding
from field to field, stopping now and then to talk to a farm-hand,
seemed to typify the ruthless and austere character of farm life in
prosperous England. It *was* prosperous, but the prosperity did not
conceal the relentless struggles with an impenetrable cloak of
comfort—as did the wealth of the Hamiltons. "Smelly things" said
Heaton when he spoke, with curling nostrils, of the car. But neither
he nor anyone else on the farm seemed to be envious so much as
aware of a different way of life. Probably I idealize them; I
certainly remember feeling that I could not live up to the enjoyment
of farm life which was genuine enough with them.

Heaton considered I would be sure to like seeing a pig
slaughtered. I, still remembering the trouble with the sheep, knew I
would never be able to stand it. This I wished to keep to myself.
Kathleen said I did *not* want to see it. Heaton, as I feared, said I
couldn't possibly be so soft as to object—after all, he reminded
Kathleen, I wasn't a girl. In fact I knew I was worse than any
girl—certainly worse than Faith or my sister, and probably worse
than Kathleen who did at least stand up to Heaton and never made
me think she was a coward. I went. By so doing I found I did not
prove my masculinity—not with Kathleen at any rate. As I kept
my eyes shut or averted I could not be sure that I had deceived
Heaton.

Less personally horrifying, but of an intensity of humiliation for Heaton, was the episode of the cow. "You two boys haven't anything to do", said Mr Rhodes briskly one fine morning, not so much formulating and reporting an observed fact as premising a definitory hypothesis. "Just drive Curly over to Mundens for me." Heaton, who expected to see his cousin Bob of whom he was very fond, dropped the caution which he usually observed when dealing with his father, and agreed.

Curly was in Bartram's field next to the drive where it crossed the Rib. This Mr Rhodes told us. What he did *not* tell us—I can hardly believe that Heaton's suspicion would have remained dormant had he done so—was that Curly had recently calved. If he did tell us he must have slurred it over to test Heaton's perspicacity. At eight in the morning we duly located Curly and set off light-heartedly enough to drive her, without her calf, to Mundens. We reckoned, or Heaton reckoned as I had no views on the matter, to achieve our task in a couple of hours without much difficulty. The first fifty yards to the gate into the drive were accomplished with such ease and speed that we were not really concentrating when Curly passed through the gate, turned sharply up the hill—that is, away from Mundens—and proceeded at a brisk trot for home.

Running up-hill is no joke, but to be outdistanced by a mere cow, with whom one does not usually associate fine athletic prowess, was a nasty surprise. Curly reached the farmyard, where her darling was lodged, a considerable distance in front of Heaton and still further in front of me. For the next quarter of an hour or so she showed that she had outdistanced us mentally as well as physically; she knew her way about the farmyard with a detail which surprised Heaton who thought *he* had been born and bred there. Then we cornered her, or, more accurately, Heaton did with myself as a stop-gap, but one which hoped that Curly would not realize that where I stood the gap, despite appearance, was wide open. Vain hope. With lowered horns she came straight for me. Without a moment's hesitation—there was no time for that—I removed myself. Curly, with frisking tail, lit out for the open spaces.

Heaton, almost beside himself with rage, hardly bothered to flash his curses at me. "Why didn't you stop her you fool?" was all his chattering teeth permitted him to say.

Curly now had a short pause for rest. This itself seemed like bravado as she was clearly the least fatigued of the three. When we drew near she moved off. We went on like this for another quarter of an hour; then Heaton's anger blazed out; he threw a clod of earth at her. It was a good shot hitting her on the head. This, she decided, had frightened her. She broke into a brisk trot and in no time at all we had her locked in behind the gate of Bartram's from which we had started. It had taken the best part of three quarters of an hour of violent exercise to get no nearer to Mundens.

Just then Curly's accursed offspring decided to moo. Curly heard, burst through a corner of the hedge and set off up the hill to investigate. Heaton set off too. Since it was not my cow my disinterest began to show. "Whoa!" I said gently from time to time—I did not want to upset Curly. As far as I was concerned Heaton and Curly could have the farm to themselves. But remembering the time when I had been hit in the eye by the cricket ball when lying on the ground fielding, remembering Curly's charge at me with lowered head and very sharp horns, I decided to consider that part of the yard and environs denied to Curly if I occupied it—that is, unless Curly wanted it very badly. By mid-day Heaton, with my help of course, had got Curly back to Bartram's field. He looked hot; I deemed it only civil to be breathing heavily.

We locked the gate but did as little as we could to upset Curly. It was not Mundens, but there were, we decided, worse places than Bartrams. We cleared off hoping we wouldn't be noticed.

In the afternoon Mr Rhodes met us. "Well Heaton how was it? How long did it take you to get to Mundens?"

Heaton gave him a wary, rapid glance and dropped his eyes. "She had a calf."

"Really!" Mr Rhodes seemed genuinely interested. "How long?"

"Three weeks."

The conversation became professional; it was carried on without a trace of sarcasm or any undertone other than interest in breeding. I could hardly believe my ears as it was unthinkable that Mr Rhodes had not all along known about Curly and her calf. Any suspicion on that score had disappeared from Heaton's mind, but I was sure it had been there.

Then, "How much will you offer me for the calf Heaton?"

"Oh, don't know."

"Oh come on!"

"I'll see it when it's ready to wean".

"I'll hold it for you. Say a pound?"

Heaton flushed up. "Nay!"—it was curious to hear the famous 'nay' in its proper context—"Nay! that I woan't!"

"Not bid a pound? Oh, come on Heaton, what's the matter with it?"

"I haven't seen it", said Heaton obstinately.

"But you've seen the dam; she's all right isn't she?" Mr Rhodes was coaxing now.

This argument went on for about half an hour, the father and son beating each other down, coaxing, wheedling, flushing angrily, complaining of being done-by unfairly. It was serious. I had never heard anything like it before, though I was to hear it again. Finally Mr Rhodes appeared to have had enough and to be preparing like a bored old cat, to dismiss his offspring.

"Old Cow"—surprisingly the herdsman's name—"will take Curly over to Munden tomorrow. You can go with him and see how it's done." And he stalked off.

We went; it was done—easily; but we did not see how.

Cow was a notorious drunk. I had witnessed a conversation between him and Mr Rhodes which surprised me, as the conversation between father and son had done. When talking cows, Old Cow was *not* drunk, however much alcohol he had on board. Mr Rhodes spoke as the Farmer whose word was law which he meant to see was observed: Old Cow spoke as a man who knew about cows and meant to see that what he observed was respected. Each was boss in his realm: each knew where the boundaries were drawn. Perhaps Curly respected the boundary that separates an expert cowman from mere men-calves.

Cousin Bob met us at Munden. He would not allow us in the pigeon-cote because "the mess had not been cleared up".

"What mess?"

"Oh, it was a bad business! One of my foremen went up there last night with a gun and blew his head off. It was a terrible mess."

This time neither Heaton nor I wanted to see.

The sun shone brightly through the soft golden haze, the doves strutted and cooed, Bob spoke quietly to Heaton and me, but 'up there' was a 'mess'. We went into the house and had lunch which was accompanied by an erratic semi-solemn conversation which was the more incongruous because nothing solemn was said. Curly spoiled our first visit to Bob; the foreman had spoiled the next one. Farming, so peaceful, so creative—'just the thing for conscientious objectors to war'—was for me violent and ruthless. Farmers taught their sons the hard way. Farmers, fathers and sons, mothers and daughters, did they not ever *love* each other? Alternatively, if they loved each other, what were the rest of us up to?

A month or so later Heaton said to Cousin Bob, "Clear it up all right?" For a moment Bob looked puzzled; then he picked up the conversation where it had left off. "Oh, *that*. Good Lord, yes." So much for *that*. Why had he done it? Who cares? He's not even news now.

As I say, it was a nice day—'Soft as Sorrow, bright as old Renown'. Rooks sat about in the fields or flapped off lazily on our approach.

"Those old beggars!" said Heaton admiringly. "If I had a gun they'd be off in no time."

"Yes" said Bob, "I've even carried my walking stick like a gun; they take no notice. Pigeons are even worse—and they do harm. Rooks are useful—well so long you two. See you soon."

We had reached the boundary of his farm and we settled into a steady stride back to Archer Hall.

8

ON Sundays spent with the Rhodes's it was understood that we attend the parish church at Standon. Heaton, Kathleen, Faith, Mercy and I walked there and returned the same way afterwards. We hated it. One day Kathleen, who had brains and spirit, announced to Mr Rhodes in the presence of Mrs Rhodes and the family, that it was ridiculous to go. We were astounded. Mrs Rhodes, who always reminded me of the Mona Lisa and derived her frightening quality from the source that Leonardo must have known, pursed her lips ever so slightly, the smile fading out of her eyes; or perhaps, since they did not alter in any other way I can describe, it was my imagination that made me think so. She asked why. Kathleen did not flinch—let me be the sacred poet who only can erect an imperishable monument to her courage—and with eyes blazing in contrast to the block of ice that her mother had become, said "I think Mr Philson is a fool; he gabbles away"— and so he did—"like an old cockatoo!"

When she had finished her denunciation Mrs Rhodes ordered her up to her bedroom. There, for the rest of the day, she stayed. Heaton and I—the men—were delighted but did nothing. I do not know what we could have done, but... well, it was her funeral, not ours. I was to remember my cowardice many years after in a situation which could not be so easily laughed off. Was I in love with Kathleen? 'In my fashion' perhaps, provided it did not cost too much.

After lunch we went to the chapel in Latchford, a tin-roofed little box with 'gothic' windows and a patch of stained glass in one of them—'late lavatory' would describe the style. Mrs Rhodes would play the harmonium to accompany the hymns. There we were, scrubbed, transformed yet recognizably the same. Saint Paul has described it beautifully: 'Behold I tell you a mystery. We shall not all die, but we shall be changed.' So we were! And though we might reasonably have died of laughing, in fact we did not dare. The change must have been something to do with religion for there was a young man who served in Fordham's shop in Puckeridge who one day turned out to be the visiting preacher. He looked so odd—he *was* so odd—that we did not dare to hail him. Even in Puckeridge we could not have done that because he was so immeasurably our inferior. Yet there he was, standing there where the minister should, as if he had not even seen us. We were surely not completely disguised—the round-faced, snivelling, red-nosed urchins that we all were had not been completely soaped and scrubbed out of existence.

There were also community secrets which overflowed the secular village boundaries, just as there were a few 'holy' jokes which flowed out through the congregational boundaries. Thus, when we sang 'Shall we gather at the River', we allowed our knowledge that the meeting house was on the banks of the River Rib to show in a few bucolic but holy leers of comprehension from which the visiting preacher, like our young man from Fordham's, was excluded; he, poor sap, had very likely not heard of the Rib.

Mrs Rhodes was not a smooth performer and from time to time we had to sustain a note rather longer than the score indicated while she searched for the next one. But we got through and at the end of the service our awareness that the religious chores for the day were over seemed to bring a certain de-tension. Indeed it was supposed that this was the occasion for the more regular lapses of Old Cow from the strict abstinence which divine service imposed on alcoholic refreshment. Eventually he realized that the obstruction could be obviated by simply staying away from service; the meeting house knew him no more.

At Christmas the farm was ruled by the festival with which I thought I was familiar. It was cold. There was ice on the ponds thick enough to bear the weight of all the children of Latchford. Latchford was a small village but more than a hamlet; at that time it was inhabited entirely by men and women employed by, and therefore known to, Mr Rhodes—'therefore', in those days, described an essential link.

When I was invited for Christmas, which was a generously frequent hospitality, Heaton and I used to arrive from school some time before midday on Christmas Eve. All the children collected to gather evergreens for the decoration of their homes, village and farmhouse alike. That was a dirty, violent and ferocious hour, exciting in itself and in the expectations it aroused. Before this, thank heaven, the pig or pigs had been killed, and sundry geese sacrificed for the pre-Christmas baking and cooking.

On those Christmas Eve excursions there would be thirty or forty of us, ranging in age from fourteen or fifteen down to eight or nine. We were armed with bill-hooks and hedging knives—ordinary pen knives carried by the small ones who invariably cut themselves rather than the greenery. Within an hour we had exhausted our enthusiasm, cut a huge stock of ivy, mistletoe from some abandoned orchard trees, and holly. This last was not popular; the leaves prickled and hurt far more than the gory, but grander, wounds of the pen knives. It was accepted that the biggest pile went to the Rhodes's farm, not least because the parents of the village did not want to have the spotless order of their parlours destroyed by mess-making foliage. Heaton and I dragged our pile to the farm where we left it to the girls to transform into decoration. We were glad to leave it to them; they were glad to dispense with any 'help' they were likely to get from us.

The arrangement worked well. Heaton and I allowed that the transformation they brought about was "pretty". Kathleen, being the oldest, took charge. The kitchen, big, stone-paved, was done first because the cook, kitchen maid and Mrs Rhodes "had work to do". By the time the girls had finished, the kitchen had become the centre from which scents of hot cocoa, freshly made bread and cake suffused the house.

Shortly, children began to collect. They were the bell-ringers and the carol singers from the village who traditionally ended up at the farmhouse exhausted, hungry and thirsty. They mostly brought their own mugs for the cocoa; the fresh baked bread, butter and jam did not require plates. Refreshed, they performed some three or four carols very creditably before being plied with more to eat and drink—this time unrestrained by fears of impairing their voices.

Then it was the turn of the handbell-ringers. They played two or three well-known carols—very well indeed they did it. It was fifty years before I heard such a performance again, at my own son's school. Then more cocoa, cake and laughter. Finally they swung off into the night—no doubt to be at home and half way to sleep in less time than it takes to remember.

The next morning Heaton and I were up in the icy dawn of an upland Christmas. Our stomachs told us we had been up for hours by the time it came to breakfast. Luckily breakfast was more than adequate to our needs. We started with porridge, sugar and cream. I still felt ashamed that I did not follow my father's custom of eating porridge with butter and salt, but sugar and cream were too seductive. This was followed by liver and bacon or eggs and bacon.

But at this season pride of place was given to a very big pork pie.

The slaughterings which had already taken place were preliminary to the making of two hundred such pies cooked in the village bakery ovens and despatched in time for Christmas to friends and relatives of the Rhodes family, and to people so poor that they would not otherwise have had a Christmas meal. In addition to this they sent off some twenty fully dressed geese to similar recipients. I did not hear anything of the poverty of the recipients to whom the Rhodeses displayed such unadvertised generosity. It was wicked that such poverty existed; magnificent that such private generosity was unostentatiously displayed; astonishing that the Rhodes parents did not own a car or a radio. I did not hear of their reading a book other than a crudely written volume on English Eccentrics which was well-thumbed and repeatedly laughed over; its humour never staled.

The consequence of appetite and opportunity for satisfaction could have been, but was not, foreseen by me. By the time that we should have been looking forward to Christmas dinner Heaton and I were feeling ill—very ill. The nature of the malady—disinclination for food, a sense of impending death, a craving for maternal love—was made worse for me by the absence of my mother. We sought the lavatories and unburdened ourselves. When we compared notes the malaise had gone and both felt completely able to do justice to Christmas dinner. Mrs Rhodes said we had overeaten ourselves. The suggestion seemed to be unworthy of her and of us.

A hearty lunch was followed by similar, less acute, but more enduring symptoms. Some slight caution during the meal—not that Mrs Rhodes's suspicion could be seriously entertained—and an eruption of the village into the fields and fresh air in the afternoon led to amelioration.

On the following day food was a prelude to beagling. A faint queasiness—of the 'art thou weary, art thou languid?' but less spiritually inspired kind—prevented me from grasping what was going on. I would rather have been at the fireside with Kathy, but my stomach clamoured for the open air and prevailed over my heart. Heaton did not like Kathy; he made no secret of his belief that no man would waste time on anyone so "wet". Anyhow, he confided, she was bad tempered. I did not think she was, but after I had heard her talking to him I could see what he meant.

On Christmas morning, before the dinner was due to start, the pony trap was loaded with toys for all the children of Latchford. The trap was then drawn very unwillingly by the pony, Puck, through the village and the toys distributed. I do not remember hearing what the reaction of the recipients was, but I assume it was taken by most to be a part of uncovenanted wages. I doubt that they consciously regarded themselves as deprived of part of their wages so the employer could buy them a 'present'. They were duly grateful but I neither saw, heard nor felt any abiding love. Mrs Rhodes did not entertain sentimental beliefs, but I had no doubt of her capacity for genuine concern for others.

The beagling, which I did not experience through my skill at evading what no one was trying to impose on me, was part of the rough and vigorous farm sport. The greater part of the sport consisted in walking the farm stalking a hare or rabbit. Myxomatosis had not then made its attack on the rabbit populations, nor was it threatening as it is today to leave in its wake an immune race of rabbits.

I have learned to look back on the kindness, of which I received so much, through a romantic haze. Nevertheless the abiding impression is one of an austere and ruthless life. Too many animals had to be killed; too much hard, unforgiving work had to be done; there were too few diversions for me ever to think of life on the farm as educative, healthy to body and mind, a painless instruction in the 'facts of life'.

9

THE Hamiltons lived an entirely different life. Although it was farming, it was under glass on a large and lucrative scale. Mr Hamilton's cultural aspirations were once expressed by buying a pianola, but he was too cultured to be able to tolerate the disillusionment this expensive toy brought him; he ceased, almost at once, to play it.

While he was away at work, the household busy with its daily dustings and cleanings, Dudley and his brothers, Stewart and Colin, and I used to try our hand at the machine. Its mechanical attributes, which were in any case more prominent than its aesthetic qualities, were then given a thorough testing. A pleasing effect was obtained by playing the Moonlight Sonata at full speed. Dudley and his brothers also found a way of making the machine play the same piece backward. But despite these novelties there was a lack of variety in what could be done. This, combined with the danger that Mr Hamilton might catch us at it, led us to abandon our experiments. The possibility that Mr Hamilton might vent his hostility to the pianola on us for demonstrating, albeit unconsciously, its maddening defects was real; it could not be ignored by boys with a sense of reality.

Mr Hamilton had a lively sense of his social obligations. He expressed these by being an officer in the Boys Brigade—the 'B.B.' as it was called by the cognoscenti such as ourselves. One day we went to an important anniversary parade. I remember how much I admired his military appearance as he stood in his officer's uniform and little pill-box hat waiting to take us all to the parade ground in his Leon Bollet; and the parade itself—hundreds of boys in their black uniforms, white belts and pill-box caps strapped at a jaunty angle to one side of the head!

It seemed to me that nothing ever *happened*; Dudley I suppose felt the same—we both wanted to *do* something.

Eventually we went off to see his paternal grandmother. She was being given oxygen; otherwise, Mrs Hamilton said, she would die. She said 'yaller' instead of 'yellow', which I thought was very uneducated. Mrs Hamilton said it was not; some people said 'yaller'; and 'laylock', instead of 'lilac'. They were not uneducated but were pronunciations used by people who were *very* well brought up. I asked Mrs Hamilton about "at"; my mother had told me when we were going aboard ship not to talk like people whom I should hear saying "'ear' when they meant 'hear', and "at' when they meant 'hat'. But 'yaller' and 'laylock', though wrong, were all right.

The Hamilton house was very big and full of nice things—nicer even than the pianola which looked so funny when the keys went bobbing up and down though no one was touching them. There was a large garden with some fine lawns and a huge cedar tree.

We played a lot in the garden. One day we bought some bird lime because *Chums* said that if you spread it carefully on twigs you could catch birds that got entangled in it. For ages and ages we caught nothing except the gardener whom we did *not* want because he was bad tempered and did not like our smashing his biggest flower pots; we did not like his not liking it because it spoiled our otter hunts. For these—years later at Oxford I read an account of the game by Kenneth Grahame in *Dream Days*, but at the time it was our own invention—you needed the co-operation of the cat. At first it used to like us, came up in a trusting way and started purring when Dudley or Stewart or I took her in our arms and made much of her. Then, while she sat and purred and smiled, one of us would fetch one of the largest pots from the gardener's shed. The next stage was a bit tricky, even from the first, because the cat seemed to think it was time to go for a walk when the one holding her put her on the ground and continued to stroke and pat her. However, without using much force it was possible to get the flower pot over her. Then she got agitated and when she had, as it were, come to the boil, one of us who had brought a croquet mallet crashed it down on the top of the pot thus shattering it and releasing the cat. So she got off to a good start—as Dudley and I tried to explain to Mrs Hamilton who said it was cruel to chase the cat round the garden as we did. We said *we* would not mind and set out to prove it by using Colin instead of the cat. We decided to use a big—enormous would be a more accurate term—ornamental vase for Colin as the pots were not big enough. The scheme came to nothing because Colin had been the youngest brother for too long; *his* suspicions were fully alerted the moment Dudley or Stewart began to say anything friendly or to use any terms of endearment less offensive than 'stinker'. The game died because the gardener complained about his pots, and the cat had become very uncooperative. As Dudley said, "It wouldn't run properly anyway."

We did have some success with the bird lime. One day when we had given up hope we found a sparrow on a bush behaving in a very peculiar way. It kept fluttering but could not fly. We thought it was ill and we were filled with compassion, determined to catch it and nurse it back to health. Colin caught it at last but immediately let it go with cries of disgust—it was covered with horrible sticky stuff which he tried fairly successfully to wipe off on his clothes. Dudley suddenly realized "It's the bird lime!" Of course! it was our first success! Getting the fatuous Colin out of the way we quickly retrieved our bird. Gone was our compassion; it was but an instant's work to wring its neck. We decided it was not really game and would not require to be hung.

Colin was sent to collect firewood while we three set about plucking the bird. At first the bird-lime was a hindrance, but after a quarter of an hour or so the feathers became a kind of amalgam and really assisted in keeping them under control. When we had finally plucked and cleaned the bird there did not seem much meat left; even what there was looked unappetizing. But we cut off the more useless parts—'beaks and works'—and cooked it. Colin wouldn't touch it, and "anyhow he had practically let it fly away"— so that left three of us to share. I chose a leg because that seemed less revolting. We ate our portions which we pronounced delicious.

10

MRS HAMILTON always had a sparkle and a smile in her eye. With her three sons she required no instruction on the need for discipline; looking back now I wonder how she preserved her sanity and her lively sense of the ridiculous. I think the cook and two housemaids used to keep her well informed of our wilder excursions. Otherwise I could not explain how she appeared on the roof just as we were about to test our essay in aeronautics.

We had built an aeroplane. The venture was surrounded by the utmost secrecy chiefly because unlike mine, Dudley's ideas about his mother had been developing in a quite different direction; he considered her to be losing her capacity for fun; in his view she was losing her nerve. Indeed her attitude to the cooking and eating of the sparrow lacked warmth. Furthermore, her appreciation of me, which was unmistakable, appeared to be based almost entirely on my least admirable qualities.

There was the incident of the rubber for catapults. Dudley and I had been given our pocket money—sixpence a week it was then—and both were stoney broke by the end of the day. Called upon to explain this circumstance Dudley pointed out that the catapult rubber had cost that amount. Mrs Hamilton said it was ridiculous to waste money in such a profligate manner, and added in an unfortunate moment, "I am sure Wilfred would never spend his money on anything so silly."

"But he has!" whooped Dudley in unconcealed triumph.

Blushing hotly I had to admit that I was in fact just that kind of ass. Mrs Hamilton's revelation of her opinion of me served to formuate Dudley's suspicions that I was really 'wet'—as his mother and everyone knew—and that his mother likewise suffered from some kind of kink that deflected her judgement in the direction of fundamentally 'wet' people. I had lost caste both ways.

Then there was the episode of the Toy Soldier War. We both had a small number of tin soldiers which we regarded as so idiotic that we did not consider them worthy of the time which would have to be spent on setting them out. Then one day we saw some little brass cannon in the window of an otherwise undistinguished toy shop. We went in to buy some sweets—cocoanut ice at one penny for a quarter of a pound of pink and white was a 'must' largely for economic reasons—and Dudley idly asked about the cannon. They were twopence each, real solid brass, "and look", said the shopkeeper, "you can fire them!" So you could! Incredible though it seems, they were pierced at the breech; through this small hole you could insert from inside the fuse of a chinese cracker or jumping jack. The crackers were extremely inexpensive. You could buy a whole mass, perhaps a pound, for sixpence. Having detached one of these little cylinders you could place it, fuse first, in the gun barrel which was exactly the right length, coax the fuse through the vent in the breech, and—the shopkeeper showed us— light the fuse. For this of course you had to have a match. In a moment the fuse ignited the tiny charge, there was a gratifying bang and the remainder of the fire cracker was ejected in a most realistic manner!

That settled it. "No cocoanut ice", as Göring might have said. "Two cannons please, a pound of crackers and a box of matches." The last item was a momentary problem because we were not allowed to have them. Dudley was in favour of my buying them because I was his mother's favourite and so wouldn't "get into a row". I demurred and Stewart hit on the obvious solution which was for Colin, who was not present to object, to buy them. We raced home and up to the attic.

All this was done in the utmost secrecy although how anyone could have failed to notice the stampede up the stairs and the immediate silence following our arrival in the attic I do not know. We set out the soldiers in two opposing armies and then Dudley said, "Can I borrow your matches Colin?"

"I haven't got any matches." But of course we took no notice of him.

"Thanks very much." He must have been surprised to be thanked at all, but his suspicions were lulled by the start of the battle.

It was truly a grand affair and though at first it seemed to take rather a long time to load and fire the cannon, this was compensated for when I landed a shot, still glowing, in Dudley's magazine. It did not catch at first, but when it did the attic seemed to become an inferno of flying crackers augmented by my magazine which had now caught. Colin, "dirty little sneak," shouting in tones of lively indignation, "my matches!", made for the door yelling for his mother. Luckily he bumped into the cook and a scared housemaid who had come, originally to see what the silence was all about, but now could smell gunpowder.

They put it out. Mrs Hamilton showed the first signs of her declining sense of humour by saying, with a tight lipped expression, that we might have set the house on fire. She did not seem disposed on this occasion to favour me. The three of us were too annoyed with Colin to bother even when Mr Hamilton confiscated our cannons. Colin, who had not allowed for the dangers of shrieking "my matches!", was, we were glad to notice, spanked for his contraband. So, we reflected, there was *some* justice in the world.

It can be seen that the deterioration in Mrs Hamilton's sense of humour and Dudley's augmentation of his capacity for secrecy proceeded on parallel but non-Euclidean lines which sloped to terminate in an eighteen-inch balustrade between us and the garden some thirty feet below. Our aeroplane was constructed from the gardener's bamboo canes, the disappearance of which he had noted and duly reported to Mrs Hamilton. The canes were tied together in such a way that they "could not possibly come loose". There was no fabric on body or wings for the sufficient reason that we could not afford any, but Stewart also pointed out that it was only the appearance that was affected; it was accordingly decided that we should delay no longer but launch it from the roof as it was. Colin was the obvious choice for passenger had he not already shown in the matter of the matches that he was a sneak and could not be trusted. We decided that the three of us would hold it above our heads, gripping firmly so as not to let go before the plane had landed us all softly on earth below, and then at a concerted signal launch ourselves from the roof. Colin, from whom we were hidden by a chimney stack, was waiting on the lawn by the cedar where he "would see something". This stirred him up so much that he nearly wrecked everything with his questions and bad temper.

We were just settling the final details when the attic door opened behind us where it gave on to the roof, framing Mrs Hamilton, a serious faced Mr Hamilton and the cook. What, they wanted to know, were we up to on the roof? Although it was lunch time, and therefore a period during which Mr Hamilton was usually back at home, his presence gave a very definite air of solemnity to the procedings. I began to wish I was not there.

Did we not know we were not allowed on the roof? Well, of course we did, but it did not sound as if the question required an answer. We had to come down "at once!" We went. I felt especially foolish; the "at once!" applied to me just as much as it did to the others. I was one of them, but this time it did not console me because I was not at all sure that anybody really thought I was 'one of them'; far from it. Later in the day, when Mrs Hamilton was talking 'in tranquility' and asking Dudley if he hadn't realized that the three of us would probably have been killed and certainly very badly injured, she ran her fingers through his hair sadly and as if she missed him. Stewart, Colin and he were very near to her. I felt I was more of a liability than an asset though she had not directly said anything to me. For the first time for a long while I remembered my mother and father and sister, and felt homesick. I even felt, for the first time, that I would rather be with Mrs Rhodes who frightened me, but had been upset when Freddie Sexton died. Though he died at school it was believed that the appendicitis which killed him had been contracted at Archer Hall one week-end when he stayed there. Who could want to go through such guilt and heart-searching on account of the son of absent parents? I never realized at the time what a responsibility I must have been to my hosts.

It must have been about this time when the unco-operation of the cat, the limited field for explosive experiments in warfare, aeronautics and cookery pressed heavily on our imaginative resources, that we dug a cubical hole in the orchard, big enough to hold the four of us, and built a small fire-place in one clay wall. We roofed it over with boards. Perhaps it was the stifling heat when we were all inside with the fire burning brightly that led to the discovery that the indignant Colin stank. He was kicked out. He was, however, good at billiards and this endeared him to his father. This time it was the three of us who were excluded; we did not, or could not, play.

We dragged Mr and Mrs Hamilton to see our 'house'. They were genuinely and understandably impressed. The next day, by Mr Hamilton's orders and without reference to us, the hole was filled in—the roof made it a skilfully disguised man-trap for anyone who had to work in the orchard.

This was a blow to us and contributed to a note of ill-will between us and the Hamilton parents. Something peculiar was happening to us all. Life was dull. Was there nothing interesting to do?

Dudley persuaded a disreputable character called Duck to buy us a packet of Woodbine cigarettes which we smoked in a field adjacent to the Hamilton grounds. The thrill was impaired by an estranging sense of guilt made worse because we were sick. 'Common diversions divert us no longer'. In short, we were bored.

11

I WAS aware that the boredom was lessened from time to time, or the mixture of guilt and boredom changed to become more interesting. A religious would have said, 'The Devil entered into us', or, at an earlier stage, 'Satan found work for idle hands to do' if—as the implication was—we did not find something to do ourselves. It was clear that the 'something' should not be interesting. But it is difficult, when you are bored, to set out to find something 'different' but equally boring.

One night when I was lying on my bed with pyjamas on waiting for Dudley to get into his bed, he suddenly discarded the towel he had round his waist and jumped astride me as if challenging me to wrestle. "*Now* how do you feel?" he said. I felt nothing physically; mentally a sense of boredom and anti-climax, which soon communicated itself to Dudley who, after a few futile attempts to provoke a struggle, got off. I was bitterly disappointed. I had no idea what I wanted, but I did know—and the realization grew with time—that I wanted it badly. I wished I had encouraged Dudley to go on and then I would have found out what he was going to do. But now I think Dudley did not know any more than I did.

When I expressed this to my psycho-analyst years later he was convinced I knew. This seems to me now to be a failure to understand the horrible and painful nature of frustration, its powerful contribution, with fear and guilt, to an absolute hatred and loathing of sexuality in any shape or form. Furtiveness, guilt, frustration, in alternation or all together—such was my experience for many years, the most impressionable years of my life, the matrix from which passionate love supposedly will spring.

Dudley and I continued to duel and wrestle with a growing sense of pointlessness. The only overt and unmistakable emotional experience was when futility flared into mutual dislike, or more correctly, hate. I did stay with him again—a visit which differed from the past in our avoidance of any tantalizing situation. We met again, once, after the war; it was the last time. At school we kept our distance.

Living with the Hamiltons typified luxury, warmth, almost sybaritic pleasure though Mrs Hamilton discouraged any idea that we should be provided with ready-made pleasures. The Rhodes family was no less well-off; they had a farm in Yorkshire, one on the Isle of Wight and the family dwelling in Hertfordshire. "In those days", Mr Rhodes said to me after the war, "you could make farming pay. Now Heaton cannot, and I'm sure I couldn't." I doubt if that was strictly true; there was nothing lacking of comfort and luxury in the farmhouse on the hill. But in summer it was not difficult to imagine that the soft expanse of field and hedgerow could change to harsh and crude under the bitter winds of winter. Heaton and his father had that winter in their characters. Bob over at Mundens had it too.

At the Rhodes's I felt a need for one particular girl in a way which would have seemed strange at the Hamiltons. Kathy was a pretty girl, tall and slender. She spoke straight; she was fiery tempered. I remember her contrasting sharply with her mother who sat by the fire-light, with her calm Mona Lisa expression, watching Kathy confronting her father with eyes ablaze.

Mrs Rhodes I feared; there was something timeless about her capacity for maternal love. But the tender feelings which I expected between mother and child took no form that I could recognize in her contact either with her sons or her daughters. Kathy with flushed face and sparkling eyes I could understand; the cold scrutiny of her mother was something I could expect to see in the farmyard outside rather than indoors in the welcoming glow of the fireside. What I might have learned at Archer Hall, but did not, was that breeding is ruthless. The graces and civilities play like a beautiful irridescence on the surface when feelings are absent or in abeyance. With Dudley our friendly tussels turned to frustration and hate; with Heaton there were no friendly tussels. Slaughter, bloodshed, cold, and Kathy's flashing eyes alive with love or hate—those were things I could see and know. But I did not know the meaning of what I saw. The Hamiltons and the Rhodes's were providing an education that was not in the timetable. I saw: and was conquered. I did not understand.

12

THE home life at the Rhodes's and Hamiltons' continued the eman-
cipation started by the revolt against the removal of Morgan.
These upheavals were probably symptoms of puberty rather than
causes of the sense of freedom with which I and my contemporaries
entered the Main School.

There was anxiety at being a new boy again. Rhodes fell on his
feet by becoming fag to Frankie Lord and Spurgeon, two mature
and friendly Sixth Formers. Rhodes had the push and drive which
made him a capable fag. Because I was thought of as a friend
of his—not through any shining merits of my own—I was
chosen to be fag to an athletic Sixth Former called Morgan
and his study mate Nickalls. Morgan had the merit of being
no relation to the prep school pest and did not resemble him in
any way; he was alert and efficient, and alas, expected me to be
so. Nickalls had the reputation, deserved I think, of being brainy
though too clumsy to be a good athlete. I was big, dreamy,
unbelievably incompetent, and though I have spoken of having
achieved my freedom I fell almost at once into the pains of
adolescence. I struggled with my duties: to make toast—"burnt
again, blast him!"; tend the fire—out? not always; and make tea. I
also had to see that supplies were kept replenished. Lack of
foresight meant that I had frequently to borrow a tin of Swiss
Milk—as our tins of condensed or evaporated milk were called. My
voice had become deep and somewhat uncontrolled. I became
famous for saying "Have you any Swizz-milka?" in somewhat
sterotyped and mournful tones. 'Swizz-milka' became my theme
call. I tried to get rid of the 'milka' but could not; by the time I
achieved 'condenny' it was too late. My nickname was 'Swizz' till I
entered senior school; then the name was used only by my
intimate, Dyer.

After two terms of fag—it had its privileges—my pair could
stand it no more. To my great relief I was sacked and returned to
the obscurity of the school common room. I was *no good*—a
failure for which I was profoundly thankful.

The sexual climate of the school could have been described as

Nonconformist Wholesome—that is assuming that sex was admitted a fit subject for description. This result was achieved, first and foremost, by keeping the school intact as a kind of gigantic sexual pressure-cooker always gently simmering away under the watchful eye of two or three masters of unimpeachable integrity and vigilance. These men, aided by a system of boys of similar but less firmly established outlook, formed the main network of honourable spying, lightly sketched in, it will be remembered, by the Headmaster in his sermon in which he spoke of the failure of boys to realize when disloyalty to their fellows had become obligatory. This network served to detect any escape of steam from any part of the cauldron and to report it at once to the appropriate authority. At this point the big guns came into action, although loosing off only small-arm ammunition in the form of a cosy sexual talk. I was privileged to watch this from close range as I myself, to my surprise, came under suspicion. I say surprise, not because of any sense of sexual asceticism, but because my own sudden illumination which had led me to realize that 'poison in another boy's food', being sent away, wiggling, expulsion and probably—but not quite certainly—poor Mrs Hirst's incarceration in the Lunatic Asylum, were all the *same thing* and made me resolve never to get within miles of that dreadful domain from which no traveller returned.

I was having a very nice confidence-inspiring tea with a master for whom I had great admiration, though I always worshipped from afar. He was the music master, Tidmarsh, a terrifying disciplinarian, widely loved and revered by all Old Boys. On Old Boys days his study was the resort of every hero of whom I had ever heard. From that room came sounds of cheerful and distinguished laughter. In that very room I was knocking back a wonderful tea of buns, cakes, toasted scones, jam. And I was all alone. At last, when all had become cosy—I would be the last person on earth to be unsusceptible to the emollient effect of buttered toasted scones on a cold winter day—with the noises of the school common room drifting distantly in, he asked me, "Have you ever had any troubles?" "No", I said at once.

In the light of the fire I could see he was watching, not intently, not curiously but sympathetically. "No", I lied, this time deliberately, certainly, confident that I knew what he meant though I could not have formulated it. The conversation became general. Thank goodness it was only firelight or he would have have seen me blushing.

In about a week guilt became too much. I asked to see him; I owned up. He was very nice about it. Did I know of any other boys? This time I did not have to lie. "No", I said. Perhaps if I had it wouldn't have been so unbearable. Did it go on for ever? How long did it go on? For a year or so; then it became less. I did not dare to ask him how long it was before one became insane, as I felt I had pretty well exhausted my ration by this time. I thought that if I could last out the next two years I would probably have escaped. I resolved to keep a careful watch for insanity—those first awful symptoms! How terrible to know *it* had come, *it* had got me. But—so far it was all right. Thank God! I did so that night, fervently, on my knees.

I avoided any more cosy talks; the reassurance wore off. I played games hard and fortunately I was good at them. Playing well became important because playing badly was not only horrible in itself, but a sign that the dread process of degeneration was active. As time went by I began to hate religion; it was ineffectual and at the same time an obstacle to sexual pleasures. My isolation was unbroken and thereby showed, but not to me then, how general this plague must have been to us all.

It seems unfair, irreverent, to say that from this time on sex achieved a certain cachet. It was a season ticket, nearly always good for a cosy chat and quite a good tea. Not all the staff believed in it. Charles Mellows, for example, produced outstanding teas but no sex talk. Just as one felt that the time had come for a slightly soulful, faintly devilish invitation to purely platonic intimacy, he would rise up, hissing through his teeth, shifting rapidly from one foot to another, and with glazing, abstracted eyes intimate that tea was over. There was nothing to do but clear out.

Sutton—Bobby, as he was always known—behaved as one man talking to another; sex or other intimacies could be discussed, if anyone wanted to, in privacy. In the meantime there were books to talk about, begonias to look at—he was a keen gardener— gramophone records to play.

Sex was not, however, so easily laughed at. One house in particular was notorious for... what? The housemaster was a huge man, frightening for his hearty good humour, his rigid, teutonic discipline, his aesthetic sensibility; his mousey, short-sighted sister acted as Matron. Some of his house were admitted to the privilege of sharing his interests. A boisterous religiosity seemed to defy anyone to storm the safe stronghold of his God—not, I would say, *the* Almighty because the impression was more of a limited co-operation, the housemaster in the foreground and the Very Nearly Almighty within easy reach for consultation and guidance. He was not popular outside his house; inside it he was deemed, certainly by himself, to be popular. At least, no one ever suggested that a capacity for sycophancy came amiss in a member of that house.

In those days early morning prayers for the whole main school were held in the School House common room. His majestic approach, rather like a great warship steaming into home waters to its anchorage, would be greeted by a spontaneous outburst of singing. The school choir, trained by Tidmarsh, was enthusiastic and very good. As befits an East Anglian non-conformist background it was naturally religious; that is to say, it had an ingrained religious quality which has, since it has become a great public school, become less raucous, less fervent. This was not so then. As the Great Man steamed up, the anthem was commenced. 'Who is the King, the King of Glory? *He* is the King of Glory, the Lord Strong and Mighty, Mighty in Battle'.

I do not know if he noticed it, or if, noticing it, he regarded it as in any way inappropriate. He was the swimming master; the school swimming bath—it must have been the only school in England to be so enlightened as to have one at that time—was under his domain. We swam for pleasure and so became extremely proficient swimmers at school. He did not swim for pleasure; he swam, so to speak, ichthyologically, natatorially, to save life. He floated scientifically, lying with his arms stretched out, his legs stretched out, his toes peeping above the surface, the Body Beautiful itself, lying there in the middle, hairy, healthy, Holy.

Poor man! After years of faithful service he and his sister one day suddenly disappeared. Sacked? Resigned? By that time war had started. I was so bored by this undetectable, undetected landmine in our midst that I had reduced my sexual life to perfunctory prayers of the "Oh God, save me from self abuse" type. I did not care what happened; one also suspected that God must have had other matters to attend to.

In the intervals between bothering about sex, cosy sex, very rare and exciting capital SEX of the 'poison-in-the-food' variety, I played games and did work of the kind that usually is mentioned in the prospectus. I do not ignore these more usually recognized activities; I am here concerned with the spiritual life of the school and its individuals.

13

THE school was recognized for its high moral tone, one of the symptoms being an absence of bad language. One boy invented and used 'blam'; 'blast' was permissible if not used to excess; 'drat' was used by masters. On one occasion the Headmaster, whose expression was unruffled no matter what the state of affairs, was demonstrating in a mathematics class while a traction engine in the lane outside was puffing and snorting and grinding gravel into the surface. It was certainly difficult to hear for the Headmaster was not given to shouting. For once composure settled on us and did not leave us throughout the exposition—which we could not hear—of the intracacies of vulgar fractions. At last he surrendered. Ruffled rather than soothed by our occasional but well placed complaints that we had not heard, he burst out, "Oh drat that traction engine!" We were aghast, both at the mildness of the expletive and that it should be uttered at all. He sent a boy out with a message to the driver, but the boy failed to convey his headmaster's wishes effectively. For the rest of the period we watched the Headmaster—we could at least watch even if we could not hear him—without his usually noble expression. For he had a noble expression which often showed to advantage, particularly when he was preaching, or making a speech on Prize Day or other occasions when parents or visitors were present. 'A fine face' it was generally agreed, except by that small group of carping critics where envy and detraction are at work. Later on, when a well-known artist was commissioned to paint his portrait, it was generally agreed by friends and foes alike that he had caught his expression perfectly; the friends averred that the fineness of the underlying character shone out from the canvas with an inner radiance; the few others agreed about the revelation, but insisted that it showed him as he might be if he were straining at stool. When I became an undergraduate at his old college at Oxford I met a don who had known him from those early days and who made to me the remark that "he was a downy old bird". I was slightly shocked because I was a supporter of the 'noble' school of thought—

and still am. Searching my mind for some criticism which would make the portrait more credible, less open to the criticism that it is vitiated by hero-worship, I think he may remind me of my ambition to soar into the empyrean without adequate down or its counterpart. In my schooldays, my fledgling period, religion provided me with a soft mental down. Such hardness of character that I had was more akin to bits of shell that continued to adhere than to the development of a character that was a 'spine'.

After tea on Sundays a voluntarily organized prayer meeting was held. The authorities provided, or permitted, the use of a classroom for the purpose. I first noticed this when I saw serious looking boys coming out of a classroom, but as there were a number of prefects amongst them it seemed as well to be circumspect with one's curiosity. I did not like being called a 'silly chump', yet it seemed to be reciprocal of 'poison-in-the-food'. I cleared off.

In due season I inquired of Heaton who usually knew everything as he was alert and did not, like me, go around with his eyes shut. Looking self-conscious he said it was a prayer meeting—*The* Prayer Meeting.

Why didn't the bell go for it?

Well, it was kind of private—but anyone could go of course.

Did he go?—I knew jolly well he didn't.

"Nay", he replied, pursing his lips and blushing as he did when haggling with his father. "You won't catch me going there." I couldn't imagine anyone catching Heaton anywhere; he was too wary an old bird, however downy.

"What do they do?"

"Oh, pray and that sort of thing."

"I saw the Prices coming out." The Prices were Sixth Formers, very good athletes. "What *do* they do there?"

"Nay; *you* ask them."

This was one way of calling me a chump, so I shut up. If it had been a pig being slaughtered Heaton would not have blushed at being questioned; some things a respectable god would know. But the Prayer Meeting belonged to a different ceremonial; to witness it would have had the same effect on Heaton as seeing a pig slaughtered had on me. Neither of us would want to be the pig—or to be 'crucerfied' if it came to that.

In the end I got there, probably as a result of asking too many questions and thereby laying myself open to the suspicion of having come to God or Jesus. One of the Prices (who some years later captained Oxford at cricket) was presiding. On this occasion he went in to bat first, saying "Let us pray." We all stood. I shut my eyes though I wanted to see what was going on. For ages and ages nothing happened; then at last someone, to my intense relief, began to pray. Otherwise I would have *had* to open my eyes to see what they were up to. For all I knew they may all have sat down except me—they could hardly have crept out without my noticing, and anyhow I could hear the chap next to me breathing. I was so relieved that I didn't hear anything after "Oh God"—not 'Gawd' or 'Gud' or any of that lot, but just straight 'God' and later 'Amen'. Then we sat down and Price read a few verses of his own choosing from the Bible. Then, "Let us pray" again. This time someone started at once, there being less nervousness in the Second Innings despite the poor score in the first. He was followed by Jones who, as I later discovered, was the mainstay of our batting strength; he could always be relied on for a good score. He was a tall, red-haired, emotional Welshman with a keen face and a powerful flow of sincerity. He spoke in a slightly strangled voice on the verge of contrition. As far as I knew there was only one thing you could be contrite about and that was linked with asking God for a clean heart. Not that, in my experience, it was the slightest use.

Jones had a peculiar walk which seemed as characteristic as the walk of a cricketer going in to bat, a walk which suggested a mixture of crisis, confidence in the outcome, anxiety mastered. In prayer meetings where movement was restricted to standing up and sitting down he managed to convey the same impression by his anguished tone. Then, as if he had somehow mentally cleared his throat, the flow would establish itself, clear, forcible—no, not clear; muddy, like a river in spate.

I found I could not easily stop attending; my presence had become noticeable. Unable to stop attending I could hardly refrain from, well... showing myself a 'good soldier of Christ'. Accordingly one Sunday I found myself with eyes clenched tight and a horrid feeling in my chest, addressing myself out loud, ostensibly to God, but in fact to Price, Jones and one or two others who formed a kind of Celestial Selection Committee. "Oh God", I said, "Thou knowest..."—then why bother the poor fellow?—"We meet here again this day to confess our faults and failings"—not on your life! Wiggling? Whining? Cheating? Hoping I would get into the water polo team come what may? 'Not', as Bernard Shaw would say later, 'bloodly likely!' However, I had 'broken my duck' and was getting into form. I was suddenly reminded of Jones, swerved off, was reminded of Price, and swerved again. In terms I borrow from a sports writer's description of my hero, the English international threequarter, Poulton, playing against the South Africans, I 'sold them the dummy, showed them the double swerve and scored between the posts', the posts being "For Christ's sake, Amen".

Afterwards I felt much better; I was not inclined to doubt Jones who assured me, coming up with his walk characteristic of impending religious crisis, that it was due to the Holy Spirit. Holy Spirit or not, a few Sundays after this, perhaps because I had got my swimming colours, I felt I couldn't stand any more of it. I *did not go* to the Prayer Meeting! Nothing happened; absolutely nothing happened. I did take the precaution of praying that I might score a goal—I felt it advisable to keep the score moderate—in our coming swimming match, though I hoped secretly for another as a bonus. I did 'hedge' my devotions by practising assiduously. I kept clear of the Selection Committee.

At the opposite pole from Jones was a master who didn't take religion seriously; it was popularly believed that he thought the boys who went to the Prayer Meeting were a lot of hypocrites. He was fat and, I thought, unathletic till I discovered he played for England at hockey. Although I knew that hockey was a sissy game which even girls played, I felt an emotional tremor; an international was an international, even at hockey. Furthermore, I respected games like cricket in which a hard ball and some hard instrument like a stick or bat was used; I disliked pain and I did not want to be hit.

Sometimes he behaved as if work was a joke. My friend Dyer had not done his Latin homework—it was notorious that he never did, so it was no surprise when he couldn't say his repetition when called up to the master's desk to do so. There sat Corelli, smiling, complacent. Between him and the window, opening on a vista of trees and lawn, stood Dyer unshaken, impenitent, floundering.

"Me... me..."

Corelli, with ever broadening smile, nodded appreciatively.

"Me... tempore... dulcis alebat..."

Corelli seemed surprised but did not allow it to disturb his composure. It was a lovely morning. Dyer fell silent. Corelli continued to smile. At length, "Don't know it Dyer?"

"No, sir... oh, yes sir! 'Carmina qui lusi... pastorum...' It's all coming to me now. Something about 'te patulae cecini sub tegmine fagi'" Dyer stopped, triumphant.

Corelli, smiling sadly, said, "Just stand aside boy, so I can see the green leaves." He stared out of the window, still smiling. "Sub tegmine fagi", he repeated, but I thought he sounded a little stern. "Not done your homework, eh Dyer?"

"Well, I had to..."

"Never mind, Dyer. Better luck next time", and he dismissed him. No impot, nothing. But I was sure he was angry. Then why did he not take work seriously?

14

WITH the exception of religion—which seemed to offer
alternations of blue skies and dark, the latter being both
threatening and exciting—I entered into relative calm. I was free of
prep-school bullying; the horror of Sundays, half holidays, night-
time, remained lively ghosts. Morgan in the main school was a
physical representation only of himself; he was a non-entity; his
relationship with all his prep school contemporaries had altered.
Whether the change was located in himself or us, or both, I did not
know. From the little I saw I did not think he had changed: his
friend Pickett had—he was more intelligent, more cruel. The
continuation of that friendship was one respect in which Morgan
showed his lack of change.

The morale of the main school was powerful enough to show up
clearly the defects of the prep school and the disastrous cancer of
Hirst's tragedy. What was done to him by the laws of his time
seems to me to be the outcome of the unspeakable cruelty of a
nation dominated by a prep-school mentality.

The main school, which I have no intention of sparing from
criticism, was well disciplined, extremely enlightened. It can stand
comparison with any other known to me since. It was lively
intellectually and emotionally, and therefore not a comfortable
place to live in for any of us, but particularly uncomfortable for
bullies like Pickett and Morgan. For whatever reason, these two left
before they were sixteen. What happened to them I do not know. It
was right, for the good of the school as a whole, that they were
removed. The question posed by their presence or absence loomed
large in my mind. I can see now that it repeated itself with
variations many times in the course of my life. It resembled a
mathematical problem set in examinations. The mathematician can
see it is the 'same' problem; not so the student who either cannot
recognize it in its new formulation, or thinks of it as 'disguised'
simply to make things difficult. I did not recognize the underlying
pattern when I became aware of H. N. Browne and 'Bilge' Browne.

They were two Sixth Formers who shared the same study. H. N.

came of a wealthy family, though I did not know this at the time. 'Bilge' was intelligent, tiresome and, as his nickname indicated, disliked. I knew nothing of either because both occupied exalted positions, but from time to time there were certain curious emotional flurries. 'C'mon", said an excited contemporary, "watch the fun!" "Why, what's the matter?" But he had gone and I immediately followed, unwilling to miss an exciting adventure.

Some forty or fifty boys were collected at the cinder track which surrounded the Old Field. It was in full view of the School House, but some fifty yards of track were on a slope sufficient to afford concealment if a boy undergoing a customary punishment of having to run ten or sixteen tracks wished to evade the supervising prefect's scrutiny. The boys had collected at the part nearest the School House and therefore least concealed from observation. Here a curious scene was being enacted.

H. N. had used pliers to cut holes in the wire fencing and through these holes he had, presumably with some assistance, inserted the wrists of his victim so that Bilge was held captive in the figure of a Saint Andrew's cross, his feet being similarly held at the other extremity. Having achieved his purpose H.N. had walked off leaving Bilge to be scrutinized by anyone who chose. As the wire had been repaired by H.N. he could not release himself. No one took advantage of his helpless position; he was finally released by two moderately senior but otherwise undistinguished boys.

On another occasion I was present early enough to see the start. It took place in an old hut which served as a gymnasium and contained various pieces of apparatus suitable for the purpose. The crowd of boys was of much the same proportion but this time, since it was indoors, the chances of secrecy were greater—though owing to the number of spectators, still slight. This time H.N. was tying Bilge, face downward, to the rungs of a ladder which spanned the width of the gymnasium horizontally. As far as I know the story followed the same course: H.N. walked off; Bilge was not molested after he had been secured; in time someone else released him.

Some time after this H.N. must have been reprimanded; the Headmaster announced to the school that it was wrong for one boy to ill-treat another. I gathered that it was particularly wrong for this to be done to a senior boy. As far as I was concerned I did not want it to happen to me.

Subsequently H.N. went to Cambridge. He was a good athlete, a fast runner, and blossomed out as a 'blood' who entertained in some style though without extravagance. Spotless napery, distinguished silverware is what I remember of a lunch party at which I was a guest. H.N. cannot have invited me from choice. I had been taken to see the University team play Newport at rugger and as I knew no one at Cambridge he, hearing of my plight, asked me to "come along" and join his groups of friends from school. Retrospectively I think he was being extremely tolerant and long-suffering; I cannot imagine anyone more gauche or less rewarding than I as an addition to a social event.

Had I been asked about bullying I should have denied any knowledge of it outside prep school; some ragging perhaps, but all good-hearted harmless fun. Many years later I met a man whom I recognized as a contemporary of mine. He had not become distinguished at work or games as I had before I left; I thought of him as a nice though somewhat uninteresting person. I felt that I, as was natural to me, was being friendly to him despite his colourless personality and lack of distinction. We had business to transact and I went out of my way to make these occasions social with some references, to which he made a limited response, to the 'old days'—I did not call them the 'good' old days. I did not think he was pleased to see me, but I attributed this to his being somewhat over-awed by me.

It took me time to understand that in fact he hated me. It is the more surprising that I was unaware of this because his feelings were not just active dislike and repulsion, but thorough going deep hatred not unmixed with fear and contempt. Yet I could remember nothing that I had ever done against him or any of his friends. There was, however, no doubt about it—I was the address to which the hate was properly directed.

While expressing freely my dislike of others whom I feared and hated, it seems to me that I failed to see activities of my own. These were obscured for me by my own efficient methods of camouflage. I do not now expect to evade my own capacity for self-deception and self-admiration; my discovery, though unpleasant, stimulated my curiosity.

At first I tried to remember instances in which I had set out to overpower another physically. I at once recalled an occasion which was more terrifying in retrospect than at the time. Three or four of us were indulging in horseplay with a boy called Greene. I had a piece of string looped about his throat, untied and loose. I pulled the ends together and at once he lost consciousness; I let go and he recovered. The event was so sudden and such my ignorance that I thought he was pretending, but I did not require much persuasion that he was not; my own observations convinced that some disaster had nearly occurred. The game stopped; an older boy told me I should never have played with string around his throat—"it might have killed him". I was too frightened by this time to admit it and laughed the idea to scorn. Later, however, I asked a master—without admitting any personal concern other than biological curiosity. I was *not* reassured. The next morning at nine o'clock, the regular hour for seeing the Headmaster, I went and made a clean breast of the matter, showing how guilty and anxious I had become. He reassured me but told me that if the string had been knotted and I had not been able to loosen it Greene would have been dead in thirty seconds. He dismissed me saying he would make an announcement to the school; he added that he was glad I had come to him. The next day in front of the whole school, but without mentioning names or any particulars, he issued a general warning that boys should never, in playing or wrestling, use string and certainly not in the vicinity of the throat, as this could be highly dangerous. I was glad he said no more—I had had my lesson. Greene, I think, had not really known anything about it—or is this one of those ideas of 'the fox likes it' type?

The next of my heart-searchings brought to mind an occasion when I was playing water polo in a pre-breakfast practice game. H. N. Browne, my immediate opponent, swung his arm and hit me in the eye. I was aware instantly of intense pain. I crawled out and began to vomit. I was too crazed with pain to know what was happening. A master was fetched and I was removed to the sick room to await the surgeon, as it was found that a piece of the white of my eye was hanging from the eyeball by a thread of connective tissue. From half past six that morning I lay till half past two in the afternoon when the surgeon arrived; I must have been only on the edge of consciousness all that time. He injected cocaine in the eye, replaced the displaced piece and put in a couple of stitches. The cocaine had stopped the pain but I could see the needle and hear a tearing as it entered my eye.

I remember waking in a confused way to see my mother by my bedside; I could not think why she was there when she should have been in London. She told me that the doctor had said it was "all right now". A week or two later I went to the doctor's surgery to have the stitches removed. I dreaded more pain but it turned out to be of no importance—a slight prick and it was all over.

I was incredulous but vaguely gratified to be assured that I had been the subject of an announcement to the whole school. The Headmaster had said I had nearly lost the sight of my eye and he urged players to be more careful in future. I could not imagine how we were to be 'more careful'; I still believe the same thing might have happened the very next day to yet another boy.

There was at school a boy, slightly bigger than I, who was short-sighted to an extent that compelled the use of thick lenses which gave him a noticeably owl-like appearance so that he came into the class of those whose physical defects made them helpless and vulnerable. He always looked miserable and this stimulated the impulse to exploit his 'miserable' resources, included amongst which was his inability to play games. As there was no outlet, as today there would be, for playing any game such as chess which might have revealed his intellectual capacity, he was reduced to working. Unfortunately for him he appeared to be as 'hopeless' at that as at everything else. One afternoon I found myself with nothing to do—a situation in which, I had been trained to believe, Satan could be relied upon to find work for my idle hands. Nor, from my experience, was this an implausible belief. And there, asking for trouble—presumably at Satan's prompting—was Maynard. He was applying his short sight to trying to read; it took but a moment to snatch his book. I did not even have to think; there was no interval between the desire and the appropriate action. To my surprise I found my wrists firmly grasped; I could not free them. I was extremely indignant; I was stronger than he, being by this time a successful games player with considerable prestige. I told him to let go. He took no notice. Luckily there was no one to see my predicament, but at any moment someone might have come in. I remembered that I had been told by friends of his parents that at his previous school he had been bullied and forced to kiss his tormentors' boots. I had been asked to befriend him and save him from similar ill treatment. In my helpless position I could not think of any way in which I could turn this to good account. He did not have to say anything; he had only to wait till someone came in to witness my humiliation.

I said, "Let me go." He tightened his grip. So—he could not read; I could not get loose. He said, "You thought I was too weak to hold your hands." This was a remark I could not refute. Finally he let go. He said nothing more and I cannot think what face-saving ritual I discovered—probably none at all.

I do not remember learning anything from that experience, but I do remember avoiding the temptation offered by weakness and helplessness; I avoided not only Maynard but any emotional situation which might precipitate another such experience. I should say it was my *intention* to avoid such a situation, but I soon forgot what I was intending to avoid. I retained only an incomprehensible vestige of the experience. I can now think only of a sense of disaster, past and impending, in which either my companion, or more probably I, was being shaken by sobs.

Misery at school had a dynamic quality. That is where Dean Farrar was baffling. In the prep school *Eric or Little by Little* seemed false. In my imagination the characters were always miserable and dying, but in my experience school was not passive depression. *Eric* was a part of the misery of school—not a good story about it.

Night in the dormitory was a time when things happened. Boys talked in their sleep, they sobbed, they cried out. In the morning, as likely as not, they knew nothing about it.

"I say Richards, you *were* making a row last night!"

"Really? What sort of row?"

"Oh, yelling and shouting. You kept on saying 'Don't' as if someone was strangling you."

"Funny! Don't remember a thing about it."

There were horrific stories of sleep-walking which were part of the saga not only of my school but, as I discovered, of school life in general. I told my cousin about the occasion when a boy had been swinging on a gas-bracket and his weight had caused it to pull out of its ball and socket joint. A master had, with great presence of mind—

"I know", said my bored and sophisticated cousin, "he rushed to the bathroom, got a cake of soap and plugged the gas pipe till it could be mended".

"How did *you* know?", I said indignantly.

"Why, that old chestnut is as old as the hills!"

"But I know for a fact it happened because it was the master himself who told me."

"It always is", said Roy, "Beaks never wash because they use up all the soap plugging gas pipes."

15

IN those pre-Freudian days sex, nurtured and cosseted and titillated by the segregation of boys in public schools, was a PROBLEM. At considerable expense of mental pain, money and time, this problem was then all set for solution. The machinery for its solution was, by a happy coincidence, the same as that used for its creation—religion and law—so that I never thought that religion had any other function than the regulation of my and other people's sexual activities. My increasing development ran parallel with increasing loathing and hatred of sex and religion and rules—all equally fatuous. It did not occur to me that there might be something wrong with a creator who created sex and did not allow you to exercise it till some unspecified date in the distant future, or that there was something wrong with sex and its rules.

There were words which were associated with the domain of 'self-abuse'. We did not use the term 'masturbation', and were too 'refined' to use others available to 'rough' boys. Even when I came to know it later, 'masturbation' had much of the same Hellish Grandeur of 'expelled'. Our vocabulary had an iridescence of terror, satanic splendour and Biblical mystery. Onan's story used to stimulate emotional ripples; the powers of Darkness, still prowling and prowling around, returned with their former glory refurbished; 'Fight the good Fight/With all thy might' also seemed to revive the dying embers of sexuality—crushed beneath the load of boredom. It must have been my first experience of the rejuvenating quality of guilt, though at the time I experienced it more as the beneficent glow of Salvation. Saint Paul was a great stand-by with his 'whole armour' of Faith.

Jones in the prayer meetings had contributed a warm, cosy, though slightly humid emotion to the sexual orchestra. "Oh God", he would start. "Oh God indeed", my sinking heart would respond. "Thou knowest..."

'Good God, said God, I've got my work cut out.'—but there had to be a J. C. Squire and a war before that phrase was available, otherwise I might have had a straw to which I could cling.

I was reminded of Jones years later when the head of a medical unit used to address the assembled medical and surgical staff at regular intervals. "I have an announcement to make. I am sorry to say that Matron has complained to me that the nurses are very shocked—" "Oh Christ" broke in an impatient senior surgeon, "has Kisch been saying 'fuck' again?" The Dean of Studies inclined his head reverently, sadly, to admit that indeed it was so.

A great hospital with its obstetric and gynaecological departments had advantages over a public school with its powerful, moral, pre-1914 traditions. We had to do what we could with a veil of modesty worn with the impenetrability of the armour of faith. By 1920, having—as my friend Nokes said—supplemented the education provided by a non-conformist school with experience extended by God's War, (Holy, soft nations, for the use of) we could go, cleansed as by fire, up to the University with a wisdom which had not been within the reach of our forebears. By 1945 the cleansing qualities of war had become too abrasive; now we are able to try LSD, marijuana ('bhang' to you my poor, ignorant, little Indian self) and other fruits of enlightenment. I am surprised to find how rigid, old fashioned, uncomprehending I have become, although I have always been naturally intolerant and self-opinionated; it is only the opinions which have altered.

As I have indicated, bullying which was overt and easily recognizable was rare; what there was of it could be, and was, dealt with adequately. But the cruelty embedded in the school system could not be dealt with because it was not possible in those days to detect it by the tentative groping methods available. What could we do? Masters and boys alike were caught in a web which we did not see even as we struggled to free ourselves. Who could recognize danger in piety, ardent patriotism to school and games heroes? There were those who suspected that the danger was not all confined within the bournes recognized by convention. Corelli was typical both in his strength and his weakness. His protest, and that of such boys as were attracted to him, would have been more likely to engender today's licence than the Golden Rule. 'Sublimation', not yet a Freudian term, was used by some for what in fact was a substitution. Games were substituted for sex; even religion was thought of by the more advanced as if it were some harmless substitute. No one thought that sublimation could mean the reaching for, yearning for games which were sublime, a religion that was sublime and not a stopper that could dam back the noxious matter till it stank, or bury the growth of personality till it turned cancerous.

When I reached the Main School I had become proficient at games. Games were in themselves enjoyable; I was fortunate not to have had them buried under a mass of subsidiary irrelevancies—such as winning matches, keeping my ghastly sexual impulses from obtruding, and preserving a fit body for the habitation of a supposedly healthy mind. I *liked* swimming; I *enjoyed* waterpolo; I could be indifferent to the rivalry with others for a place in the team. I was equally fortunate in rugger. It was soon obvious that I was good; I was first class at every game but cricket—at which I was so bad that it presented no problem. I could, therefore, come nearer to playing the game for the sake of the game than I ever came to working for the sake of work. My excellence meant that the prospects of captainship began to appear over the horizon. That would mean that games for the sake of games would no longer be a feasible aim. In fact I became a very bad captain, but by that time war had come and captainship—but not leadership—had become irrelevant. My failure, in so far as it was noted at all, was excused in the prevailing disaster—'it's the war'. No one had told us that the games were a prelude to war.

Before that day—dies illa, dies irae, calamitatis et miseriae—I had one triumph, one great pleasure even though not unexpected. Athletic contests took place in the Easter Term—a bleak arrangement, inimical to athletic success, but so it was ordained. Distinguished from the rest was the Senior Cross Country Run.

16

THE day of the Run was sunny and clear. The hedges showed the green blush which in southern England I had come to expect within a day or two of March 25th. In School House lunch was over; we runners ate sparingly, believing that a big meal produced 'stitch'. The sky was blue and cold; I felt taut in the pit of my stomach for I was expected to win. My rival was a sprinter, stories circulated about the high speeds he had reached in practice runs over the distance. They were faster than mine, but I judged it prudent to keep my mouth shut. It was time to line up. At last—the start. There were thirty or forty of us, too many for the lane to hold us conveniently, so I had to run faster than I cared for to avoid being held up half a mile from the start at the narrow gate at the top of the hill.

I was distressed by the sprint up the hill, as I knew I would be. Nevertheless it seemed more severe, more sinister than I had expected. I was first through the gate, my rival second. How smoothly and easily he ran! I felt awkward, clumsy, laboured. The stitch had started; as we had drawn away from the others I felt sure he could hear my distressed breathing. I quickened my pace to draw away so he could not hear me. There was the Farm, sharp and bright in the sun. I was drawing ahead; the sound of his foot-fall was fainter. Long Meadow and the stitch gone at last; no more sound of feet to torment me. I was running easily when I saw the gate leading into the road in front of me. As I came up to it I had a sickening feeling that I had lost ground. A scrap of hedge enabled me to snatch a glance back without being seen by my rival from whom I wished to keep all knowledge of my fear of his success. He had closed right up; he must have seen my furtive glance, hawthorn hedge notwithstanding. I vaulted the gate though I felt I could hardly spare the effort. As I turned left-handed on the other side I saw him check. I fancied he had been disconcerted and had fumbled the catch of the gate in momentary dismay. I had regained a few yards I was sure; how had I let him catch up on me unawares?

The road was hard and uneven; it was much further than I

expected before I reached the field where the run left it for the slope down to the Plantation. He was close behind now and I knew he would pass me. I sprinted down the slope, but he did the same. I so desperately needed to reach the shelter of the Plantation before he could pass me. He was breathing easily; I was sure he could hear my gasping distress. I hardly realized I had entered the Plantation before him, but what use was it to me? I needed to be screened from him to put my despairing plan into action.

Though the path through the coppice was a series of short winding turns I did not think they could serve my purpose. The Plantation was notorious for this path, narrow, almost overgrown and of a glutinous mud at any season. It was known that any runner would take the chance to regain his breath there where nobody could run. I decided not to take the chance. At the first twist of the path where I could be sure of being hidden from sight I would... I lengthened my pace. He was too distressed to notice. At last I had a few yards to spare, under cover, disguised. Throwing all I had into the effort I began to sprint—if I could call it that when every step was an agonizing pull to release my foot from the squelching, cloying tug of the mud.

At last I saw light at the path's parting from the wood. If he could see me then he would know the race was his. I came into the clear light of the afternoon sun, gasping and without the energy to spare even for subterfuge. Here the path was firm and dry. I ran for the point where a left-handed turn interposed hedge between me and the path he yet had to run. As I reached it I saw he was out of the Plantation and had me in view for the second before I turned under the shelter of the hedge. Once behind it I lengthened my stride and ran as if the fiends were after me. No fiend could have spurred me more than the knowledge that my rival could not see me for at least seven seconds. I wanted to be sure that when he saw me next I should have gained so much that his hope was destroyed. I was now running up hill. Though the firmness of the ground more than compensated for the slope, I knew that this effort would punish him more than it did me. He had lost ground in that terrible Plantation; he cannot have expected me to gain on him there. I had a chance to see him again, about a mile later; he was a hundred yards behind. There were another thousand yards before the finishing line, yet I was sure I could not now be beaten. I was not.

I did not like my rival; he was the hero of his house, the athletic champion on whom they relied to defeat me. He was favoured by the classics master who was a popular man and a fine cricketer; his status as a scholar was similar—a fine classicist with a genuine passion for Virgil and Homer. He would expostulate with me in class, "What is there difficult about Latin? You have the brains; you only have to follow the rules and there are so many of them—"that", said I finishing the sentence for him, "you cannot possibly remember them." This pert answer annoyed and puzzled him. It puzzled me; there was more of jealousy and envy than I realized—jealousy of the boys, the athlete being one, with whom he had friendly tussles; jealousy of his glamour which dated in our eyes from Cambridge University days, and which was enhanced by his association with the senior classics master, Colman.

Colman was of established English stock; he looked like an Elizabethan statesman of the kind with which I was familiar from portraits in history books. His enthusiasm for sport was intensified as he was debarred from it by an injury reputed to be due to falling from a lamp post in a boat-race night rag. He liked me sufficiently to invite me on one of his schoolboy parties on the Norfolk Broads; on another occasion to his home in Peterborough.

The envy and admiration of English Society—so different from my ayah or dhunia—grew as it had with the Rhodeses. The religious rituals of the family surprised and impressed me. His parents, both deaf, filled me with awe and dislike. Before breakfast the whole family—domestics, visitors and any relatives who might be near—gathered for prayers. Before they all knelt, after the Bible reading, the sister whose duty it was would deftly slip the lighted spirit lamp under the egg-boiler so that the termination of the prayer—three minutes for lightly boiled—would coincide with the readiness of the eggs for consumption. This economical arrangement kept piety, gastronomy and common-sense in harmonious combination until one day the guest of the family was a gentleman of great piety and distinction whose claims to represent the family before the Lord could not be ignored. He was asked to offer up a prayer. Whether he was overwhelmed by the thought of the August Personage whom he was invited to address, or whether he was modestly aware that the family were wealthy members of his congregation, never became clear. Martha slipped unobtrusively to the egg-boiler; all knelt, and the petitioner slipped into what might be called 'top' or 'Jonesian' gear.

'Lightly boiled' was passed easily; 'hard boiled', and still he showed no sign of weakening. Martha began to have a spiritual crisis: to extinguish the unspiritual lamp, or not? Martha, true to her name, was troubled about many things.

The family, knee-sore and flushed, rose; prayers were over, the eggs—boiled. They had lost their savour for the family; all refused except the guest. Unfortunately it appeared that he could not take hard boiled eggs. Could he, perhaps, he asked modestly, have a 'soft boiled egg'? He could, and did, as he didn't in the least mind waiting. The guest must have been spiritually inspired—perhaps by a spirit with a sense of humour.

The walls of the parental home were covered with painted leather. I was not able to see what was depicted, nor, I was surprised to find, was Colman. The home possibly had oppressive memories and the power to evoke them, for when he proposed a walk across the fens he seemed as pleased as I with the prospect. We had previously visited the cathedral. Although he and I both took an amateur interest in identifying ornaments and their styles and periods—to which he in fact had introduced me—the cathedral seemed to evoke similar feelings to those of his home.

Colman was a personality as complex as his physical body but his patriotism was simple and unwavering. It did not suggest to him the roll of drums, the clangour of martial music, but the great expanse of the fenland sky, the soft glow of hazy sun, Ely riding the landscape like a huge ship, a shadow matching the procession of clouds above. He was a man of the Fens, of Elizabeth's England, of Hereward the Wake, of Cromwell, of Milton.

The walk to Crowland Abbey enshrined in an England which I was never to know again. It was hot; the air formed a shimmering screen between us and the landscape; the song of the yellow-hammers had crickets to form accompaniment; the bells of Crowland came over the land before we saw the remains of the abbey. The threat of war was upon us as an exciting actuality for me rather than the source of exasperation it was to Colman. The joy of fenland skating on the peculiar hooked skates, the shimmering bare landscape of summer, the small life of Wicken Fen, the glory of the skies—the thought that these were in jeopardy from robbers and violent men made his detestation of the German threat. The similarity to the Rhodes farmers, although outwardly they could hardly be less alike, was unmistakable. The Rhodes family did not read books; Colman, Oxford graduate and scholar, would not go to a performance of Shakespeare for 'religious' reasons. The beauties of nature were hard and bitter like hoar frost, the bleak winter scene, the slaughter and sale of animals; for Colman there was no beauty in international brotherhood, the ideals of peace on earth. These were matters for those who liked conversation.

Colman knew every inch of the Fens; his friend Will Mellows, Town Clerk of Peterborough, knew every street and alley of that city. He was able to point out that the Victoria County History had, in its painstaking survey of the Peterborough streets, made one great error—the streets described were those of Stamford, not Peterborough. The error had not been acknowledged, —nor had the receipt of his communication—perhaps a sign that the rot had gone too far. We discussed this in sight of Crowland and ate our bread and cheese.

17

THE walk to Crowland, the visit to Peterborough cathedral, Ely swimming through the heat of the unsheltered fenland—as I write of them I am distracted, aware of some change which meant 'nevermore'. In the light of later events it is easy to suppose that it was war that brought about great changes. I do not believe that my sense of loss derived either from changes in myself or the world I knew. The expertise of Will Mellows, the fiery yet controlled patriotism of Colman, the calm security of Hereward the Wake's country—I was dismayed, resentful of a past so filled with renown that it both stimulated and imposed a dead hand on my inchoate ambitions.

The Agadir crisis: what a nuisance these Germans were! "Wake up England!" King George V was alleged to have said. Well, what for? I *was* awake; so were lots of others. I would soon be going to Oxford or Cambridge—how wonderful it would be if I became an *International!* Wonderful indeed, but so ridiculous that such thoughts had to be kept secret.

I had no money so, I thought dully, I would have to win a scholarship. I knew no subject in which I could aspire to a scholarship except history—and that I did not like. I wrote half-heartedly to my parents, but I knew the answer so well that I could hardly bother to open the envelope or read their letter. No—I knew it—they had no money, unless £50 a year would be enough. It was awful to think that they imagined that £50 a year would do. Euston at Trinity, I told my father with such civility as I could muster, said I might be able to scrape through with £300 a year. I did not want to scrape through. I wrote, rudely, to my mother to tell her to get some sense into my father. She did not reply; even if the money was available I would need good manners too if I were to 'scrape through'. To them I could express my ambitions while exposing the bankruptcy of my equipment; I did not anticipate a welcome from less tolerant observers.

I had to go to sit for scholarship examinations at Oxford. I was overawed by the Queen's College hall where the exam took place.

I knew I was not worth a scholarship—it was one respect in which my estimate of my chances was correct; the result showed beyond a doubt that they could not give me a scholarship or an exhibition, even though an exhibition took into consideration the poverty as well as the worthiness of the candidate. Damn them! They said I was not even poor enough. My relief at slinking out of Oxford was tempered by despair at what was to happen to me. Without influence I could get nowhere; I had no influence.

I told Colman. "Never mind", he said, "better luck next time." No money, no manners and no luck. I despised having to depend on luck instead of on—myself? It did not inspire me with hope. Colman comforted me, not by anything he said, but by what he was. His crippling headaches could come on him so suddenly when he was in class teaching that he would have to leave, dazed and almost reeling, to return to his house and his bed; his temper, so quiet that its intensity intimidated the oldest and bravest of us, never quite obscured his gentleness and stealthy kindness. Though it was many years later before I had an idea of the extent of his benevolence, I could feel it and be sustained by it.

A new spirit was abroad which began to obtrude upon me and gradually to obscure my anxieties. The pre-occupation of all the staff seeped through to pervade the senior school. At first they seemed only to be uninterested in us and our world; it was not clear why they were attaching so much importance to Agadir, the Panther, the Germans. It was interesting of course. Did they think there would be a war? They didn't know. Probably not. Perhaps. Maybe. But it would be short. Someone—Norman Angel—had proved no one could win a modern war so, clearly, no one could be so foolish as to start one. I felt my heart sink; even a short war would be interesting and it was depressing to feel that it would be smothered by common sense. Colman thought it would be a relief to see the end of war scares. "Do you think there will be a war sir?" Our questions became more frequent, more hopeful that there *would* be a war; perhaps a great naval battle. 'Your glorious standard raise again to face another foe', we sang at the end-of-term concert. Our music master laughed. "No", he said, "it was pure coincidence." He had chosen *Ye Mariners of England* months before he had any idea that there might be a war. Still, it would have been nice if only he had owned up to some premonition, something which we could have boasted about—a psychic counterpart of the leak of gas from the torn-out gas bracket so magnificently plugged with soap.

ENGLAND

The war became a bore. The fleet had sailed under sealed orders. Even 'sealed orders' was something you sailed under with the inevitability with which you conferred behind 'locked doors'. Where the hell had the fleet gone? After a few days I stopped rushing to the paper for news of the Great Naval Battle.

Term ended. I went off for my holiday to the Thompsons' with Laurie Lawn whose parents, like mine, lived abroad. Thompson and his wife ran a prep school. He had a boat, an untidy, dirty, dilapidated old yawl which he kept tied up at a mooring in the river Deben. There was no nonsense about Thompson; he was an unpredictable, bad-tempered tyrant—unlike my loved, unhappy, ghost-haunted failure 'Nigger' Hirst. He hated boys who were soft, loutish, half alive, half dead—a perfect description of me. I felt he could have saved time and words if he had simply said "Bion". Manly boys, morally clean boys, did not make a fuss about dirt. They liked his indescribably filthy boat with sails whose brownish red pigment came off on their jackets. They liked being up at the bow working the foresheet while icy cold seas broke over them. So did I, but I was determined that I would not be in debt to that hateful old fool. I liked it because nobody was there except myself alone.

Part of the pretension of manliness was to turn up for the day without any food—being indifferent to hardship and food was manly. In my soft way, nurtured on the luxuries of Colman's boat on the Broads, I thought—but did not say—that it was not manly, merely incompetent. Years later, when I read a book describing the dreadful winter of the South Polar exploration, I felt I knew it all—the manliness, the incompetence, the utter futility, contrasting so nobly with the sneaking, unmanly clockwork precision and success of a rival team. In my soft feminine way I preferred success. I certainly preferred success that fine blustering day at sea when I was invited by the effervescent Thompson to make do with a hunk of stale, musty cake; search had revealed that there was no other food aboard.

Mr Thompson's wife, unlike Hirst's, was not in a loony bin. Mrs Thompson was beautiful; she wore smart, frightening clothes; she liked manly, intelligent boys like Laurie who won a lead over me which he never lost. One or two of the boys of Thompson's school who were staying after the end of their term were already far in the lead. They looked tremendously scruffy to me; it was hard to realize that they were superior beings.

I was in love with Mrs Thompson; with hang-dog look and

downcast eyes I worshipped from afar. And then I realized… it was quite simple really. She could not understand how a great big boy like me, who could easily be taken for military age, did not run away and join the army. I couldn't understand it myself. Whenever I thought of doing so I felt such a fool that I dismissed the thought. It would have been fine to run away, join the army, go to the front and… I couldn't quite make up my mind about getting killed and finally settled for winning the VC and coming back to see how Mrs Thompson took it. Even so I had doubts; one glance at my woe-begone face in a mirror showed how ridiculous I would look as a hero. Subsequent events proved me right.

Anyhow, there in the evenings I sat—a great boring lump of dog-like devotion. Poor Mrs Thompson! My heart bled for her. I could *not* make out why I didn't run away and…

The holidays at last came to an end. I didn't run away; I didn't join up. And the bloody fleet did not have a Great Naval Battle. Laurie and I on our last day did, however, put aside our school caps—so as not to bring dishonour on them—put on sailing caps and amidst some furze bushes pulled out two brand new pipes and began to smoke them. We admitted that it was better than fiddling around doing nothing in particular; tobacco was a solace. After a bit I told Laurie I thought I would take a stroll. He, damn him, agreed with alacrity and offered, almost insisted, on coming with me. It was the last straw; war, pipes, Grand Fleet, Mrs Thompson—they could all be at the bottom of the sea for all I cared.

On the second day of term someone rushed into the studies. "The Army! Quick!", and vanished. At first, with dignity sufficient to show that we of the Sixth would never be influenced by scum like boys from the Lower Sixth, we moved towards the gate. But… That was band music! Those powerful throbbing pulsations! We ran; we reached the gates just before the head of the column. It was the army!

As column after column passed I was overawed. "North Midland Division", someone said. North Staffs, South Staffs, the Leicesters… I had never heard of any regiments in my life except the Guards, and they were only something to do with Tuck's postcards, Buckingham Palace and other fairy-story furniture. But the Leicesters—they were real. I was converted; in an hour or two I spoke with professional ease of regiment of the line, gunners, 'figurez vous en plein Sahara'. I was not brash as I had been about India, cannibals and such exotic fry in my first term at the prep school, for I did not even know this was a Territorial Division—nothing at all compared with regulars. My pride, though immeasurable, was not based on knowledge. Later this same division, incompetently handled at Neuve Chapelle, arrived at the Line worn out and unfed only to break when its attack met the withering fire of German machine guns. They said it never recovered; this I can believe even though I never heard any supporting evidence. When we saw them the division was at full strength; the marching columns could have gone on marching for ever without tiring me.

From then on I could not work. I was captain of the 1st XV; I was a prefect. Dust and ashes. At last, at last—I left school after a year which would not move. I went to say good-bye to Bobby Sutton. I was miserable, and angry at being miserable. I said something rude and hostile about being glad to leave. I then burst into tears—to my surprise and embarrassment, and I suppose to his. Bobby was not a sentimental man and I expect it was as well for both of us that I immediately removed myself, collected my traps from the School House and went to the station. I had been at the school for ten years; the last year, my year of glory, the culmination of one of the longest school careers, ended in anti-climax. My captaincy of the XV had been a succession of cancelled matches, frustrations, gloom. My captaincy of swimming, the same. Visiting teams were composed of abstracted and bored men who had made great efforts to come together to give the school a game. Their efforts were understood, but not appreciated; our lack of appreciation aroused no sympathetic response.

As the train drew into Liverpool Street station I knew I would shortly meet my father and mother. Thank God, thank God! And then I thought, for what?

WAR

1

THE world was all before. The iron gates of my Paradise clanged to behind me as I walked, alone, solitary in my anonymous glory to face the dawn of the freedom for which I had waited so long. Were there not millions of others? No; I only knew what it was like to be me. No one knew that terrible fear; no one could know how it felt, how awful that first night at the prep school, Search-the-Scriptures Sunday classes, the Sunday 'tuck' in the gym, crawling over the horrible bar with the concrete floor below, the 'summer suns are glowing' but *not* for me. "Oh, not again!" Exactly; *not* again. No more; no, never more.

I knew that tunnel at Bishopsgate. Once it used to open out into the sunshine. There breaks a yet more glorious day. And this— dark, sodden, sulphurous Liverpool Street—was *it*. Surely it *must* be a pool whose stench-borne waters close over one for ever. So like the shell-hole—no, no; not yet. That was later; or long ago; take your choice. Now I stepped out into the glorious company of the umbrella-bearing Saints. England at War. Myself with nothing but my tiny little public-school soul. "Let us run with enlarged hearts", the Headmaster used to beseech our inconsiderately unmedical Maker. "Animula, vagula, blandula..." Did Hadrian really feel like that? That was a long time ago, and not in Liverpool Street with the rain pouring relentlessly, icily down. A great big boy like you! These buses! Not one... ah, here—Russell Square? "T'other way chum". Someone's umbrella emptied itself down my neck. Mustn't say "damn", damn it!

I got there. In my parent's bedroom the electric light cast its livid warmth; they were glad to see me—that I knew. But I could feel that her boy's precocious departure for the war left my mother kissing a chitinous semblance of a boy from whom a person had escaped. But I was imprisoned, unable to break out of the shell which adhered to me. 'Couvre-toi de gloire!', but how loudly my unjesting soul said, 'Couvre-toi de flannelle', despite the prickiness of those hated Indian stockings. The roar of traffic in the streets below 'bore all its sons away'. Although fanned by its waves yet I remained tenuously held by a thread, my father praying that I would join the Church's communion; my mother praying, as I knew she must be, that I would not be swept away and lost. Often I have wondered whether it had not been better if those invisible bands had not been so steely strong, or whether, had they been any weaker, I should have lost my hold on sanity. "'and, 'and" I would weep as a child when asleep in the throes of terror. "A great big boy like you!", sneered Miss Whybrow and Mrs Thompson. And here... would the evening never end?

One morning—it may have been the next—I presented myself at the recruiting office of the Inns of Court OTC which, being a territorial unit, had been embodied at the outbreak of the war. Although it was technically liable to be sent abroad for active service, by this time the authorities had learned from experience with the UPS that it was not a good idea to put all potential officers together where they could in one short disaster be destroyed or captured. There were two such units; the Artists' Rifles and the Inns of Court. The Artists no more consisted of artists than the Inns of Court consisted of lawyers. It was understood, however, that men considering themselves to be officer material would join one or other of these units. Who 'understood' that I was officer material I do not know; it did not occur to me that I was not. Thus I found myself in a queue of similarly aspiring officers and gentlemen waiting to be interviewed so that our credentials might be scrutinized. I thought we looked a rum lot including three or four elderly desk-bound men who had been swept into the army as the national authorities—Lord Kitchener of the piercing and accusing eyes, Asquith with his unsheathed sword—combed ever more deeply into our reserve of manhood.

One face I recognized belonged to the captain of the rugger team of a famous school—one far better known and prestigious than my loved but unadorned institution. He, I noticed to my horror, was wearing a bowler hat! Of course, already and by nature a 'gentleman' and therefore as good as commissioned, whereas I—loutish as usual—wore the gaudy school cap of our 1st XV. 'Soccer' (not 'rugger'), moon-faced and school-capped (not bowler hatted), I, already demoralized, faced two majors. They were red-faced as true alcoholic epileptics should be, but with piercing eyes. These were not as penetrating as the accusing finger of Lord Kitchener, but like gooseberries in a strawberry tart—more appropriate to an OTC. "Come back after lunch", I was told. I came, but had no lunch.

"You there—you with that college cap—'op it."

"Can I go?"

"Yus—that's wot I said—napoo, finished, rejected."

That blasted cap! I knew it. But I also knew that I had no base on which to stand. Why hadn't I run away and joined the army?

2

MY father and I were trying to see into the shop window. A large woman suddenly stepped back into me. She turned her angry face up to mine. "What the bloody hell!" Although only eighteen I was heavy and solidly built, but a moment's scrutiny of my moonface as I raised my cap and stammered out an apology satisfied her curiosity. She and her companion laughed, linked arms and moved off. My father, who had drawn in his breath sharply as if to say something, thought better of it; we went back to my mother at the hotel.

It was November 1915, gloomy and drizzling. We went up to our rooms, ostensibly to change but really to pass the intolerable hours until the evening meal. One cannot make a change of clothes last for ever; I found my parents in their room waiting.

My mother looked up, but her affectionate greeting could not hide her anxiety. There was plenty of time before dinner to continue the family debate. Their debate and mine differed but overlapped in a way which seemed to make each an interference with the other. Their debate, I suspected, was about me, my hostility, misery, resentment and self-centredness. After a while my father picked up the paper and pretended to read; my mother knitted, which was awkward because it did not remove her from the scene enough to relieve my guilt that she was available for conversation; I did not want to talk.

My idiotic cap! Of course the woman, being sensible, laughed. Anyone knew it was a symbol of humiliation—not officer quality. My father had been flabbergasted by my rejection; he was very good at being flabbergasted. But the 'stout party' of the kind of Punch joke with which he was familiar differed from the kind who had bumped into me. Two flabbergasts in one day had put him out; I could feel him wondering which one to start with.

He put down his paper. He had decided to start at the "Cannot possibly understand how you could fail to be accepted by a nation at war" end. The storm beat around my head. Finally it let up enough for me to hear my father say, "I wonder if Marsh could help." I would not have noticed it if my mother had not laid down her knitting as if something worth pondering had been said. She listened, but my father had nothing more to say. I kept my mouth shut.

At length my mother conceded that it was 'an idea'; we went in to dinner in a frame of mind which was surprisingly and unexpectedly cheerful. It was clear to me that my mother set great store by Mr Marsh. I think my father was as much surprised as I was to find he had dispersed so much gloom.

The relief was more my parents' than mine. I did not know who Marsh was and I found it difficult to imagine how anyone could help with me. Not that I had any opinion that I was worthless, but rather the contrary; I felt it would be difficult to demonstrate any grounds for my conceit of myself. I was furious at my humiliating failure to be accepted; I was humiliated by the humiliation which I vaguely felt to be my own fault. Adding sharp detail to my drab and sordid state was a memory of August 1914: a green meadow and on it drawn up, brave and shining, the guns of a territorial regiment. The men looked fine, so keen, like a materialization of Glory itself. 'Quo Fas et Gloria Ducunt.'

A day or so after the Marsh conversation, loafing along Russell Street, I heard a band. I could hardly believe my good fortune when the excitement, the craning of necks told me they might be coming my way. Then—there it was; distant khaki moving rhythmically. All too soon it was passing. How fine they looked! Who? What? Royal Fusiliers! City of London! Why didn't I go and join up and get done with the whole damned business instead of messing around with... respectable people? While I could take wings and 'finish the damned thing' mentally, I felt as if I had feet and a body of lead. I could not finish the damned thing; I was rooted in a ghastly, unimaginative, unromantic slug of reality. My feet would not lift off the pavement; paralysis from the pelvis down. I felt that anyone could see I was not walking but shuffling. I hauled myself, iron rail by iron rail, to the Russell Square hotel lunch and Russell Square paternal moral nurture.

My eyes glazed, my ears were filled, my venturesome dream of joining the army gave place to the following dialogue in which I could distinguish my own voice, clearly and distinctly—so clear and distinct that I could not understand it. Had I not been familiar with my father's voice and the very sentiments expressed I would have said that I did not know either of the participants. Was it really about joining the army? To fight? Was it to make the world

safe for Non-conformity? 'Like a mighty army... Onward Christian
Soldiers...'—shuffling as to war? The trumpets sounded an
ambiguous note. 'Come to the cookhouse door boys.' The needle
had stuck in the groove of a very old recording.

"There's one thing I don't like", said my father. I knew the tone
of voice.

"What's that?" I said flatly and with an enthusiasm to push the
answer as far away from my understanding as I could.

"Why do they call it 'The Devil's Own'?"

"Oh that", I said carelessly. "Well you see, George III or
somebody once asked where these troops, or trained bands or
whatever they then were, came from, and he was told they were
lawyers. He said, 'They should be called The Devil's Own'. It's a
kind of joke really."

"But", said my father turning this over in his mind, "surely they
could drop that now? After all, one can't fight under that banner
when our cause is just."

"We don't use banners now", I said, playing for time, but I knew
I was going to be defeated; his eyes had glassed over which meant
paradoxically that the game was up. "And anyhow they don't
fight. It's only an OTC."

"You know very well what I mean", he said with some warmth,
unglazing his eyes for the moment. I realized you can't be angry
and keep your eyes glazed. "This is very dear to me; we should
fight with clean hands."

It *was* very dear to him. I remembered when I was small and had
in an unguarded moment bragged of the daring with which I and
another boy had broken bounds and gone down town without
permission—'skunked' down town we called it. "The very term you
use shows that you think it is mean. The skunk itself is an
animal—" "It doesn't go into town at all Dad!"

But my Dad did, at great length, morally, biologically,
theologically. I tried to avoid these conflagrations in which he
extinguished me with a moral foam that made it impossible to
breathe. If only I could join the Royal Fusiliers! They were
probably made up of boys whose mothers said, "What the bloody
hell!"

"Have you heard from Marsh?", I said, hoping to deflect the
flow. To my surprise it worked.

"As a matter of fact I have. That is just what I was coming to
when I was saying the one thing I didn't like was its being called—"

"What did he say Dad?"

"He wants us to come to dinner." It was a struggle, but he abandoned the Devil to tell me that I was to go with them so he could introduce me to his old friend. Dark suit—but no school cap, I thought.

3

MAHOGANY, silver candlesticks, two maids and plenty of white starch. The conversation was uneasy; I could not believe it would be anything else with me about. My father was trying to ask me something—I imagine it would be by way of getting me to explain why I had been such an oaf—but my mother gave him a look which stopped him.

Mr Marsh did help. On January 4th 1916 I was being sworn in as a member of the armed forces. The officer had thin sneering lips. "So, you are Mr Marsh's friend?", he inquired. Was I? Luckily he wasn't wanting an answer or heaven knows what I would have let him in for. A few days later I was in uniform, baggy, itchy, hot. I felt so unsoldierly that I had quite a shock when a girl who had given me a white feather a few days past didn't give me another as I passed by her beat. I thought she must have been pre-occupied or worried about something to have missed me. Then I realized that she had mistaken me—taken me?—for a soldier. My mother was proud of me.

I enjoyed the Inns of Court. We drilled in Lincoln's Inn Fields. We were very bad; even my feeble cadet corps experiences at school were enough to make me shine—or at least 'glow'—rather more than others.

We graduated to Hampstead Heath and to Leffman, an amateur—like us—CSM, an intelligent, efficient, drill-book performer—unlike us—who prided himself on the distinct and elocutionary exact pronouncement of his orders. One of us, a professional singer, Topliss Green, was contemptuous; "He thinks his voice carries!" Lunch—coffee and cheese at the Express Dairy—and 'home' in the evening.

Once, when we had been dismissed early, I went to evensong at St Paul's cathedral. It was a gloomy day. The non-conformist Sunday had eaten deeply into the soft remnants of my soul; it brought back the queer sense of Doom from my prep school days which had confirmed my fundamental timidity. Many regard timidity as the disposition of a 'milksop'—flimsy, wayward, unreliable. In me it is the toughest, most robust, most enduring quality I have. 'All we like sheep have gone astray', but at least Handel's sheep seem to be a cheerful lot. Not so my 'ewe lamb'. I was tough, timid, gloomy and infectious. It was a hideous foundation on which to base one's warlike hopes.

I do not now remember when or how the period at Hampstead Heath came to an end. In retrospect it was pleasant and short—at the time never-ending. It was spring; it was warm; it was exciting to be in camp. In my tent were Baker, my bowler-hatted rival school rugger captain; his older friend Hunter, who shared with him a common background of mancunian origin; and Howells, who was of an age with Hunter and who dwells in memory as a man of sense, humourous and kindly. I was separated from them by my immaturity, queerness, nonconformity; drawn to them by the same difference.

Typical of the trifles I remember is of being on parade with Baker immediately behind me in the second rank. We were inspected by our platoon sergeant to see that we were correctly turned out. One item of 'correct' dress was having the safety catch of our rifles in the 'on' position. As we stood immobile at attention Baker mischievously used to reach forward with the toe of his boot and trip the safety catch of my rifle to the 'off' position. So when the sergeant reached me I was detected as being 'improperly' dressed—much to the amusement of Hunter and Howells. This was often repeated so that 'Private Bion improperly dressed again' became a stock joke: so did my fury at the 'unfairness'.

Two great pleasures stand out. On most days we had a route march of some fifteen or twenty hot, dusty and thirsty miles—"Don't empty your water bottles; only wet your lips. Save the rest." Once we passed a garden with high lavender hedges and roses in profusion; an old gentleman reclined in an easy chair reading his newspaper. The faint blue, the soft glow of roses, the scent of England ruffled my hot and sweaty face. The 'past' was etched in my mind more indelibly than the grime which our communal showers could wash off. Later—so time as it is measured by calendar and clock told me, but not my sense of smell or poetic ear—perfumes known as 'Quelques Fleurs' and 'Temps de Lilas', a line of verse, 'Soft as Sorrow, bright as old Renown', set music vibrating in me. Another scent was introduced into my life by Quainton, a recruit nearer to me in age and social culture. Though a Quaker, he had joined the army with a view to fighting. One pleasure to which he introduced me was Pear's Attar of Roses scented soap. From now on I washed away the sweat of the route march with Attar of Roses. Quainton's fate almost washed away the joy of life I learned from him.

My second delight was acquired in 'night operations'. Tring station, our operations orders told us, was on fire, having been captured by 'the enemy'. Perhaps the enemy was unimaginative or my memory deceives me by leading me to believe that this was a frequent event. It introduced me to the experience of creeping through the woods at night. Here I learned what it was to be alone with the sound of deer belling. Blessed peace! Blessed wildness in England's cultivated calm. Tring station is on fire? Not yet; only make-believe so far; schoolboys of all ages playing soldiers, rehearsing for the real thing, but never learning that war and yet more terrible war is normal, not an aberrant disaster.

We had a field-day against the Officer Training Corps of the Public Schools. The authorities had issued us with blank ammunition which our 'patrols' handed to the boys so that they had plenty to fire. Blank ammunition makes a rifle dirty; as we had to clean ours we kept our barrels unused. I do not remember the lessons which were drawn from our exercises; they cannot have been profound. They certainly did not bite into the substance of my mind as the love of Stokes, the South African, and Quainton (the quaint'un) did. Stokes is dead; Quainton has left only the sound of his name. 'Gone are the gypsies but where, who can say?' Perhaps memory can throw a flickering gleam—firelight that teaches gloom to illuminate the dust.

From Berkhampstead I passed to an Officer Training Unit in transit for Bisley—change at Brookwood, the London Necropolis, for the few miles to Bisley. Before this I was amongst equals for none of us had combatant experience. I remember only a Jewish cadet who made fun of his Jewishness by singing—very competently—comic songs about Jews. The songs were well received. I did not ask him a question that bothered me—why did he make fun of Jews? It was no business of mine; I was learning not to ask questions. A Jew was entitled to make fun of Jews if he wanted to.

Bisley was the final school for aspirants to commissioned rank in the Machine Gun Corps: for me it was only a transit camp on the way to the Tanks for which I had applied and which were known as 'Machine Gun Corps (Heavy)'. The men there had almost all seen active service at the front. There was a difference, which was palpable, dividing us from them. They were tolerant and kind—as if we were children; you weren't cruel to children, nor did you take them seriously.

The camp was understaffed. We had two officers—at once known as Gona and Diah—the brothers Rhea. There were one or two warrant officers from the Brigade of Guards; and there were two or three hundred of us. The understanding between the men from the front was spontaneous, instantaneous, complete; it was in no sense favourable to co-operation with the authorities unless pursuing parallel aims in a wish to say good-bye to Bisley Camp.

We learned the intricacy of the Vickers machine gun. We practised stoppages by using American ammunition, thoughtfully supplied by our American allies but withdrawn from combatant use as soon as its unreliability became apparent. Clearly, as it invariably led to the jamming of the machine gun, it was ideal for training soldiers in how to deal with emergencies.

My first and only week-end pass from that camp was a horror which plucked harshly and cruelly at chords which I had forgotten—my week-end of respite from the daily misery of the prep school. I loathed it; I hated every moment of it. I have no recollection of how I spent the day; I must have been conscious—my psycho-analytical bible tells me so. What it was like for my mother I do not know and cannot remember caring. I was cut off from my base. And the enemy was in full occupation of my mother. 'Tomorrow to fresh woods and pastures new'. Yes, *woods* you fool! It is there alone in the jungle that you have to learn to live.

4

WHEN it was time to go back to camp my mother was pre-occupied; she stroked my cheek; she said it was soft. I was furious and about to remind her that I was not a baby now—I had begun to feel smart, like a kind of soldier, by this time—when I noticed she was crying. I kept my mouth shut but fumed inwardly.

Waterloo was horrible. Khaki everywhere, blanked out and anonymous. Brookwood. The London Crematorium. "Nearly there boys—any more for the London Crematorium?" As we neared Bisley the whole train became active. I thought it was because they were all on leave and we were approaching camp. But they were not all on leave—I doubt if there were more than a handful like me who were. Someone pulled the communication cord, the train came to a halt and the passengers, all in uniform, swarmed out of the carriages and onto the fields to make their way back to camp without running into the Military Police. I stayed where I was, feeling foolish for all my military grandeur and wishing I did not always feel a milksop. At Bisley the few of us who had stayed because we had leave passes started to slush back to camp. Why was it always dark? Why was it always raining?

Mutt and Jeff were there; they at least were always cheerful and had earned their nicknames because of their resemblance to two comic characters in one of the daily papers. They made life bearable in camp—not beyond. There was no anaesthetic for those suffering home leave, the worst being before embarkation.

After what seemed an eternity of anxiety about the chance of being commissioned I was eventually posted to the 5th Tank Battalion. I had applied to go to Tanks as it was the only way to penetrate the secrecy surrounding them. I was ordered to report to Bovington Camp at Wool where I saw my first tank—it blocked the road to camp. The day was hot, sunny, still. The queer mechanical shape, immobilized and immobilizing, was frightening in the same way as the primitive tiger trap near Gwalior; I wanted to get away from it. A metallic hammering came from inside; a soldier got out and the day sprang into life again.

It was a good camp, well disciplined—not ramshackle, temporary and amateur like so much I had seen in my feverish and irritable progress. This I felt was *it*. The officers were men you expected to obey; even a second lieutenant, though known as 'a blot on the landscape' as I soon found, was expected to behave like one in authority. We were drilled by a senior NCO and our manoeuvres were intended to impress other ranks with our efficiency, not as evidence of our unimportance.

Drill, technical courses, revolvers, machine-guns, 6-pounders, and above all the mighty tank itself, filled our days. Then Mess; still a ritual. Not so wonderful—how could it be?—as the Royal Naval College, but still not bad for mere soldiers. Then Lights Out, the deep evening glow, the nightjars.

I became re-united with Quainton and Stokes who had been parted from me at Berkhampstead. They had taken a different route to arrive at their commissions—in Tanks and, by a curious chance, the 5th Battalion. Health, good food, intense concentration on guns and courses, and on one occasion a ramble with Stokes, Quainton and Bayliss through the hot, humid, rhododendron-studded parkland far from the devastation of the tank driving area, seemed to stretch out the carefree minutes into hours and days. It was known, but like all else we knew we hardly dared believe, we were to go overseas as a battalion; we were proud of it.

Embarkation leave and a lovely sunny day—how I wished my mother could see us as we marched down to Wool Station. But she preferred to stay in the cottage she had rented in the village. I was sure she would hear the band when the special train drew in—it played Auld Lang Syne and Home Sweet Home.

Le Havre, 'rest camp'; this time no courses to hide our frustration. Close by was a VD hospital and about this there was a 'funny' story. The 'funny' story belonged to the VD camp as certain adjectives belong to words; tired adjectives, tired words, tired stories; as tired as the diseases that belong to wars. "What are you doing?", asked a padre of an officer who kept dodging from one camp to another. "I've just seen my son here and I don't want him to see me." A little later, to his surprise, he saw another officer behaving in the same way. "May I ask what you think you are doing?" he asked. "Nothing; only I've just seen my Dad in here and I don't want him to see me."

Cohen, Bayliss, Stokes, Quainton and I were religious; in the view of other members of our company we were 'pi' or just plain humbugs. As far as I was concerned, though I kept to the disciplinary code, I felt that religion had not 'taken' even as effectually as medical innoculation. There were reminiscences of night-time fears when I was small in India, linked with a harmonium played very carefully by mother while my sister and I sang 'Jesus loves me', or 'There is a green hill far away'. The parched Indian landscape must have drained all its green into that hill which retained its city wall like a crown within which were tiny spires and towers huddled together against the foes 'without'.

Again, and for the last time, we marched as a battalion to entrain, the band creating a mild stir by playing the Marseillaise. As Carter, our company reconnaissance officer, remarked, the people of Le Havre must have hated the sound of it by this time. "On the other hand", he said, "it does drive the point home in the unlikely event that any German spy might fail to notice and report our arrival to Boche HQ." This indeed was unlikely, but then the enemy also made extraordinary mistakes.

Le Havre, though undamaged by war, was stark and gloomy to march through for all the music the band was blowing through its streets. "We are quite near Agincourt", I wrote dutifully to my old history master at school, feeling as far from the thin skin of my patriotism as I could be. 'This quarrel honourable'—of course we all 'did' Henry V—seemed to be some quirk in Shakespeare rather than anything stable in the English character. No one could have been so 'unpatriotic' in the glorious days of Elizabethan England. Patriotic, had I realized it, was all I could be.

Our destination? A mysterious place called The Front. Maybe for half an hour—time had already come to mean something that could not be measured by watches—we travelled slowly but in a manner reminiscent of railways in pre-war England. The coaches bore a resemblance to those on trains going to the East coast—Norwich, North Walsham, Cromer. Then the train stopped. Novices, we wanted to know why. After a while some of us *asked* why. A railwayman came along the line; he seemed a decent fellow and he stopped to give the matter some thought. Finally, though we were not sure as we only spoke public-school French, he suggested the train had stopped. Even in french French it sounded unenlightening. Later we became habituated; we did not ask questions requiring answers. It was wiser to sleep.

It sounded like the rumble of an approaching train. What was remarkable was the speed with which it came, out of the silence as from a ghostly world. Then it was upon us, so material, so evidently an express that in that context it *was* a ghost,

117

shimmering, brightly lit, it passed with its rhythmic beat. It was not blacked out; in that innocent age the International Red Cross needed no protection other than to make its presence known. A faint smell of iodoform came through our windows.

"Lucky sods", said Yates feelingly. The rumble died away in the distance till silence swallowed us again. Yates was one of our few veterans; he had been in the landing of the Royal Lancashire Fusiliers on Gallipoli. It was said that the survivors tossed up to decide which of them were to receive the Victoria Crosses which had been awarded in 'bulk' to the battalion because it was invidious to make distinctions when in valour all were equal. Yates was not quite our hero. One of his friends joked about his wearing his second lieutenant's star on a shoulder strap already pierced for the stars necessary to mark his promotion to captain. "After all, I have already worn the stars!" he replied with what to us was more eloquent of a chip on his shoulder than of a badge of rank. Poor Yates—he looked worn and his attempts at putting a brave face on the prospects now looming were threadbare. The Colonel, he confided to me, had given him a damned good talking to. "I tell you he gave it me straight. He's a fine chap!" The Colonel was a handsome young regular who had been jumped from captain to command of our battalion to match the DSO he had been awarded on the Retreat with his original infantry regiment.

"What's the matter with this damned train?" said Carter. The brilliant flashing special with its suggestion of spotless linen, nurses, cleanliness, against the anonymous dark had cast a gloom on us all. We were many hours, days, weeks from the Line; what was the trouble? Too far and too near.

5

WE woke to a fine sunny morning, stiff and cold from having slept on the concrete floor in our uniforms without bedding. Carter, who must have been nearer fifty than thirty, stoically did not show the pain which must have been much worse for him than for those, like me, who were nearer eighteen than twenty. "What a rum smell", I said sniffing the sweet and rotten air. Carter drew in his breath through compressed lips and spat it out. The nearest, I thought, he ever gets to a smile. "Must be a corpse somewhere—that's what that smell means." We hunted vainly, four or five of us when that many had woken. "It's not a Boche—they stink; not the rotten sweet smell." 'In death they were not divided'—much. We could not find it so we had to endure it till we moved off two days later.

The trains were for men or horses, forty or eight, and with one or two coaches or compartments for officers; not just broken down third-class compartments such as we might have used in our youth when we ourselves were civilians, but grand, shabby, broken down *first* class, thus making unmistakable the gulf that separated US from THEM. Our men, my men or *The* Men? Or perhaps "Men!" as one would address them before battle. It seemed queer that Sergeant O'Toole, Hayler, Allen, the other Allen, Richardson, Gee Colombo should suddenly have become estranged and separated as we now approached the Line for which we had prepared so long. Much later I had a similar crisis of etiquette when cheerful, jolly Smith suddenly became 'It' when a shell splinter entered his brain and we could not get his limbs to pack properly into the grave. 'Him', 'Corporal', 'Matey', 'Smith'—time was getting short and it made things awkward if we had to make a grave to fit him (or It).

We sat in our superior comfort. I felt uneasily that my crew might not see or realize that I was entitled to travel first class because of my graver responsibilities.

The afternoon landscape through which we crawled was scrub-covered. It grew dark. We went more slowly. Then stopped. "Is this the Line?" "No chum, it's not." "Then what?" "Nothing.

We've arrived—that's all." We got out and I went to find my crew. They wanted to know too. They were wet and cold. We were standing outside the trucks and coaches which were forlorn and bleak. And the rain came down in sheets; rain which was destined to be 'mentioned in dispatches', to become famous later, but which for the present was only wet. We stood there and waited for something to happen. We had not even begun to realize that nothing happens in war, or—which comes to much the same—nobody knows what happens. I would have thought I was being made a fool of if I had been told that, even years after that war and yet another like it, I still would not know something so simple and obvious as who had won.

"Fall in!" The word began to pass along to us from the distance; then stopped without reaching us. After another fifteen minutes there was a flurry. An angry voice, agonized—Bagshaw's—"That you? What the hell do you think you're doing? You're supposed to have fallen in years ago! Oh, never mind, get fallen in now anyway!" Boots squelched in the mud; the rain poured down our faces and necks; the sound of it mingled with sniffs and coughs and curses. We moved off, too well disciplined to 'slouch off', too raw to achieve a semblance of a march.

Oosthoek Wood they said it was, tangled undergrowth which our advance party had made an attempt to slash down. It was a quiet night. The distant gun flashes made it impossible to do more than guess that there were branches between us and the teeming sky. "Put down your bivvy tents where you can and turn in." We used them mostly as ground sheet cover; in the blackness and rain it was foolish to pretend to pitch anything. Tomorrow we would put up proper tents. Then and there it was a tangle of knotted twigs and roots and rain which we churned up with our heavy ammunition boots preparatory to lying down on the patch which we fancied that we had trampled flat. When we could stand it no longer we seemed to arrive at a simultaneous agreement that it was 'tomorrow'; therefore time to pitch our tents.

After a few days the wood was filled with irregularly spaced tents laced together by a network of paths. "Luckily for us", sneered Cook, "the Boche couldn't recognize it as a camp even if he could see through the trees." "If we were the ship-shape Guards", said Carter, "it would take hours to make them look like this. As it is, our natural flair of warfare needs no schooling; we are just spontaneously military." He swore as he tripped in the remnants of a shrub.

We all felt excited though it would be hard to say why. The prospect of action at last, the fear of being afraid—all the phrases were true but empty if uttered. For me fear was the central fact made worse because I could never even try to escape. I remembered 'Popsy' Brightman inviting me to get a commission in the Corps and his feeble, off-putting inducement, "You won't get a Military Cross you know—just one of those little wooden ones." How absurd to think that any such commonsense could carry weight. And now, here we were in the bleak, grey desolation of rain which seemed to have a quality of garishness.

One evening the company was sent on a route march. 'You're in the army now' was the catch phrase to sum up such exercises in forgetting our incurably civilian outlook. It was wet, cheerless and dark. The vitality of the desolation broke out of black night, mud and abandoned gear like the bubbles in a cauldron. As we stood 'fallen out' in one of our regular halts, the horizon changed from uniform black to dazzling, shimmering white. We stood, stupefied. Then on the breeze came 'drum fire' in which no individual gun could be heard any more than the individual flashes could be seen. The white was now penetrated by the red of bursting shells, the enemy's return fire.

The order to 'fall in' came down the line and we continued our aimless march. The raid, for that was all it was, was not even mentioned in *Comic Cuts*, the army paper, and since we were not marching in that direction we could ignore it. There must have been few who did not, like me, wonder how anyone survived exposure to such hell. One day I would see in broad daylight a German battery position with the legend 'Hurricane Fire', guns wrecked, German bodies around, some half-clothed as they had been surprised by our gunfire. The scene had the meaningless neatness of a war correspondent's drawing.

Our march was sombre, irritable, mindless, as if to keep an appointment with reality emulating a popular weekly; headlines exciting a languid curiosity—'Fall of the British Empire'; 'The Umpteenth Royal Irish Grenadiers' drawn up in regular lines at the Ypres Salient, kneeling with heads devoutly bowed, 'Receiving Holy Communion Before Battle'; 'Tanks Storming the German Lines'. The pictures might have repaid careful study; our march seemed unlikely to reap any reward at all. It was just a bore spoiled by hideous mis-shapen blobs of fear.

Then—we were going into action. At least, my section was going into action—not Battle. A division of infantry, a section of Tanks, simply to clear up a couple of pill-boxes.

We were urged, ordered, to reconnoitre. This was exciting, frightening. Soon we felt, we should *know*. Our section commander, a young, bespectacled captain, addressed his officers and men. The talk was designed to tell us of the nature of the operation and, I suspect, enthuse us with the lust for battle. His appearance reminded me of the Mock Turtle; this, combined with a sense of reality, militated against a would-be forceful address.

"As you all know we shall shortly be going big-game shooting." He sounded as if he was talking from the bottom of a heavy cold. We were listening with such intensity that the mirthful response which a stage direction would have indicated was absent.

"The red line on the map"—here came a crackling of papers as officers, four of us, with the crews craning their necks to see the shared papers—"marks the starting point. We have to take Hill 40. Got it?" More rustling. "And the village behind." Gunner Harrison, our cockney, looked serious which usually meant a witticism was coming, but none came.

"Bion, you take Hill 40 and patrol it till the infantry have consolidated. You must watch the sunk road—marked just to the north-east—because our intelligence have told us that the 'umptieth' Division have just moved in. You will see on *this* map which is secret and must not be given to you"—he held it up for us to see—"the sectors held by the individual units are marked and will probably remain unaltered for three or four days—that is till after your show. The chap in command of your sector always likes to counter attack down sunk roads; so, when you are patrolling after taking the Hill, watch for this bit"—he indicated the sunk road—"and let them have it. Despard, you'd better watch it too. The village no longer exists, but Quainton, you and Cohen have to take it and hold it. You can tell when you are there by the brickish stain of the mud. Any questions?"

"The pill-boxes sir!" It was my tank sergeant O'Toole speaking. His large protuberant ears, red shiny face and permanently indignant expression suggested that an officer should have asked the question. Perhaps he was blushing for us.

"Ah yes; I nearly forgot those. Well, you know they have usually six or more men in them—some people say a dozen. As they are solid concrete and over a foot thick all you need do is fire at the gunslits and go round to the back door. The gunners are concentrating on them so don't go too near. If you fire at the gunslits you may stop the Boche firing."

It sounded most improbable, but he had to say something. We all knew of heavy howitzers, 9.2's, that had registered direct hits and done no harm. Our questions had little to do with a thirst for information; it was a mindless activity, the individual becoming merged into a primitive brute, an army.

On our journey to 'the Salient' we came first to a crawl, then to a halt. After a long pause someone said we were outside Hazebrouck and couldn't go through because the station was being shelled. The train, like a stupid caterpillar, waited. Finally it went through, slowly, ponderously, between shell bursts which continued rhythmically like an animal chewing the cud. The tail of the train waited breathlessly for the front to get hit; the front waited for the tail. We listened, searching the air as if to get some clue.

We were to parade in a quarter of an hour to start our first reconnaissance. The remnants of evening sun—its appearance after weeks of rain had precipitated the idea that the battle commenced on July 31st could be continued—lit up a watery sky as we scrambled into a lorry. Our captain was in front with the driver; the four tank commanders and men in the back. We rattled, roared and bumped our way at a good pace for half an hour. Then stopped.

We could see we were at the beginning of a ruined city—Ypres; unusual, for buildings still stood. "Military Police", said someone. At that instant he appeared at our tail board. "All gas masks to be worn at the Alert from now on", he said. "Gas and HE shells mixed, but they have slowed up a bit now." We set off with a jolt as the driver let in his clutch. "God! He's going as if all the devils in Hell were after him", said Despard as he was thrown against me by a particularly violent jolt. Cohen, who had known action and wounds before, shouted through spasmodically clenched teeth, "So would you if you knew Ypres."

6

'WIPERS', Ypres, the Salient. It had to be held. Gaunt, echoing
streets, empty but for an occasional soldier, always hurrying. This
I was soon to know was a peculiarity of the Salient—no one in sight
other than the solitary hurrying figure; uncharacteristic were the
standing walls and masonry forming a pattern which made it
possible to speak, still, of streets. We were soon done with it and
were standing on the banks of the 'Canal'. Like 'Wipers' and
'Salient', the word needed no qualification.

These words have little meaning to anyone today, but as an
ancient this is the only way of making my voyage through time;
from now on it can be only to islands in the mists of memory.
Thus, though it must in fact have been dark as we stood there, a
few dream figures about to traverse a narrow causeway from one
bank to the other, a black puff uncurled in the sky and expanded like
the Japanese flowers of my childhood. "A woolly bear; they are
quite harmless. If the nose-cap hit you it would kill you, but as you
can see, the shell bursts about fifty feet in the air and it would be
very unlikely for any of the bits to damage anyone. No, they're
quite harmless."

The Canal was not the place for chat; we moved on impelled
partly by doubts of the harmlessness of woolly bears, but also by
the state of mind engendered by that dreadful place. Even now the
menacing streets of Ypres and this nightmare Canal can return
to me and leave a stain of foreboding on the brightest day.

We pushed on in silence till it became too dark to see more than
the mud at our feet in the light of gun-flashes. As we were to
continue the reconnaissance in daylight the next day, we returned
to our waiting lorries. They wasted no time on the journey home,
thankful to be getting out.

The scene in daylight had its peculiar horror, contrasting with
the blackness of night and the unknown it covered. We went in
twos, I with Quainton whose cheerfulness, though unspoken, was
a change from the more usual silliness with cliché and foul-
mouthed continuo. The sky for once was blue and cloudless, the

land a glistening ochre. There were in the distance some scattered stumps which we decided was a wood, since one was marked on the map. We were walking down a slope supposedly to the Steenbeck from which the ground rose to a series of gentle rounded slopes, one of which was Hill 40. The enemy line, between us and the hill which was to be my objective, was clearly marked on the map as a series of trenches in great depth, redoubts and machine gun posts, all in red and dated the previous day. It was meticulous and a marvel of the work done by the Royal Engineers. We walked on a duck-board track, shattered here and there by a recent shellburst. Otherwise there was nothing to be seen; no trenches, redoubts, fortifications or machines. Even so I had enough respect, never diminished, for the Royal Engineers, to know that what they had marked was not a flight of imagination, but a reality.

We stopped and sat on a piece of duck-board to study the map. As I fumbled with it I found my hands were trembling; I was exasperated to find I could not control them. I was grateful to Quainton that he seemed not to notice them. A sudden scream and almost instantaneous explosion made us both flatten out. The enemy had fired a salvo of three. We picked ourselves out of the mud as we realized the burst was some hundred yards away, in no sense dangerous. Then we noticed a group of three men between us and the shell bursts. They were standing; their teeth shone white in a mirthless grin; our reaction had been observed. I was too obsessed with fear of cowardice to avoid flushing with humiliation. We walked on with as much swagger as we could muster.

And now a fresh anxiety—where was the Steenbeck? At this time it was as deeply graven and marked in our minds as the fortifications were clearly delineated on the map. It was notorious as an obstacle that had presented an insuperable barrier to attack after attack of our armies which were supposed, on August 31st, to have swept on over it and beyond to 'open warfare' in what I had imagined were green fields where the German was to have suffered a blow from which he would never recover. It has now become at most a name without meaning except in the minds of a few old men.

We looked at the maps again. They were exact and clear; the cursed place where we stood was not. As far as one could see, even in the direction from which we had come, was a rolling desert of mud where shell-holes intersected shell-holes. We were in a hollow from which the ground sloped upwards; water trickled from one shell-hole to the next, or lay stagnant at the bottom.

Quainton asked one of the party of men with whom we had now drawn level where the Steenbeck lay. Still grinning inanely he pointed down to the quag where we stood. So, that was the Steenbeck. Quainton then asked where Hill 40 was. He continued to grin but said nothing.

Haig and his Staff have been blamed for thinking that such terrain was suitable for tanks, for not reconnoitring the ground personally, for not understanding the capacities and limitations of tanks. Well, we three *did* know the tanks and we were reconnoitring the ground on the spot. But I do not remember that any of us for a moment thought that a forty-ton tank could float; the mud must have seeped into the place where our minds were supposed to be. The army, of which we were part, was mindless. "One of these lumps", said Cohen vaguely indicating the horizon, "must be Hill 40. The German line is between us and them, about a hundred yards away." The slow quacking machine-gun note and some whining bullets were at once answered by a burst of rapid fire. "Lewis guns; too damned close for my liking. Come on, let's get out of it." Cohen with his wound stripe could dare to say this, but neither Quainton nor I could. The working party had disappeared. We had not seen them go and this intensified the sudden sense of loneliness. The sky darkened. "What about Hill 40?" I asked. "Look for it tomorrow", said Quainton sarcastically.

My anxiety to be gone made me particularly guilty about not having identified my objective. The ochreous slime, glistening, featureless, stretching for mile after pock-marked mile scared me. Some guns over on our right began to fire; more machine-guns, the slow German rhythm as from a squat animal, mingled with the faster hysterical chatter of our Vickers and Lewis. So this dead place *was* alive; this was what armies concentrated for battle looked like. "Come *on*", said Cohen. "Come on!" said Quainton. I was not afraid; I felt as if my nostrils quivered, scenting danger, watched by thousands of eyes, animal eyes like those in the Indian night of my childhood.

A man over to the right where the guns were firing was hurrying along a path; while I watched he disappeared. Then I noticed we were hurrying with short, quick, staccato steps. Later I realized that any figure, every figure, walked in the same way. Even our faces had become standard, strained, covered with a slimy sweat.

The ochreous mud became reddish. "*This* must be that blasted village we couldn't find." "Blasted is correct", said Cohen.

Things seemed to be livening up; many more guns were firing.

Machine-guns, five-nines—"What did you do in the Great War Daddy?... What are five-nines Daddy?... What..." "Oh, eat your damned bun..." I still feel I am in too much of a hurry to explain all that. And anyhow it is out of date; they do things better now. Even atom bombs, nuclear fission and such 'trash' have been replaced by... the successors to the human race, at present an unknown, undetected, but what we would call particularly dreadful disease.

But, to return to happier days—we were once more at the Canal. The woolly bears, great black question marks in the sky, were more frequent. "I hope we get across before they start shelling the bloody place properly with something harmful like HE." (Not His Excellency—High Explosive, you fool.)

7

IN the darkness we could just distinguish some remains—possibly
they had been sheds. English Farm they called it. This is where our
tanks were to rendezvous for the battle. The timing was exact and
we went on without having to wait for each other, but not before
some German bombers unloaded. Meant for us? Did the enemy
know of our impending attack, or was it just a routine raid on
English Farm because it was there? Then a star shell fell on our
route. We stopped instantly, or so we liked to think; no man
moved. The entire line of tanks, eight of them, was glistening,
brilliant metal against the velvety blackness of the night. It burned
on and on. What an age they took to open fire. Bayliss, at my side,
suggested they were just having a good laugh as they watched us,
standing to attention there like a lot of military dolts. We had not
recovered from our first bombing; dread of the immediate future
weighed heavily on our attempts at being carefree. No weight so
leaden as the weight of freedom from care. Perhaps Miss Whybrow
and Mrs Thompson had been right—I should have run away. Too
late, too late.

In another ten minutes we could not be affected by what
happened to English Farm. Suppose, though, the presence of the
tanks had given away the impending attack. It is difficult now to
believe that our anxieties were of so little substance.

The route we were pursuing now became jammed with traffic;
suddenly without warning troops came from nowhere. We waited.
Nothing happened. I ordered Allen to switch off the engine. On
that packed road no one spoke. Occasionally a mule whinnied or
harness jingled.

As I write these words I know that I have not forgotten what
happened that night at English Farm, what was going to happen on
the St Jean-Wieltje Road at Cambrai, at Amiens, in the 'train bleu'
after years in the black areas of a second world war; I see them still
in the watch fires of a thousand sleepless nights, for the soul goes
marching on.

"If the Boche start shelling we shall be for it." It was Quainton,

1897

1900 With his parents

1903 With his sister

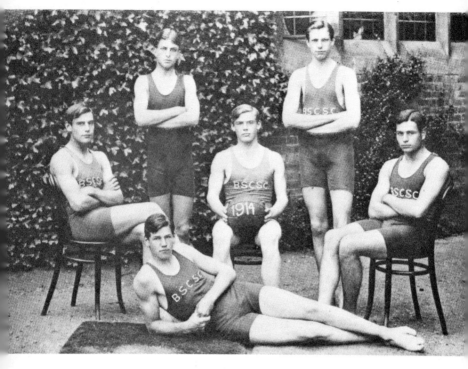

1914 School Water Polo Team (sitting right)

1915 School Football Team (back row second right)

1916

1978

1979

whose tank was some thirty yards behind mine, who had come up to see what was the matter. He had always had that kind of initiative and I envied him his easy, uninhibited way." I think I'll go forward and see what's up. After all, they told us this road would be kept clear for tanks."

"Don't be a fool", I whispered back, "If anything happens you may not be able to find your tank again."

Bagshaw came up. "What's up? We ought to get on." I told him I had no idea. Infantry, gunners, ammunition limbers were all stuck in a solid mass in the silence and darkness. Every so often a red spurt of sparks and an explosion marked the fall of an enemy shell. It was a quiet night, but for how much longer? I had visions of a chaos of plunging mules, overturned ammunition limbers, and above all, tanks with their ninety gallons of petrol aflame.

There was a sudden disturbance; a young staff officer had appeared. "You!"—he was speaking to me—"What the hell—is this your tank? What the devil do you think you're doing? Get on man! You should be at your starting points by now!"

"I can't sir...", I started to explain.

"Good God man!" he cut me short, "Drive through them! Push them off the road!" I realized I had fallen into some peace-time form of manners. "This is a *war*—get on!"

With sinking heart I told Allen to start the engine. We edged and pushed. A gun limber went over amid the curses of the team. "You fucking bastards!" they swore at us. I felt they were right. I tried to get off the track but the tank began a fearful slither into the mud. Allen stopped the skid with difficulty—only the fact that he was a fine driver made him able to do it—and we pushed, surrounded by curses and hate every foot of the way.

At any moment, I thought, the star-shell which must have discovered us at English Farm would flame out in a barrage to blow us all to hell. And then suddenly our guns opened up their preliminary barrage. All around us the mud became alive with the white flashes of our artillery. These were not field artillery—they were 6-inch howitzers in position fifty yards behind our front line. In a moment or two the enemy counter-barrage started. Our 'road', inevitably, was the target of their fixed lines, calibrated over the weeks, automatically registered. The nightmare was now fact. I signalled Allen to turn at right angles off the road. The shelling was now uniform, as heavy off the road as on it. Yet it was a comfort to feel we were not now a pre-determined target. At least I did know what was happening on that road.

I judged we had reached our starting point, signalled again to Allen and pointed our tank towards the 'hill' which somewhere in shell-illuminated night was our objective. The tank commander's private fear now possessed me—that I would fall wounded, unobserved by the crew and so be driven over by the tank. Just as I reached our side door a shell-burst blew me over. The door opened and my crew pulled me in and slammed the door to. "I thought you was a gonner sir", said Richardson. I worked my way to my seat in front next to the driver Allen. We shut off the engine; we had another forty minutes to go before zero.

With the engine's roar silenced we could appreciate the racket outside, like an inferno of slamming doors. And now I was aware of a novel sensation; the tank with which I was familiar as a solid mass of steel was shaking continuously like a wobbling jelly. No protection more solid than a figment of the imagination.

I was not aware of being afraid, which, from the point of view of comfort, is as good as not being afraid. The tank continued to wobble and the doors to slam; sometimes the slam and the wobble were instantaneous. When I realized that both violent slam and wobble occurred at intervals which were rhythmically connected, I knew we were very near the bursting point of a heavy shell. I felt we should move; there was nowhere to go.

Since it was dark the enemy were firing blind on their established barrage lines and, so far, we had not been hit. Could a shell fall short or over? It could—so I gave up thinking about it, thus taking shelter instinctively in mindlessness. Allen had nothing to do, but I could order Hayler and gunner Allen, a youngster whose face I could see by the dim interior light of the tank to be glistening with sweat, to get out with me and release the pigeon reporting our arrival at our starting point. I recorded the time and Hayler stolidly fixed the message to the container on the carrier's leg. With only five minutes to zero Hayler tossed it into the air. It promptly settled on the edge of a shell-hole and began to walk about. Exasperated, frustrated, we watched its deliberation. "If it's going to *walk* to HQ it will bring very stale news." "It's not daylight yet sir", Hayler reminded me. We started to throw clods of earth at the bird as if that would disturb a composure which could not be shaken by the now intense shell-fire. "I wish I had its bloody wings...", shouted Allen. "You want the best wings: we have them", it seemed to say.

It was nearly time. "Get in and start up", I ordered. The crew began to swing the starting handle. Nothing happened. Then, just as despair began to settle on us, the engine sprang to life with a roar.

Dawn; and we were moving into battle. Through the front flap I could see the contours of the 'hills' and that was all. We were in low gear; even at full power we could only lurch at a mile an hour from shell-hole to shell-hole. The tank began a list to the right. We could not correct it and the six-pounder gun filled with mud as it ploughed through, not over, the ground. The flying earth made it impossible for Allen or me to open the front observation flaps more than a thin slit. When I tried to use the periscope it was shot off.

Once, to our front and right, I saw the stumps of trees. It was a great relief as a wood was marked just to the right side of Hill 40. So far so good—if only the tank would right itself, but it would not. We were on rising ground, but with drainage gone the higher ground was a morass worse than the Steenbeck.

Should the staff have known? Of course; but nobody had told the Etonians, the Harrovians, the Public School Elite, that rain on a summit emerged at the surface just below the summit. Or had they—when I was not attending? In Geography class perhaps. No, that was only 'jute and flax' growing somewhere or other. Not on Hill 40. Where the hell was Hill 40?

It was time to try to check our direction. Opening my flap wider I was relieved to find the shattered trees more or less where, according to my guesses, they should have been. Bothered by chunks of earth each time I opened the flap at all widely I found it difficult to make my fleeting glances cohere. "Shells seem very close sir", screamed Allen in my ear. He was right. With the increasing daylight the rhythm of shells I had noted before we started had given way first to the drum-fire of zero hour, and then to something more discriminated. The enemy could see us and his artillery were aiming concentrated fire at us. He could not miss. Yet miss he did, and this contributed to the delusion of safety. And then I realized, in one of my repeated glances in the direction of the trees, that they were not trees but our infantry advancing in line with their rifles slung on their shoulders. I had imagined that infantry used their rifles for shooting; not so—not in Ypres Salient. Imaginary security; imaginary aggression? Yet men died.

8

WITH sinking heart I pulled out my map and looked at it. It was the same map so it was hardly surprising that it looked the same. But what the devil had it to do with the mud bath in which we wallowed? My hands were not now trembling although I was certain of death, probably of the whole crew, but certainly for Allen and myself. What happened in the back of the tank I left to Sergeant O'Toole, that brave, ugly man with red face and protruding eyes and the biggest protruding ears I had ever seen issue from the sides of a man's head. The first time he introduced himself to me as assigned as second-in-command to my crew he had stood as rigidly to attention as a knock-kneed man could and announced defiantly, his habitual expression, that he was an orphan.

Something heaved up in the middle of the tank with a grinding noise. I signalled to O'Toole. "Get out with Colombe and fix the unditching beam." The two clambered out—to certain death I thought. The huge balk of timber, iron shod, had to be belted to the tracks so that they were locked to revolve together carrying the beam round under the belly of the tank and giving the track additional purchase.

They did revolve but the tank did not budge an inch. The beam scooped the mud out from under the tank; we were digging ourselves deeper into the mud. A louder, more raucous grinding than before—"Transmission has gone", shouted Allen. The engine was racing, free-wheeling. He shut off the power. "Get out!" I ordered, and the whole crew tumbled into the mud. O'Toole yelled and pushed me away from the door. A bullet had spattered, missing my head. I had not heard it or been aware. The near miss they said, unlike the whining more distant bullet, made a loud crack—or killed you.

As I looked at my map and hands in the tank I felt I was floating about four feet above my self, Allen an interested and unfrightened spectator. This dis-association, de-personalization was a way of achieving security—spontaneous, automatic, but potentially costly as it involved not knowing of the imminence of death.

132

We formed, according to our training, a 'strong point'. We scattered in a rough line between the tank and the position in which we thought the enemy lay. We had our Lewis guns and ammunition. If rifles were not used by the infantry, what could we do with our guns? If I knew where the enemy, or even Germany, was we could have fired in that direction. I got out my compass. I could hardly believe my eyes when I saw we were facing in the wrong direction. Luckily for us I retrieved some capacity for scepticism; it delayed me enough for suspicion to ripen into certainty that the compass was disturbed by the mass of steel of the tank. We crouched in our shell-holes, fiddled with our guns to see the mud had not clogged them. Morning passed to golden afternoon; the sun came out, the gunfire seemed less and our tank, now sinking out of sight without help from the unditching beam, no longer attracted gunfire.

"Triplanes!" They were said to be Royal Navy reconnaissance machines. We showed our identity by putting our three discs on the ground. The planes, we had been told, would thus learn of our position. It seemed a miracle that they were not hit by the shells which, though fewer, were hailing down on us and must be weaving, with those of our guns, an invisible pattern in the air. "Shouldn't think they will see these things or our tank", said Colombe. "I would have other things to think about if I were up there." Indeed, their loops, dives, steep climbs into the sky looked more like an exercise in evasion of an unseen enemy than a part of our life.

It was now 12.30; I could have believed we had been there timelessly. There was nothing to see but the unchanging mud, the faces of my crew, the spotless sheen of the guns contrasting incongruously with our caked uniforms and filth. There was no doubt of it now—the gunfire was less. Richardson produced some photos of his wife and children for me to look at. He was the grandfather of the crew—thirty-eight, twice my age, and much older than the rest of us. His wife, motherly looking woman, and the two rather lumpish children were displayed with pride, discoursed upon in detail and in confidence of a sympathetic hearing—I did not know why. Now I suspect it was more out of a feeling of compassion for my youth and inexperience than belief in me. Could anyone, outside a public-school culture, believe in the fitness of a boy of nineteen to officer troops in battle?

I had no idea what was to happen next. No one said anything about tanks sinking in the mud or men like trees walking—except in religion. Battle orders I wanted—not Bible stories. There came a time when I began to feel that religion could likewise do with battle orders and fewer fairy stories: God is too much of a devil to be dealt with by the fairy stories of Birmingham business men. Krishna made Arjuna see that long ago. Would nobody tell *me* what to do?

Richardson fell silent. We watched the wastes of mud. Nothing, nothing, nothing. 'We are Fred Karno's Army, What bloody use are we?'—the words of one of our marching ditties seemed to fit our situation. "And, boys and girls", said the parson, fresh from a conducted tour of the front at government expense, as he warmed to the peroration of his children's sermon, "what do you think they were singing? All those brave marching men" (not sentimental Sunday school softies as you might think, but soldiers) "were singing, 'The Church's one foundation is Jesus Christ our Lord'."

"Sir!" It was Sergeant O'Toole, asking permission to speak; battle or no battle, the conventions, the rules must be observed. "Yes sergeant?" "I think things are livening up over there." His voice was urgent.

They were indeed; a flurry of figures, the first I had seen since the early morning 'wood' had appeared; some seemed to stumble. "I think they are our chaps retiring sir!" They were about a hundred yards in front and slightly to the left. Had I managed to direct the tank to the wrong side of the hill? German machine-guns were now joined by the rapid high-pitched note of ours. Down came our barrage and the whole inferno broke. Cursing our luck we 'stood to' our guns.

An officer appeared and ducked down by my side. "B Company? Your orders are to withdraw to forward Company HQ", he shouted.

"Oughtn't we to stay—Lewis guns, plenty of ammunition."

"Do what you bloody well like—I've told you the orders." He was cross. So was I. Why the devil start arguing? I wanted to be cleared out; the Angel of Mons itself could not have been more welcome than this apparition. In 1940 it would have been said he was a German spy dressed as an officer, causing the gallant armies to fall back.

The officer had gone. I knew—I still know—I should have stayed, orders or no orders. Even junior officers are supposed to show initiative. "Come on chaps!" I yelled, waving them back. Breathless, hot, worn out, we got back to the Advanced HQ in a German pill-box. Victories, said Churchill after the terrible defeat in Malaya, are not won by retreats however glorious.

Despard, a tank commander rather older than the rest of us, was waiting to go in. A bullet, God knows from where, hit him in the belly. He sank down.

"What's up?" I asked. I was surprised; more surprised still when he said he was "finished". The pallor of his face increased.

"I knew it. When that bloody... magpie... came this... morning", he gasped, "I knew my number was up."

I felt stunned. I could not think what to say to this queer fatalistic Irishman. How could he possibly be convinced, as he was, that a magpie was more obviously the cause of death than a bullet? He died some two hours later.

I was called in to the Company Commander and saluted. "Despard has just been shot sir."

De Falbe looked pained. "Nothing serious I hope."

"He thinks he's dying sir."

"Dear me, dear me. Poor fellow."

The pill-box was relatively quiet though the door-slamming went on and the rat-tat-tat of machine-guns reminded one that the front must be near—if a bullet could kill a man it must have been fired from nearby.

"Sit down my dear chap." The major's voice was soothing. "What a pity; such a nice chap too. You did say Despard, didn't you?"

"Despard sir."

"Yes, yes of course. That's what I thought you said. I'm not deaf you know. Have some port my dear fellow."

On the table shone half a dozen beautiful port glasses of a size unknown to me. He was—had he been an ordinary officer—what I would have called 'drunk'. But the fruity voice, the gentle, melancholy tones, were no different from what they ever were. How like the White Knight in *Alice* he was.

"Thank you sir."

"What? What did you say?"

"I said 'Thank you sir'."

"Don't mention it my dear fellow. Now, we must get on. Where was I? Oh yes. But do have some port first won't you? Sergeant, just pop out and see what it's like will you?" He leant confidentially towards me. The blast as the door opened and shut again prompted his next remark. "Very rough night. Doesn't do to have these chaps hanging around when we have secret stuff to discuss. Now, tell me, what was it like?"

I told him, and explained that I had lost my tank. He nodded sympathetically.

"I knew it was rough. I was afraid it would be."

I said I regretted having had to withdraw during the counter-attack and after we had formed a strong-point. He was getting bored. So was I. I felt I was beginning to believe we really had formed a strong-point.

"It was really very good."

"What was sir?"

"The strong-point."

"Not really sir." I was trying to struggle back to the world of fact.

Was my Company Commander drunk? These 'old seasoned casks', as Mrs Jorrocks said, are not easily made drunk. I had not—then or since—known what it is to be seized by the joy of battle; taken 'by the throat' as Julian Grenfell described it. My sense of reality made me too leaden-footed even to run away.

Mercifully the Major's boredom and my fatigue asserted themselves. "My dear boy, you must be tired out. Get back to camp now. Carter, get these chaps to camp."

Carter drew me aside. "Tomorrow the brigade intelligence officer will be interviewing you. Your chaps are in the trench outside. Get them together back to the Canal. There should be a lorry there—if it hasn't been blown up."

Outside I thought the shelling, though heavy, was less than it had been. Our bedraggled and exhausted band stumbled together and shuffled off towards the track leading to the Canal rendezvous. It had become lighter. Just time, I thought, to get to the track before dark—maybe even to the Canal.

Harrison, Quainton's driver, had attached himself because Quainton and his crew, also without their tank but otherwise intact, had gone off in front of us without him. About ten minutes later we saw them a hundred yards or so in front. We could not catch up. In fact, as we stumbled and floundered with our heavy loads of guns, ammunition and equipment from one water-logged shell-hole to the next, I felt increasingly afraid that we could not get to the track. Dread of spending the night in that bog made me drive myself and the crew desperately to reach the track, now an incredibly long fifty yards in front. I relieved Allen of his load which was now beyond his strength.

At last; we threw ourselves onto the duck boards while it was still light. I decided to check our direction by compass; to my amazement the compass showed I was about to lead the crew back to the enemy lines. Unable to think and with no one to ask I followed the compass instead of my sense; it was an age before I was assured that I had been right to do so.

We were joined by a couple of tommies escorting some half dozen prisoners who were carrying two stretchers with wounded. Harrison, without any warning, broke under the strain; he had seen the Germans. "You bloody bastards", he screamed. "You bastards, you killed my brother." He had drawn his revolver and was blazing away at the stretcher party. Luckily O'Toole and I managed to disarm him, still fighting violently. We got him down and two others pinioned his arms with webbing belts from our equipment. He was frothing at the mouth. No one had been hit and his ammunition was exhausted. I stuffed his revolver, empty, into my pocket.

After some minutes he stopped struggling; the fit seemed to have passed. I told O'Toole to keep by him and not let him out of his sight. When we had re-loaded ourselves we all stumbled on, Harrison morose and sullen with his hands tied. Somehow we found the lorry and scrambled in. I managed to count our party, found the numbers correct, gave the all-clear and off we went with the usual jolt which threw us into a jumbled heap on the floor. I suppose we slept, but beyond the jolting and rattling I knew little more till the driver said we were at the camp.

9

THE Intelligence Officer sat on one side of the table and I sat facing him. "Can you show me whereabouts your tank got stuck?" It sounded simple, but though it was early afternoon I seemed incapable of thought. I said it was a bit to the right of Hill 40, that is, east of it—or was it west? It could be...

He waited patiently, "Here, show me on the map."

Obviously it could not be west—it would be in the German lines. Nor east, because we would not have got into action. But, come to think of it, I was not sure we *had* got into action. I kept thinking of my shell-hole which I shared with a corpse from a previous engagement.

"Here", I said with a wobbly finger.

"Or", he said with scarcely concealed sarcasm, "possibly here... perhaps?"

I agreed that it was very likely. The corpse was lying andrews-cross-wise. It was thin, dessicated, not blown-up, and the green skin was stretched tight like parchment over the bones of the face.

"Sir?" He was asking me something.

"I said, did you notice when the alluvial changed to the cretaceous?"

I could hardly believe my ears. "I didn't notice any change", I said truthfully.

"There seems to be general agreement about *that*." I was unable to interpret his intonation. Anyhow I was not alone; the fellow in the shell-hole had his mouth wide open, the skin stretched—*by* the mouth? Or did the tight skin pull it open? It—or was it 'he'?—didn't stink, for which I was thankful.

"You say the tank sank out of sight?"

I considered this. "No, it sank level with the ground. You could probably see it if you stood up."

"But... didn't you *look* at it before you went?"

"Not standing sir. I had nearly been shot through the head just before."

"Well, yes, I suppose there is always the risk of that... in battle I mean."

I was getting cross. "This was supposed to be a battle... sir", I added.

He looked at my face for a moment and then studied his map. At last he said, indicating that the interview was over, "Well, thank you very much. I think that will do... Oh, by the way, did you see any infantry?"

I said they had been falling back when we left—a small bunch of them under counter-attack. "Here, pretty well on the top of the hill, a bit to the left I should say."

"Ah! That's very interesting". It must have been my only intelligible remark. I saluted and left.

The Intelligence Officer was Clough Williams Ellis whom I was to meet after the war when he designed the War Memorial to our school dead. At this meeting in 1916 he could hardly have failed to realize that I was typical of the damned fools that were made combatant officers. We were not impressed by our highly intelligent staff, or I might have congratulated him on the arrangements for the blockage on the St Jean-Wieltje Road. No fool could have arranged the battle I had just seen for myself.

Cohen met me outside. As always he was pallid, skin drawn tight—oh God, not that again—sweating and tense. Seeing my face he laughed.

"What did he say? I liked the bit about the alluvial didn't you? Or didn't he ask you?"

We joined a small group. Despard was the only casualty. Cohen and Stokes, both twenty-two and so much more experienced than the rest of us, were exchanging notes on the 'show', 'stunt' or, as I hoped, 'battle'. Broome, pink, baby-faced and foul-mouthed, joined us. His eyes wide open and innocent, he described how he had tripped over a bit of barbed wire.

"Before I knew what had happened I began to slither into this ruddy shell-hole. Must have been a 9.2—huge, filled with water. I didn't stop till I was up to my waist. It stank—full of arms and legs and blown-up bellies. I tell you, it was a kind of human soup."

"Liar", said Stokes.

"It's gospel truth I tell you; if you don't believe me ask my batman—he's just had to throw my uniform away—the whole lot—it stinks so awful. Kind of horrible sweet..."

"Oh shut up for Christ sake. We don't want to hear about your swimming gala."

"I tell you, it's absolutely true." He was getting annoyed. "The belly was ripped open and the guts..."

"Stank—they usually do", said Cohen crisply.

"But—" expostulated Broome.

"Oh, put a sock in it. Shut up—we don't want to hear about your battle. What did you do with your tank?" Stokes tried to stop the flow.

"It blew up. Direct hit."

"A direct hit?," said Stokes incredulously. "What happened to the crew?"

"Dead", Broome simpered. He began to snuffle and wiped away a tear.

"What's the joke?" asked Carter joining in.

"There's no joke. These silly bastards don't believe..."

"How did you get out if the whole crew was killed?"

"I don't know."

"You were having your soup—swim I mean—I suppose."

"Well, that was afterwards... I think... I caught my foot in the barbed wire and before I could stop I was slithering waist deep into this sort of human..."

"Oh God! You've started him off again." Cohen, Quainton and I had had enough and drifted away. "Do you know", said Cohen, "I really believe that little bastard is speaking the truth."

"He's got the story pretty pat. We can find out—I'll ask in the orderly room about his crew."

It was true; they were dead—'missing', they called it, 'believed killed'.

One day, years after the war, I was swimming at a popular road house and was accosted by another swimmer. He had recognized me, but it took me a moment or two before there emerged from out of the matrix of the firm businessman's face the pink baby-face of Broome.

"Those days of the war—when I look back at them", he said, "were the happiest days of my life."

"Impossible!" I replied.

"They were. I enjoyed every moment of it."

Every moment; fancy that. I really believe that prosperous businessman was speaking the truth.

"How's Harrison?" I asked Quainton.

"Oh, he's all right. He's simmered down again. Sorry you had all that fuss. I don't know how he didn't see us going off. I should have noticed that he wasn't in the party. Talking of parties, here's the *Daily Mail*. Do you think the papers will mention the show?"

"How about 'We carried out some adjustment of our line', or 'We took X-thousand prisoners and reached all our objectives'? I haven't a clue what happened but I did see about half a dozen prisoners."

"And we seem to have captured a lot of mud", Quainton replied, "even if it's only what I've got on my uniform. I think I'd better see what Perkins has done about it." He went off to find his batman.

Cohen came up; he and I started to walk off down the road outside the camp when an orderly said the Major wanted to see me.

"Oh Bion, sorry, but I've got bad news for you I'm afraid. Will you take your crew up the line this evening and see if you can bring your tank back? It wasn't knocked out when you left was it? We are supposed to salvage any tank we sent into action."

"Sir, I don't think we can do it without special equipment—it's buried in mud, up to the roof before we left." I was going on to tell him that the transmission had gone too and even if we could dig it out something would have to tow it back, when my eye caught the expression on the face from which the soothing tones and quiet voice proceeded. His moustache drooped, his face was flabby, but his green eyes were hard. This unmilitary figure had always frightened me.

"I know my dear boy"—he still frightened me—"Silly isn't it?" As he spoke he reminded me of the soothing, almost oleaginous tones of the parson—he of the 'and-what-do-you-think-they-were-singing?' infamy—when he pronounced the words, 'Hear what comfortable words Our Lord saith'. ("I know dear boy, something humorous I think—with boiling oil in it.") I thought it best to hold my tongue.

"Don't risk the lives of your men", he added, "If the fire is too heavy come back."

I saluted and went out. The aristocratic—and he was aristocratic—alcoholic—and he was alcoholic—is not to be treated with the sort of familiarity which one might dare to assume with a man-eating tiger.

"What luck?", asked Cohen who had waited for me.

"Going to fetch the tank back."

"Mind you don't get your feet wet—I should take an umbrella if I were you."

I went to rout out Sergeant O'Toole.

10

THE lorry was waiting, so was the Canal, so was Number 5 Infantry Track. I was disappointed to see it was an unmistakably quiet night. If we found the tank again… what? We could beat it with shovels so the enemy would open fire. "We got there sir, but the enemy fire was so heavy they beat us off it every time…" But in fact I was too green to think of it. Later one became more of a veteran liar.

This time our journey was easier. We had only revolvers, the heavy service Colts, and little ammunition instead of those Lewis guns which seemed both flimsy and made of lead. At one point the ground became dark and lumpy; there were men resting or sleeping—a relief party.

A lump detached itself and came up to me. "Who are you?" it said. I told him. "And you?" "Number 17XY battery—gunners." "What's it like forward—do you know? He told me it was very quiet. Of course I could see that for myself. In any case we were on one of the well-worn infantry tracks so clearly marked by the duck boards that the enemy gunners had registered it weeks ago. If it were not 'very quiet' the track would be spouting with high explosive and the air above whining.

The clouds parted and a shaft of moonlight revealed us momentarily to each other. "Good God! It's you Bion isn't it?" "Bonsey! E. K. Bonsey!" I remembered him at school, a couple of years older than I, studious, wearing spectacles; I neither liked nor disliked him.

Now, sixty years later, that momentary moonlight contact is etched on my mind. We walked a few yards. In the quiet a groan came from the mud in the distance, followed by a cry further off. I was listening—but not to Bonsey. How queer! Like marsh birds, innumerable bitterns mating. Or perhaps, a more comfortable vision, the moonlit plain near Avignon bathed in light, alive with the cheerful songs of nightingales spreading a web of sound.

"What's that?" I said—as if I didn't know!

"I was just telling you", he said, exasperated. "Don't go off this track. You may get wounded, or just sprain an ankle and you will sink into the mud and drown. No one will ever find you. Listen!"

We did. Sometimes it stopped for a minute or so and then the chorus broke out again, not raucous or crude—gentle. Dante's Inferno—but how much better we do these things now.

"Do you mean no stretcher bearer gets them?"

"No stretcher bearer would be such a fool. *Your* unit might save you, the regimental stretcher bearers. Haven't you heard of the RAMC? The Rob All My Comrades boys?"

Of course I had—and have many times since, particularly from the RAMC itself which is determined that the particular stain should not be forgotten by its members, though it cannot turn it into an honour like the spats of the Royal Highlanders, or the muzzle on the Bear of the Warwick family.

"Shut up! Shut up! you noisy sods, you bleeding pieces of Earth."

But they didn't; and they don't. And still the warning voices sound in answer to the sufferers of bereavement, depression, anxiety. "Don't go off the beaten track. Don't do as the psych-o-analysts do. Haven't you heard? Pay Stills Your Conscience Here. Don't go off the beaten Church. Remember Simon Magnus. Leave your mind alone. Don't go down the Unconscious Daddy: Let the Gold Mine come up to you." How wise! How very wise!

Those guns would *not* fire. "Good-bye old man", we said to each other. "Good-bye! See you in Peace-time!" What morale! What poppycock!

We trudged on. Now, not for the first time, I wonder why. It was most unlikely we could find the tank; if we could there was nothing to do. Eight men cannot lift forty tons of steel out of the mud. You can't win a war by retreating, said Churchill. But you can't win a war with a bullet through your head. And yet I knew a very cheerful man who had a bullet just there—through his brain. It must have been the only place where it cannot have done any harm.

Some shells fell; it shut out that damned groaning. I called to O'Toole, "What the hell are we doing here sergeant? You saw that bloody tank!"

He gave the matter some thought. "No idea sir." At least he remembered to say "sir".

"Sergeant, that is the fourth shell I've heard fall in the last five minutes. It is too much. We must not risk the lives of our men. At any moment the place will be aflame. My orders to you are to fall in the crew and march back."

"Very good sir."

It seemed like bravado: it seemed like common sense; a combination which was a luxury indeed.

I thought I would have a last word with Bonsey on the way back, but he had been killed. Requiescat in Pace—"See you in Peace-time old man". I was shocked; I was shocked to find I did not care. I was to become more familiar with the intense comradeship of war, every scrap of gesture, intonation, etched apparently indelibly. A week later it was over and yet not so. One still seemed to know the stout heart, but the name, the history, the parts that lay outside the limits of time and space where he entered into the sphere of one's own life, they did not exist. Married? Single? How many children? Military Cross I see; university graduate. Father as rich as Croesus since he is head of that firm. Accounts for his uniform. *Nice chap.*

Married? Not yet. Related to that Celebrated Swindler. His father? Really! What does it feel like to have a Dad who's in gaol? Shut up—or you'll say it aloud. Doesn't even wonder if I've heard of his Dad the notorious swindler. But—savoir faire. Fine presence. Hello, hullo, hulLO! What are those nobs under his tunic? Well, I'm damned! A steel waistcoat! Of course, if your father is a notorious swindler he can afford to buy toys like that. I didn't know they made them now. Perhaps he had it made specially—by another swindler of course, because it would not keep out any ordinary bullet. No more use than the ordinary prayer books and Bibles which are always keeping bullets out according to the press. I'd rather wear my Bible over my shins or my balls. Obviously officer material—and anyhow, think of the row the press baron would make if he didn't get a commission. Promoted at once— tank commander! Such an outstanding fellow. Promoted again—company commander! Such an outstanding officer—must send him home to organize a new brigade. We want men of experience. England, Flu and Dooty. Dead in a week—the 'flu got through the waistcoat. Nice chap. *Shifty as hell.*

I did not see the Major when I got back; he had had to go to HQ. He saw me the next day and was kindness itself. When I told him of how we had been unable to get through the barrage he said, without a trace of sarcasm, "Ah yes, I was afraid you would." Where did he think the barrage was? "No good risking the lives of highly trained men. I am glad you used your judgement." He looked at some papers—some officers thought he kept these papers especially for looking at. I saluted. "Goodbye dear boy—crew in good heart?" "Yes sir."

For my part I had learned to keep a crew who wore their good hearts on their sleeves—for inspection, part of their kit like boots or blankets. I went out wondering why that man made me sweat with fear; perhaps he could see the 'very heavy barrage' far better than I could.

11

ON an exercise march a few days later we came under shell-fire. A lorry in front of us was picked up and thrown into the ditch; one man was killed, but the driver escaped. After the march was over I saw Harrison had been on the parade.

"How did he get on?" I asked Quainton.

"Oh he's all right. When we were passing the lorry he shouted at the driver leaning against the upturned engine, 'What's up chum? Won't it go?' He's back to his usual."

"What was all that about his brother?"

"Well, apparently he thought he was a great hero and he got done in at Gheluvelt. He's been sore about it ever since."

Harrison came up just then, pink, bony-faced and upturned nose. He saluted me and said, "Sorry about all that fuss the other day sir. I was upset."

"You upset *us*. Never mind—try upsetting the German army next time. Those were unarmed prisoners you know."

He looked downcast and examined his boots. "All right—off you go—but don't do it again." The sound of my voice impressed and reassured me.

I felt no such assurance about that battle, but according to the press a few days later we had made big gains in guns and taken three thousand prisoners. Well, that was a comfort at least. Not so my discovery that, as I suspected, I was a coward and that there was no chance of running away—while observed. But what if there was no one to see? Then no one could say you were lying. Oh shut up! My conscience was dying, but like the Dead it would not lie down.

I did not realize that fear was an irrelevance; there is no question of being able to 'run away' in so far as such an expression is related to muscular activity. That there are other expressions of fear was brought home to me by one ludicrous and painful event.

Cohen, Quainton and I had had some talk of religion and prayer. Both of them were religious, even fervent as I had been until the powerful effect of school services and those conducted by our parson ate deep into my soul. But after our talk I decided to make a public affirmation of my faith. About half a dozen of us slept in one officers' marquee. Cohen and Quainton used to kneel publicly with the support of Gatehouse our company commander who was huge, an ex-boxing champion of Sandhurst and used to bending his powerful frame in devotion. I was not so lucky and the ritual was something of a strain. Still, down I flopped. The absolute lack of comment or ribaldry left a gap which was immediately filled with an emotion which might have been solid. I found I had nothing whatever to say to My Saviour who, I felt, shared in the general stupefaction. There were some surprises to which even the Almighty should not be subject.

How to get up? Obviously I could not stay there on my knees all night. I could not pretend I had been doing up my boots because I had no boots on. I got up. Never, never again, I vowed, would I make such an utter fool of myself. My fellows would not even believe I had 'wind up' at the prospect of fighting, for despite my preoccupations I was not usually regarded as that kind of person.

The previous night the Prince of Wales had dined with the Major, Gatehouse, and Gull the adjutant of the battalion who introduced him as an old friend of his. The Colonel also had been present. Gull was an intelligent man, but liable to talk with a peculiar nasal bleat when mentioning Royalty. He wore very shiny boots and well-cut breeches.

This evening the mess, separated from the main tent by a canvas partition, was the scene of an altercation. Gull was speaking; then the Major; Gull again; and then the angry voice of Gatehouse. "If you say the Prince's name again I shall thrash you." We pricked up our ears and I at least regretted that I could not see beyond the screen. Again Gull's voice, still somewhat nasal; something about "an old and dear friend of my Oxford days". "Damn Oxford!"—this was Gatehouse—"and all the rest of your arse-licking sycophants!" Then the Major's oily voice; the quarrel stopped at once, but the Major's voice had not sounded emollient, however oily.

Gull diminished now that there were no battalion parades and no call for shiny boots; the Colonel too seemed redundant for much the same reason. But God? I thought that most people would assume that my precipitate raid on religion had been a flight from fear. In fact fear, real fear, seemed to diminish the God, in whom I sincerely thought I believed, to colonel-size vestments, rituals, like tossing up for innings before a cricket match—impressive to the elite who knew the importance of shiny boots.

The time for heart-searchings, religious and others, was suddenly cut short by strong rumours that the battalion was to go into action. By the afternoon the rumour was certainty. I vowed that this time not even the Angel of Mons in person would cause me to clear out of the battlefield. I would keep my mouth shut and use my judgement about forming strong points, retreating, returning to HQ.

We had drawn new tanks the previous day. Mine appeared to have something wrong with it so the crew sweated feverishly and continuously to get it into perfect condition. The 6-pounders were overhauled; the Lewis guns cleaned and oiled till the whole shone like sombre jewellery. Every scrap of ammunition was sized, that is, dropped into the barrel to see that it fitted and rejected if it did not. Short of firing there was nothing more we could do to be sure we had none of the defective American ammunition.

As we slaved and sweated I wondered if this battle would be for another invisible hill made of mud, or whether the staff had found a dry patch somewhere. At last all the chores were done. As near perfect as maybe but for one thing—the tank would not go. The engine would start perfectly and would move the tank for a hundred yards, though with a seeming lack of zest. Then, backfires, overheating, *stop*. Obviously a timing defect, so we retimed it. The Major turned up and watched our feverish efforts. Had I not by this time learned better I would have assumed that he was captivated by the spectacle of our enthusiasm. Then he drew me aside.

"You are not preparing for action are you?" I admitted, somewhat surprised, that we were. "Oh my dear fellow—quite right of course, ready for action at any time and any place, quite right—but er... you don't mean this show?"

I was furious; as relieved as hell and furious to find I was so relieved.

"You see, your lot have already been in action, so Bagshaw's and Clifford's sections will be in reserve. Of course that means you won't be called on for action."

It was like a tug-of-war when the opponents suddenly let go; there I was—on my bottom. When I had recovered we went on fooling with the engine. Then I boiled up and went to see the Major to protest at being left out of the action. It was, in its way, nearly as bad as saying my prayers. My keenness was terrific; the Major's appreciation of my keenness was also terrific. When I finally left I felt as if I had been taking part in a little dramatic dialogue. "You know that I know that you know that I know the whole thing is a lot of damned humbug." Perhaps there was a shade of a shadow of doubt in the Major's mind. Was it possible that the extreme youth and stupidity of one of his junior officers was reducing him to enthusiasm? If he had any such disturbing doubt he soon recovered. Not so myself. I had resolved to do or die and felt as if the tombstone had been suddenly withdrawn from under me—a most undignified posture in which to find oneself.

The rest of the battalion went into action; same mud, same non-existent objectives, same victory, but a different lot of names. Their name liveth for evermore. "If I should die, think only this of me..." wrote Rupert Brooke. "You did and we don't", ran the postscript of the second war on the heroes of the first.

12

THE conditions for the further employment of tanks at Ypres were demonstrably so unsuitable that we began to feel we should not be used there again. The last battalion attacks had hardly been able to flounder into danger. Our casualties in men turned out to be slight. Nevertheless I had one more jaunt, a reconnaissance of the Poelkappelle-Pashendaele front. By that time I was sufficiently angry and fed up to condemn in plain English the bit of the project on which it was my business to report.

And now officially-originated rumours began to circulate; we were to prepare for a new battle on ground 'suitable for tanks'. We were given special maps of our area printed without names. We were to rehearse on land similar to that on which we were to fight; we were not to know our accompanying troops till the rehearsal; above all we were not to talk. The last injunction has by this time become a grim joke with reference to the Royal Navy as the Silent Service. Certain actions co-ordinated with the Royal Navy had become, first, topics for fascinated and fascinating women to discuss in luxurious hotels and clubs, and next, matters of serious concern to the German secret service and staff. For these the Army paid in blood. "If tea is the price of Admiralty, Lord God, we'll pay in blood."

The section and tank commanders of the battalion were taken by car to some country of chalk downland. We waited at a cross-roads at the bottom of a declivity; on higher ground was a small group of officers including Gull and the Colonel "wearing a French letter", as someone said about his transparent raincoat. He was as usual immaculate. Sometimes such dress is an expression of the personality; sometimes a substitute for a personality that is not there. There are times when it is imperative to know which is which. I think most of us would have endorsed the views of Yates: in England it seemed to matter; now, seeing the group on the crest the old aura still clung, but it was diminished. The 'fine' face, the handsome regular features, the clipped military moustache, the haughty demeanour and studied negligence of his pose were not sufficiently often displayed; yet too often to be safe from revisions of estimate. Later that day he was to lecture the division's officers on tanks and tank warfare. Of this he knew less than our Major; he lacked the tough ruthlessness of our alcoholic. There was, when I went to the Royal Naval Barracks at Chatham for my gunnery course, a story of a destroyer captain, one of the Dover Patrol, who was reputed to be in a state of permanent alcoholic stupor. The harbour entrance was notoriously dangerous and difficult to enter or leave. It was made more difficult because the war meant that ships had to leave without warning, without fail, at any hour of day or night and without regard to the weather. The naval men said the captain was the only officer who could enter or leave without any possibility of error. Having done this immediate chore no one would dream of asking him to do anything more—he would return to his stupor. Our Major had a similar gift.

This morning he was present, jolly, rubicund, at peace with himself and the world. The fresh November morning seemed an incongruous setting for him. Yet he had a Bacchus-like quality. He exuded an aroma of old port which civilized the rude rusticity of the scene, pervaded it rather than subdued it.

"Hullo Quainton dear boy", he said affectionately, like the Duchess when she met Alice in her 'and-the-moral-of-*that*-is...' mood. "Do I hear something?" His eyes twinkled.

"Sounds like bagpipes to me sir."

"It *is* bagpipes", he said archly, putting his finger to his lips. "Listen!"

It was faint but clear, the skirl of pipes coming nearer. Over the crest there presently appeared the first files of marching men, battalion after battalion of kilted troops.

We watched the rhythmical sway of the kilts as the battalions went by. Nothing was said, for we all knew who they were. In that war the 51st Division, Highland Territorials, had won a reputation second only to the Guards. In their own opinion, and many could be found to share it—even amongst the enemy—they ranked even higher. For steadiness and reliability the Guards, as we ourselves were soon to see, could not be matched. But the virtue that was their strength also led to the defect of rigidity in some situations where the flexibility of the 51st would have been more valuable.

The music of the pipers was extremely moving. Whatever gibes can be levelled at the pipes no one as near to action as we were could possibly deny their heartwarming power. We had already learned in our very slight and brief experience that our lives depended on the stout hearts of the infantry who were in action with us. The coming battle was to bring this home to the Commander-in-Chief himself. We watched in silent relief the troops who would be in action with us. The 51st Division? Someone meant business—at last!

We rehearsed. Our part was to provide small flag parties to represent tanks. At the end of the day officers and NCO's of the division, with some sixty officers of our battalion, assembled in a long hut for our Colonel's lecture.

As always he looked the part. We, his battalion officers, must have changed since our days in Bovington. The magic of his uniform had lost its potency; we listened with attention diverted from his looks to the content of what he said. But after the revelation, at the start, that he did not know what guns a tank carried, we listened no more. We were consoled by the thought that in action the Colonel had nothing to do.

Afterwards he picked out Quainton, a favourite of his, to speak—ostensibly to display his soldierly comradeship, but I who stood near felt he was looking for reassurance. Quainton seemed embarrassed; I shared his feeling.

The day was over. Exhilarated and expectant we returned to our gloomy, muddy camp. We could not and did not say, even to each other, what we had learned on our day's outing.

I routed out O'Toole. How about the tank? Was the trouble sorted out? O'Toole was gloomy. It was as bad as ever. Alarmed and disappointed I said, "But Sergeant, it is obvious that the timing is the trouble." He went over the symptoms in detail. "It cannot possibly be anything else!" "I know sir. We have checked it up completely; at least six times. It came out the same each time. After a hundred yards it would be red-hot, back-firing. No life in the engine at all—and then—stop! The crew are tired out."

The next morning confirmed his report. Allen the driver and I went through it all. There was nothing more we could do. Orders came through that we were to entrain that night for our unknown destination. In desperation I told O'Toole to ask the workshop officer to come. Luckily for once he had no other job and came round immediately after lunch.

Williams was a wiry, wizened man, no soldier, but an engineer to his finger tips. He was cheerful and reassuring.

"Well old man, what's the trouble?" He listened intently as I told him the story in detail, missing nothing. "Well, thank God! I

thought it was something serious. It's obvious—the timing's wrong."
I told him about the timing.

"I'm sorry old boy, it's obvious. You've just made a balls-up of
it." He spoke with the pitying superiority and confidence of the
engineer talking to the usual amateur bunch of boobies. But I
wasn't going to let him go.

"Would you mind checking up on it yourself?" He was a good
sort.

"Well, I haven't anything to do for once. Give me a spanner",
and he set to work while we stood round and acted as assistants.

To my secret relief he found no obvious mistake in our work. He
seemed a bit less assured when he had finished. "Now—give her
another try."

At that moment the order came to entrain. "Never mind; I'll
come with you and we can check it as we go."

It was about a mile to the railhead, but I remember little of the
journey. I spent it watching the engine anxiously. Its behaviour was
an exact repetition of its previous performance. It had no guts, it
became hot, backfired and after about a hundred yards we dared
not drive further and switched off. Williams looked anxious.
"Never mind. Get it onto the train and we will see to it at the other
end."

It was touch and go whether we could reach the train before it
had to steam off. We did—because we were so late we were out of
order and drove up the ramp onto the last truck. It was just as well
for otherwise we should have had to drive almost the length of the
train and though it was easy I always hated the sensation of driving
on an unstable platform of flat trucks marshalled end to end, just
wide enough for the tanks and their tracks, but often with an inch
of the latter overhanging.

It was still light when the train left. Any reconnaissance
plane—and there were plenty at the Salient—could and probably
did see us. But in the hour before night fell they would not be able
to find out any more about our destination than we on the
ground could. White puffs of anti-aircraft shell bursts showed we
were as usual being observed. Our last taste of the Salient was the
flash of wings and bursts of machine-gun fire from a 'dog fight' high
over our heads in the fading light.

13

WE stopped after an hour. The officers of our company were to go along the rail track to the Major's coach, a dilapidated first-class compartment. Officers *must* travel first class I remembered, though it was an age since we had known any luxury other than the snout of the tank looming above us as we lay on the boards of the tank trucks. A shaded hand torch was our illumination as we strained to catch a glimpse of the map in the circle of light. We knew it by heart anyway—except for one word clearly visible—CAMBRAI. Where the hell's that?

That was where there was a great railway junction, a nerve centre of the German army communications which, when we had broken through... Not *again* surely—all through those beautiful green fields? Ouderdom, Vlamertinghe, St Jean—one bit of mud is very like another whatever the name—had destroyed military fairy stories. And we were not to know that the secret operation could be discontinued at any time since there were no reserves available. Just as well perhaps—one tank was worry enough for us.

There was no port. As no one had ever suggested that the Major was a secret drinker—that was a fault of which the old rascal was incapable—we were agreed that things must be pretty serious. We dispersed to our trucks after one parting injunction.

"Remember; between the time we detrain, in about an hour I should think, and half an hour before dawn, say six o'clock, every tank must have disappeared so the enemy can see nothing, *nothing*, between rail-head and Harringcourt Wood." Another blasted wood. I hoped it didn't look like men walking.

As we were last on we came off the train first when we arrived at our rail-head. Williams was there. "It may be carboned up; if so, with a bit of luck it will burn itself clear as it goes. I'll give it a proper doing when you get to the wood."

There was no luck. We had five miles to go and in the best conditions we were unlikely to make more than five miles an hour. Certainly the ground was dry and chalky—was that what the intelligent fool called cretaceous? I hoped I was not going to see it

154

change to the alluvial—but after that the conditions were not the best. We were utterly tired out.

A party of some ten men was approaching with a curious shuffling, somnambulistic gait which yet reminded one of men marching. As they came nearer it was clear that they *were* marching. Harrison dared to ask the question the rest of us seemed unable to voice.

"Who are you chum?"

"Coldstream Guards."

"What! The whole lot?" said Harrison facetiously.

"The whole bloody lot—and mind your own business!" He was angry; so they were alive and not a delusion.

Now we felt unable to be certain of our own reality. During one of my turns at driving I became aware through the open flap at the front of my seat that the sky was lightening. Dawn! And heaven knew how many miles to the nearest air cover. As far as I could see the country was bare; just the rolling downland in front silhouetted against the pallor of the sky. Suddenly someone I could not see was yelling through the flap. It was O'Toole and Allen. "Stop! Stop!" I knew the engine must be about red hot and stopped at once.

"Sir, you've nearly driven into a house!" I got out to find we were in a village street, the nose of the tank almost touching a sturdy brick building. Thoroughly awake I got back to my driving seat to find that the 'sky' was the dim torch light, which they were using to watch the engine, reflected on the flap of the observation opening. At least we still had time.

Remembering the Coldstream experience I said that when it was time to take fresh air the crew were to do it in pairs, both men walking together. I did not want anyone lost through falling asleep.

Far behind the tail of the battalion we eventually limped into a village. We had to stop. I drew in as close as possible to a ruined cottage. We draped sacking over the sides and placed empty petrol cans on the roof so the tracks were hidden. We piled up some cans to simulate a chimney.

The Major came up. "Quite a nice little country cottage you have there. I'll have to warn the infantry you may not be able to operate. Luckily the rest of the battalion seem to be at their stations." And off he went, affable, rosy-cheeked, cosy; there are worse states of mind and I felt comforted by his matter-of-fact state.

As for the crew, they were as near mindless as fatigue can make men. I told O'Toole and Allen the driver to check up the tank and its guns so that nothing we could do would be left undone for action. The rest were to go under the tank—there was a space of two feet between the lowest part of the belly and the ground. Then I went off to find Williams and the other company officers in the wood.

The wood had real trees with thick foliage and its quota of magpies. Why, I wondered, was it not a name on a map? Why had nobody been fighting? Nobody had been fighting because this was a position to which the enemy had retired after the Somme; it was untouched country and we were now lying before the Hindenburg Line. Or so somebody said.

Where was Williams? The mess corporal gave me a note. 'Sorry—can't do anything now. As soon as it is dark get your tank into the wood under the trees where we can work at it properly. We shall have nearly twelve hours. Sorry you had a bad trip.'

Quainton, Cohen, Bayliss and all other tank commanders had had a virtually trouble-free trip. "You look tired", said Quainton. I felt oily; the cool morning fresh air emphasized the greasy, unshaven sense of being encased in a film insulating me from fact. My skin was tired, my eyes bloodshot. Quainton was not being funny. Both he and Cohen were clearly concerned and I wondered why.

"Where's Williams?" I asked.

"The corporal has a note for you from him."

"Oh damn it; of course, I've seen it."

"Go and get some sleep."

"Where?"

"Anywhere; I'll wake you if you are wanted", said Quainton. Then in a low voice, "I'm sorry old man—are you all right?"

Of course I was all right—but we were still inexperienced and had not seen fatigue close to, let alone felt it. Later I learnt more of that terrible infantry fatigue of men tried beyond endurance, pasty-faced, almost as if their very eyes had become grey. In tanks we knew nothing of that unending 'world without end' fatigue. In April the next year... but that was mercifully hidden.

I went back to the crew; they were now all asleep except O'Toole who was keeping watch.

"Do you think we shall get into action sir?"

"I know we shall Sergeant; but I have no idea what we shall do when we get there."

In his fatigued state he looked more horrible than ever. "Hard luck if we miss this sir. After Ypres this looks like proper tank ground."

It told him it was part of the fortress-like defences of the Hindenburg Line.

"It will be pretty tough fighting then. But Jerry always is a tough job."

Particularly for a lot of amateurs, I thought—and I was one of the amateurs who said the words without knowing what they meant. There were many catch-phrases endlessly repeated. Those in vogue at this time were, 'Remember Belgium', a sarcastic use of an official formula; 'The first seven years are the worst'; 'Remember the Hundred Years War'; 'Oh my, I don't want to die! I want to go home', a tuneless song sung in the English manner—tunelessly.

"Rout out one of the others and get some sleep yourself Sergeant. I'm going to the mess tent if you want me, but I will be back anyway. As soon as it is dark we must get into the wood where we can see to this properly. Oh, and keep the men from wandering round the tank when they do wake up." He saluted and I went off.

The Quartermaster's men had managed to set up a marquee, part of which was divided off by a screen to serve as the mess. No one was there except the Quartermaster, a short, smooth-faced man, a peace-time Territorial who I think must have been a grocer. He was not given to talking because, I suspect, he had not much to say to executive officers. I seized the opportunity to show him my lunch, a tin of bully beef made by a well-known foreign firm. "This", I said, "is all I have left of my day's ration. It's got to see me through the show tomorrow." The next day's battle was a 'show'—probably indicating something more important than a 'stunt'. He saw one third of the tin was finished; the 'unconsumed portion of the day's ration', the official title, was a solid chunk of translucent gristle. Without a word he pulled out his field service notebook and entered into it the name of the firm and the date. Then he handed the tin to his orderly. "Get this weighed and tell me the result." Peace-time grocers are not used to being surprised. War-time (embodied) territorials of his experience did not sentimentalize about patriotism or the loyalty of our Allies.

"How about some bully mutton?" he asked me. I told him I would try anything once, but I would like to know what was the worst part of a sheep that could happen to me. "Ah, I didn't say anything about 'sheep'", he replied, "but it could get you invalided back to England if you are lucky in the draw. That chunk of bully wouldn't even get you into hospital." After a moment's thought he added, "unless you've got very good teeth."

The arrival of our Company Quartermaster made him terminate the conversation by telling his orderly to get me a tin of bully mutton from the store. "Make it two tins", he shouted after the man. "Do you want some biscuit too? Captain Tipledy could let you have some."

"Sorry; no teeth", I said and took my leave to a chair in the corner to have a snooze till I had to go back to the tank.

Tipledy, our Quartermaster, was a motherly old woman, competent and with exactly the right name and temperament for the job. Unfortunately he was the wrong sex and this led to a number of coarse jests which tended to a mild and uncertain irrascibility of manner.

"Why? What's the matter with the biscuit?" Tipledy was mobilized. I had no inclination whatever to engage in war about biscuit.

"Nothing. It's OK I was just telling the QM about some bully and he wanted to know if I wanted biscuit. If you've got a decent tank to spare I'd be glad of it."

"You know damn well I have nothing to do with issue of tanks."

"I know you haven't. I was only joking." I felt the conversation had taken the wrong turning. I was desperately tired and wanting to snatch a few moments of sleep before going back to that nerve-racking tank. He glared at me with twitching moustaches like a very large, suspicious and bloated rat. A bit like the corpse-fed rats in our billet up at Ypres I thought—and then his good-natured smile reappeared.

14

I WAS woken from an uneasy sleep when the sound of voices stopped. The silence disturbed me. It was still another quarter of an hour before I need set out. It was hopeless to try to sleep again so I set out for my tank. How dark it was and gloomy! The crew I found awake. They said they had all slept and were fit for anything. I felt they were glad to see me, and I felt glad to see them. What the devil we were all so glad about I could not imagine.

The crew cranked up and we drove some six hundred yards to our rendezvous. We had to stop five times in that short distance to let the engine cool down.

Williams had a reputation for talking bull-shit. So we were not impressed by his optimism and assurance.

"First", he said, "we will check up once more. Has it been any better? No? Just the same in every respect—no power, short run, backfiring and finally red-hot? You're quite sure?"

"Damn fool", I thought.

"Positively no deception, ladies and gentlemen—you have heard what these gentlemen have said? Very well then. *This* is a defective tank. Now watch me very carefully. First we shall retime it because it is obvious that there can be no other explanation. But this time we shall do it by measuring—from the cylinder heads. All right then—first remove the cylinder heads—"

"You mean first remove the roof of the tank don't you? We can't take the cylinder heads off without." Williams checked up and saw this was true, but he was not going to be deterred.

"We shall have to do it through the exhaust ports. Not so good, but good enough. I always said these bloody petrol engines were no good. They should have used steam."

It was popularly supposed that Williams was an ex-naval engineer who had never recovered from the day the navy went out of sail. Now it was the change from steam to the infernal combustion engine.

It was a long job and time seemed to race by. Eventually Williams stood up. "Jesus wept! I've got it! Do you know what's wrong? Those bastards have marked dead centre wrong on the fly-wheel!"

Bastards? What bastards? Not Americans who had provided us with plenty of small arms ammunition—or tins of bully gristle to eat? It *is* called an iron ration so it is really very generous to have given us animal substance and not mineral. But who are *these* bastards? They gave us plum and apple jam, they gave us one fly-wheel with dead centre marked wrong. In fact they were patriotic Britons who one day would be rewarded by their grateful country. For the present they had to be content with making their fortunes. Later—the Honours Lists. For us—sleep you perishers! A Military Cross for your officer; "Art thou sleeping there below?"—a 'wooden cross' certainly seemed more likely.

"Finished!"

I felt too tired to care. We said nothing. I did not believe the job was finished; I was beyond profanity, depression or anger. Now, when the entire crew was exhausted, our troubles were about to start. Williams was surprised, even hurt, at our reaction to a very arduous and finally successful job of work. Looking back, I wonder if the journey from Ypres to our starting point at Cambrai killed the spirit of our crew.

The job was hurriedly tidied up—there was now no time to lose—checked and passed by Williams for the last time. He wished us luck and disappeared. The engine was now running sweetly as she should have done from the moment we had drawn her from the Tank Central Workshops. I left a message to be taken to Advanced Company HQ and a copy to the Battlion HQ of the Seaforth Highlanders to say we should be operating after all.

At last we were clear of Harrincourt Wood, out in the open and on firm ground. It was dark and silent. The last tank had reached its starting point long before and I imagined dawn was beginning to pale in the east.

The engine suddenly overheated and stopped. I think I must have ground my teeth with rage, but all I said was, "Give her time to cool." After a few minutes it was evident that either it had not cooled enough and it would be blown to bits, or we should be dangerously late, caught in the barrage if we waited.

"Swing her!" I ordered the crew. A splutter and then a roar as it sprang to life. "Throttle down for God's sake", I said to Allen. It seemed noisy enough to start the enemy barrage at once. This time the engine went on running till we reached our starting point with a couple of minutes to go. We left the engine to idle as I thought it would be tempting Providence to stop it and hope to start it again.

Night had turned to pale grey. My watch hand crept on to zero and there were three individual bursts from our artillery. Then at once a moaning in the air. The enemy's trench system was picked out along its length by our barrage, unregistered yet bursting, at most, twelve feet above ground level in a precision I have never seen equalled. I could have cheered as I saw the white puffs shot through with white sparks picking out the pattern in the pearly light.

A and C companies, forming the first wave, had already gone through. Our company, B, were to support and go through A and C at the Grand Ravine. We went through to avoid the enemy's counter-barrage and then lay waiting beyond his barrage lines till our turn came.

As the light grew we could see our first line forging ahead. To us it looked as if the enemy's surprise was complete. We could even see the Highlanders signalling the tanks on at crossing point of trenches and other obstacles.

It was our turn; soon it was the Grand Ravine which turned out to be no obstacle at all. A and C companies halted while we went through to take the lead. The ease and orderliness of the operation after the chaos of Ypres induced a sense of unreality. The battlefield was set out like a diagram; the functions of infantry gunners and tanks slotted together with such perfection that it seemed as if we were more pieces of a Staff Officer's dream than soldiers at war. Small pockets of German prisoners were being marched back, filled more with curiosity than fear as the spectacle unrolled before them. It was as if the British Army had decided to have a mock field day on territory already in use by enemy troops. They seemed awfully decent about it and indeed quite keen to watch what we were doing.

I raced my tank—in those days four miles an hour—towards my objective, the village of Flesquieres. The firm ground made it easy and exhilarating. The ground sloped upwards to an enemy strong point. As we came nearer I could see how formidable was the barbed wire—at least six feet high and ten yards thick surrounding the fortification proper. As a routine I closed my flaps and plunged into the wire; for a moment I felt a slight tug as it gripped us. Then we broke through and over wire which at Ypres would have held fast for weeks any attack no matter how powerful the artillery support, and probably for as long as we cared to go on hanging our corpses on it.

161

I still had not got over my exhilaration when an appalling din broke out. It was probably only one gun left out of the depleted garrison, but there may have been as many as two. It sounded, each bullet, like a sledge hammer stroke against a sheet of cast iron held against one's face. There was no way of seeing anything. Taking control I drove the tank so that the bullets struck in front of me; they could do no harm against our armour, and I argued that so long as the bullets were striking on the armour in front of me we must be heading straight for the machine-gun. As each bullet struck off a red-hot splinter from the armour, we had an improvised direction finder provided by the bullets themselves. Feeling my face pouring with a greasy sweat I put up my hand to wipe it away. Allen looked white-faced and scared as I saw him looking at me. I noticed that my hands were covered with blood. Another wipe with my hands showed me why Allen looked scared; my face was streaming with blood. 'His gory visage down the stream sent.' The words repeated themselves in my mind monotonously, rhythmically, like 'Around the rugged rocks the ragged rascal ran.'

The gun stopped. The silence seemed to flow back with a suddenness that hurt one's ears. The roar broke out on my left side.

"Put it in reverse! Fire the left six-pounder"—at anything, anywhere, to make them think we're fighting someone, I thought to myself.

The moment the breach was opened to load, such a storm of bullets came up the barrel that gunner Allen left it in panic. At once the inside of the tank was an inferno. Richardson managed to close the breach and thanks to him we had nothing but a couple of flesh wounds amongst us.

"God damn your soul Allen you bastard!" I yelled at the cowering boy. I was blubbing with rage and fear myself.

No sooner had the gun causing us such havoc been silenced, or had silenced itself, than an explosion from the rear of the tank rocked us all. The tank stopped.

"What's up?"

"Won't go", yelled Allen.

What on earth had happened? I had no idea and couldn't think.

"I think it's catching fire by the petrol tank", reported O'Toole.

"Every man with a Lewis gun and as much ammo as you can carry. Now out you go! Richardson first—we've only one door—the left one. Fall out, firing your gun as you go. Into the trench!"

Richardson tumbled out with only one bullet through his thigh. The enemy must have been as surprised as we were; all eight of us arrived safe in a bay of the enemy's trench system.

When I could look back I saw that the tank had a shell hole where the right rear driving mechanism had been; it was effectually out of action, but the destruction of the gears had saved the petrol tank and ninety gallons of petrol from exploding in flames.

So—we were in the enemy's strong point, holding a short bit of trench in a veritable fort. In front was a high brick wall. At right angles to this, and on our left, was a low wall about a copse of tall fir trees. As we and the enemy recovered from our surprise so the sense of menace grew. My utter ignorance of fighting, as contrasted with the professional soldier's knowledge, was mercifully hidden from me. I could feel it, but I did not know it; subsequent events conspired to postpone my enlightenment.

15

W E were under fire, but I had not the slightest idea where the bullets were coming from. They were in fact converging on us from all directions. At the time the most obvious seemed to be the high wall in front, but I had no clear reason for concentrating on that rather than any other possible target. I told O'Toole to take charge in the trench while I tried to deal with our tormentors.

Taking four drums of Lewis gun ammunition attached to my waist and a Lewis gun, I clambered clumsily onto the top of the tank and set up my gun under cover, as I thought, of the fascine—the bundle of faggots about four feet thick which had taken the place of the unditching beam as a special equipment for crossing the deep trenches of the Hindenburg Line trench system. I was not aware of any danger and therefore experienced none of the fear which might have served as a substitute for my common sense which was wholly lacking. I commanded a good view of the little copse behind the wall, this I proceeded methodically to spray. I soon exhausted almost the whole of my four drums of ammunition.

By this time my escapade had stirred up a veritable hornets' nest in the copse. I do not know what I expected would happen—probably nothing—but I was surprised to find German troops, led by an officer, pouring out of a gap in the left distant corner of the wall. An officer pointed his swagger stick to direct his troops to me. I swung round and opened fire on them as they were coming through the gap. At the same moment my gun jammed.

I saw it was a simple stoppage, could not clear it, and realizing that my drum had no more ammunition left fell rather than scrambled back into the shelter of the trench.

By this time I must have been thoroughly scared though I was unaware of it. My crew were standing about nonchalantly doing nothing.

"Why the hell aren't you firing?" I said to Lance Corporal Forman—he and O'Toole were the only men left. Allen, the driver, had been sent back with gunner Allen to take our two wounded, Pell and Richardson, to the trench on the perimeter. "For God's sake man! Fire at them!" I pointed to the enemy now lying in the open. O'Toole was fiddling with a German gun.

"No ammunition left", said Forman.

Before the enemy had recovered I said "Get back!"—to the trench about a hundred yards distant—"short rushes!" O'Toole struggled with the German gun.

I remember our short rushes; Forman and I with our last two Lewis guns. I remember being hauled by a Highlander into the trench. Safe at last, I thought as I realized that all three were present, still unwounded. Otherwise, but for a vague sense of being under fire, I remember no details.

Gradually I took stock. Richardson and Pell were in good shape, but both were too badly wounded for further fighting; the two Allens were very badly shaken and as there was nothing for Allen to drive I decided to send all four back under O'Toole who was to report to Advance Company HQ after handing over the two wounded to the first advanced aid post. The Allens he was to hand over to the Regimental Medical Officer. Forman and I stayed with our two Lewis guns and the German machine-gun which now was ready, after O'Toole's ministrations, to fire again.

I reported to the Seaforth captain, Edwards, who appeared to be the only officer left in his company. While I was talking to him in the trench there was the loud crack of a near bullet. He fell forward and I saw blood and brains bulge out at the back of his skull.

I was too stunned to know where or how the bullet was fired; it might have been chance but the infantry had no doubt it was aimed fire. As we were occupying the enemy trench system there was no parapet to protect us from fire within the planned strong point.

Search showed a suspicious thickening near the top of one of the tall pines; on this our Lewis gunfire was at once concentrated. Under the intense fire the thickening began to disintegrate, a body detached itself, caught in some branches, hung for an instant and crashed onto lower branches, was again halted and finally dashed to the ground. The Lewis guns continued their chattering search of all tree-tops in the radius of our segment, but there was no further result. Edwards was avenged. What does 'avenged' mean? Think it out—later.

At Ypres, and once again later, there was a sniper posted at least a mile within our lines. In each case it was clear that the end for the sniper was death or, very improbably, capture. Such cold-blooded bravery, if there is such a thing as bravery, I could envy but never emulate.

There was one similar act which was unknown to me at the time (but of which I learned from the Commander-in-Chief's dispatches) which had led to the destruction of our tank and seven others. The Commander-in-Chief, in addition to all his other crimes, was much criticized for having given comfort to our enemies by having made known to the world the bravery of the German gunner officer whose devotion to duty, when all his men had fled, was responsible for our disaster. For my part I am glad that, even if one cannot oneself be capable of such courage, our C.-in-C. had the courage to acknowledge courage in our enemies. In 1976 I learnt there was no such German officer, but in 1917 there was a hole in my tank.

The Highlander senior NCO reported to me that there were no officers left. Would I therefore take command of the infantry? As I knew nothing of infantry fighting I asked him to stay near and advise me on my new duties.

They turned out to be insignificant. It was obvious that we had to hold our positions which we did against one powerful counter-attack on our left flank. Although the troops of the infantry battalion on our left were forced to yield some ground we held our pivotal position. We lit our marker flares when one of our reconnaissance planes came over.

That was the end of my part in the Cambrai battle. Shortly after, the Colonel of the regiment, hearing my report of the position rapidly summed it up.

"Since you have no tanks you and your bloody Lance Corporal are no good to me. Get back to our HQ."

I reported to our Major, was kindly received and told to turn in. My batman had produced my sleeping kit: I lay down and in the slight drizzle that had started fell fast asleep. Some time the next day we went back to the comforts of our bivouac in the wood.

Through the day I heard, bit by bit, what had happened. Quainton had escaped injury and so had two section commanders, Bagshaw and Clifford. Stokes was dead and so was Bayliss. Broome had not been in action. Cohen had been very badly wounded and it was thought was now in the hands of the military hospital.

Of the rest of the company one-third that had gone into action had been killed. As usual there were few wounds as the nature of tank warfare meant that most casualties were killed outright by direct gunfire or the almost instantaneous fire caused by the burning petrol.

Looking back I am surprised that these casualties had so little impact on us at the time. In the next few days Quainton and I had plenty of time to talk. His tank had broken down just after the Grand Ravine; he and his crew had been holding a position ready in case of counter-attack when their tank was knocked out. It blazed up at once and for the rest of the day could not be approached because the exploding ammunition made it a spectacular but dangerous firework. None of them was hurt and as no counter-attack developed and nothing could be done for the tank they were ultimately withdrawn.

Quainton, Carter and I were thrown together with very little to do. Quainton was a comforting person to be with, partly because of his Quaker origins and secure religious outlook. Carter, the tough, wiry, colonial intelligence officer, was also good company, but for different reasons. He was supposed to have joined the army, coming to England for the purpose, when he was still at the permissible age. I am sure he was nearer sixty than forty, but his great physical fitness gave a mild degree of plausibility to his fictions. He strode about his duties, in action or out of it, with a stout walking stick which he said was not so heavy as a rifle and "a damned sight more use". We did not discuss the casualties; they had gone and that was that.

We few survivors were summoned to say good-bye to the Major. We went down to the road where the car was going to pick him up. There the old aristocrat spoke a few words.

It appeared that he had been dismissed from his command. There seemed to be no good reason to suppose that he ought not to have been—and equally no good reason to suppose that he should have been retained. I could only suppose that it was in keeping with a stereotype of the Colonel's idea of efficiency. To be efficient you must be ruthless; if you were ruthless it proved that you must be efficient.

"You mark my words", muttered the Major, "I'll get that tailor's dummy"— meaning, we all assumed, the Colonel—"You see if I don't."

Shaking hands with our small party and wishing us luck he clambered into the car and drove off. He was in a very bad temper, only slightly alleviated by his assumption that he was beloved by his troops—of whom in fact he had only the vaguest impression. Still, I was sorry to miss the healthy countenance and exuberant moustachios. He was a link—with the past.

To anticipate: before Christmas our Colonel also went— dismissed. Quainton saw him on leave reduced to the rank of captain. Poor man; the blow to him must have been infinitely worse than if he had never been promoted to a job for which he had only one qualification—his looks. Gull went at the same time.

16

THE removal of our company commander had one immediate consequence for us; the interviewing of officers reporting their part in the battle fell to Major Gatehouse. He was a powerful, ambitious and not very intelligent regular. I loathed the prospect of having to explain the action; I did not feel very clear about it even after several talks with Quainton and Carter. To make matters worse there was a rumour, fortunately quashed in a day or so by the capture of Flesquieres, that Highland troops had been fired at by a British officer from on top of his tank. I could not see how I could have made such a mistake because the troops who counter-attacked were German. We could not, all three, have been mistaken—nor yet the Highlanders who had witnessed the action. But anything seems possible in retrospect after battle. The evidence of German dead had not become available at the time.

I was called to see Gatehouse. I was far from being at ease as I stumbled through the interview. It was a long one and I was relieved that my account, which was substantially the same as that previously given by O'Toole and Forman when the men's account of the battle had been taken, seemed to reassure him. Then, right at the end my confidence was shaken; Gatehouse congratulated me on a 'stout show' and said he was going to recommend me for the Military Cross.

I could not easily say why I felt dismayed. Even the rumour about the 'officer on the tank' could hardly account for my feeling. Why on earth couldn't they leave me alone? But so it was. Quainton congratulated me and was surprised that I was annoyed; I said I wished I had never heard of tanks.

Quainton told me that he and Bayliss had talked before the action, wondering whether they should not tell the CO they wanted to become conscientious objectors. He said he had spoken to Gull after the action and put his doubts to him. I said that in any case after action 'they' would say that it was 'shell-shock', and before action that he did not know what he was talking about. We were still discussing this when Carter appeared. Affecting a jaunty tone he said he had just heard my good news and congratulated me.

Quainton went on, "Obviously the whole business is flat contrary to the Christian religion."

"Well of course it is", said Carter, "But", he added, "I don't believe in the Christian religion. I've never understood what all you pious people are doing here. I think the Boche are a lot of dangerous maniacs—if we don't stop them it's all up with everything decent."

"Why do you bother with its being decent then?"

"Because I prefer dealing with decent people. In my business before the war"—he was a coffee planter—"I preferred dealing with people who didn't lie, stuck to their bargains and didn't rob you if your back was turned. Or murder you", he added meditatively, "but I don't see what this has to do with Christianity."

"Christianity has a lot to do with *it* though", rejoined Quainton. "If there had been no Christianity there would not be any decent people to deal with."

"Oh rot! The biggest liar I ever knew was a 'Christian'. By the way, did you know that poor Yates lost one of his 'pips'?"

Yates had, before leaving England, been promoted to Lieutenant, a step nearer getting back to his mourned and coveted Captaincy. Carter told us that at Ypres he had broken down and hidden, weeping, in a shell-hole. He was now a second lieutenant and a tank commander. He was all right again and had been all right at Cambrai, perhaps because A Company in reserve had seen no fighting after we had gone through them at the Grand Ravine. Our debate ended for the time being, leaving me to bear my impending Military Cross alone.

Two days later Gatehouse called for me. He seemed curiously excited—I wondered what was up now. It was not long in coming.

"I have had a long report about you from the 51st Division." (My God, not shooting up their men for heaven's sake?)

After an impressive pause he went on, "They have said they want to recommend that you be awarded the Victoria Cross. With their report I absolutely agree. So I am putting you in for the Victoria Cross, not the MC."

Not a court martial, I thought. Not for shooting their men or losing my tank. I was immensely relieved. "Did you say from the 51st Division sir?"

"Yes, entirely their idea. My recommendation has not gone

through to HQ. So it can go in 'for Military Cross read Victoria Cross'", he said with heavy playfulness.

I could not think of any suitable reply, so I saluted and went to digest this turn in my fortunes.

In fact I did very little digesting; the recommendation was so utterly unlike the experience I would have expected had I been told two months earlier that I should receive it. Gatehouse managed to be completely unconvincing; it sounded as if what he was saying had nothing to do with me, but a great deal to do with some story of which *he* was the hero. The story, I could see, was quite a good one even if somewhat unconvincingly dramatic. It was odd that it fitted so closely the facts as I knew them, and odder still that nevertheless it was not the experience I had had.

Yates looked in, disgruntled, red-faced and red-eyed. Was I supposed to know, to say something?

"Congratulations old man—wish I had had your luck. If I had the luck of the draw..."

It was obvious he had not—he was drunk. I did not hear from him what had happened. Indeed he was so oblivious of any personal disaster that I wondered if the story I had heard had any truth in it. I judged it prudent not to ask any questions. I murmured something suitably nondescript, but I need not have worried; he had staggered off.

He was immediately followed by another A Company officer, Collinson. He looked at me with frankly jealous, envious eyes as if hardly able to believe that *I* of all people should be on the way to a decoration—and such a decoration! His eyes kept on returning incredulously to have another look. No; there was no clue; nothing at all.

"It's no good looking at *me* like that—I haven't done anything. You'd better ask Gatehouse."

He checked his wandering gaze, quickly, guiltily. His eyes settled on my face again. He was not really listening to me, suspecting that I was probably being modest, or, more likely still, that I was a bit soft in the head. "Why Bion? Why not me?" he seemed to be asking himself vainly. Then he sheared off.

The baffling old problem—why do the wicked prosper, and not decent, worthy fellows? I could not help him. I was obviously all set to be turned into a war hero though I could not bring myself to believe that anything so ridiculous as my having to wear a VC would come out of it.

Yet—I hoped... But what for? I longed to be a VC. It would be wonderful... but I dreaded it. The worst part of it was facing my crew. They were there damn it! They *knew* what had happened; they had seen what I had seen and had been in the same danger. They did not know—I did—that it was my bungling incompetence that had driven the tank into the strong point *before* time, before I was due. Had they all forgotten that I shouldn't have been there at all? Ought I to remind them? Or should I keep my mouth shut and get a VC? How marvellous it sounded!

I had to face my crew; they would have heard by this time. Booby Bion. How humiliated I had felt when F. M. Kingdom—the master we called Bim—ticked me off, with the background of sniggers from the form. This was worse. I faced them: Hayler, the farmer who was no more likely to be fooled than Williams was when facing Henry V; the two Allens, my driver and the one who was shortly to be charged with the crime of 'dumb insolence' for his curious archaic smile.

"Of course I realize", I stammered out my guilty embarrassment, "that we were all in it and it's silly to single me out as if I were..." (Bloody fool, I said to myself, what the hell did you get those pips on your shoulders for? You knew you wanted to be 'somebody special', and you knew you weren't.)

I think it was Colombe who recognized my embarrassment and came to my rescue. "We are all very pleased sir", he said. Hayler said nothing; Allen the Australian said nothing; Allen was not insolent but was with his senses shut.

Gradually in the following days I grew a protective skin and my fellow officers shut me out. I was not ostracized—it was as if they had become reconciled to my peculiarity, a 'rum bird', always a bit queer, more queer even than Cohen and Quainton. In this unpleasant turmoil of feeling I faced the prospect of further investigation. How I hated them all! How I longed to avoid them all. But I loved my crew and resented being cut off from them.

I was hauled before the General. I had to go through it all again. It seemed a bit of a job to find someone to be a VC. It was clear that not just anyone would do; on the other hand, if it had to be someone brave—'for valour'—how was that to be found? He looked at me—a bit reminiscent of Collinson I thought, but with somewhat different anxiety. Would I do? Could I possibly be made to look, with some degree of plausibility, like a hero? He seemed to doubt it. So did I. I had not forgotten that ridiculous college cap and the moon-face under it. To make matters worse I was feeling in a bad temper. If the General or Gatehouse wanted someone to be a VC why the devil didn't they go and win one themselves?

"But you say you didn't actually *see* any enemy falling?"

I considered this for a moment. "Well, there *were* some people falling, but I thought they were taking cover."

He looked very disappointed and distressed. I felt sorry for the poor fellow— in so far as it is possible for a second lieutenant to be sorry for a General. I could see it was a terrible job to have to find war heroes out of people like me.

"You couldn't—you are sure?—be sure any of them were killed?"

"No sir; they looked far too much alive for my health I thought."

For a moment he almost smiled, though he must in fact have been having an anxious time.

"Somebody said there were a lot of German dead where I had been firing over the wall, but of course I couldn't be sure how they got there."

He didn't seem to feel that this was very convincing. Nor did I. It had all the elements of a first class drama but obviously a hopeless cast.

He tried again. "The 51st Division sent a report about you..."

My mind went back to Edwards with his brain oozing out. It was too much. Though I had only had a few words with him I had seen his men's response to his death; it was not all hate.

I looked at the General. He seemed a decent sort; quite different from Gatehouse whom at that moment I hated.

"Yes sir, Major Gatehouse told me. I thought it was exaggerated sir. I am sorry; I don't know why they put in such a report."

"Do you *know* the report?"

"No sir. Only Major Gatehouse said that after he had read it he decided to recommend me for a VC. I thought he meant the infantry report suggested that."

"Well, don't you want one?"

I wanted to explain that I thought the VC should be kept for people who deserved it. But all I could manage was, "Oh yes sir, very much... well, not really sir", I finished lamely and miserably.

He did not seem entirely uncomprehending. "I shall of course have to send the report in—but it doesn't rest with me." He pushed back his chair. I felt it was a sign to me to leave and out I went.

I was exhausted. Probably the prolonged strain before action, screened by the battle itself, was now coming to the surface. Carter met me.

"Well, how did it go? Did you get a VC?" he asked ironically.

"I shouldn't think so—I couldn't think of anything to say."

"You ought to have learnt up your past properly beforehand."

I could not guess what was in the mind of this strange, grizzled, disillusioned but determined man. "See you later", and he loped off with his long walking stick and swinging unmilitary stride.

17

T H E next morning Carter, Quainton and I were having breakfast just below the Gouzeancourt Ridge by the edge of the wood. A gun limber with two panicky horses came over the ridge and raced towards us. "Looks as if someone's in trouble—lost his limber for good I would think." We went on with our breakfast.

I began to feel that something was wrong with the morning. It was rather like a bad dream without a dream. "Do you know", I said to the others, "I keep on thinking I hear machine-guns. Like having goose flesh—"

Gatehouse appeared from his tent.

"I think something's up sir", said Carter. "Why, what's..." Before he had finished his sentence an all too familiar sound froze us into silence.

"By God! You're right!" Carter said to me. 'You *are* hearing guns."

We listened, taut, to the slow unmistakable pulse of a German machine-gun. The whine of bullets overhead clinched it.

"But the Line is a good ten miles away!"

Carter was grim. "The Line is now *here*. Back to where we started from—or further."

The news, when we got it during the next hour or so, was this: the enemy had attacked the Salient formed by the successful attack on the 20th. After bitter fighting the Prussian Guard at Bourlon Wood had held our advance. His counter-attack was expected and his main attack on our left had been bloodily repulsed. His feint attack on our right had broken through our flimsy defence and what we were now watching as helpless unarmed spectators—we had two men, no tanks and the four of us—was the clever exploitation by the enemy of our disaster.

Watching from our cover at the end of the wood we were now able to see a sight that I have never forgotten—the Guards Division going into action. The operation was almost nonchalant, it was unfolded with such ease. Right across the plain to our right front the Guards advanced in open order. But for the rattle of machine-

175

guns one might have been watching a troop exercise. They moved steadily up the slope, reached the Gouzeancourt Ridge and disappeared behind and beyond it. The sound of German machine-guns, so threatening, so close and so insistent, died away.

The Guards had been ordered to retake Gouzeancourt; they had done just that.

The battalion, though not our company, had been continuously engaged since November 20th. Now, ten days later, it was without tanks, having suffered very heavily at Bourlon Wood and after. It was therefore withdrawn to winter quarters where it was to be brought up to full strength and re-equipped.

It was a 'permanent' camp, that is, one made up of wooden huts. It was disposed on the slope near the crest of a hill and lay within the devastated area of the Somme battlefields. By the time that the remnant of our battalion was installed the rains had started. In the usually pouring rain Quainton, Hauser, Carter and I did our parades with a handful of men, and in between whiles visited the rest of the battalion to gather news of how they had fared.

We knew that our company casualties were exceptional; but for three tank crews who had not gone into action, and Quainton, Hauser and myself, we had been wiped out on the advance up the slope from the Grand Ravine. What we did not know was that the exceptional nature of the disaster lay only in the speed with which it had occurred.

Our visits showed us that news was hard to come by; only a few newly-joined subalterns seemed to be about and they could not answer any of our inquiries. The battalion officers' mess was not yet in being, officers messing in the quarters of their respective companies; therefore there was no way of meeting the officers assembled as a whole. However, I met a Sergeant Robinson of A Company. He could not tell me much as he had missed the action through illness, but his officer was a man called Green — in peace time a barrister, intelligent and with a kindly but acute wit, with whom I had spent a Saturday in Bournemouth. There had been nothing to do, but it was a fine afternoon and we wandered about the lifeless resort. He, and his barrister friend Ball who was with us, made the desperate nullity pass easily till we could at last decently return to camp. If I could find him we might even relieve the ugliness of this desolate hole. I asked Robinson how he was; I cannot imagine why I was surprised to hear he was dead. I did not ask about Ball. Later, when I heard from Gull about other officers, I was glad I had not, for Ball was said to have broken down and crawled underneath his tank and refused to move.

Later in the afternoon I met an officer of C Company, Dawson, whom I knew by sight. Yes, he had come through all right. No, he didn't know about the others; he thought one or two may have been wounded—no use to ask about the ones who had not possibly been wounded. I asked how he had got on. He appeared vague. What had impressed him most was the Prussian Guard. "They finally got right on top of the tank, trying to shove their bayonets through our loop holes. Twice I got a Mills grenade onto the roof and blew the lot of them off. Do you know, they got our Lewis guns under their arms so we couldn't fire! I think the whole damn lot were doped. They came at us in mass formation and while we *could* fire it made no difference." Dawson was a solid unimaginative man; when he said these things had happened I was sure they had. He began to repeat himself, reciting monotonously bits of the story I had already heard.

Quainton and I disengaged ourselves to see if we could find anyone else. We met the Colonel, spruce and soldierly as ever, making the rounds with Gull who was equally dapper. Quainton was wearing a beautiful beaver lamb trench coat. The Colonel looked at him enviously. Next to the Prince of Wales, Quainton was more likely than anyone else to cause the bleating note to come into Gull's voice. He tolerated me because, like Cohen, I was usually in Quainton's company. The Colonel who knew all his officers by name—"a truly Royal Attribute", said Gull—spoke to both of us. We could not very well ask how things had gone with him and we did not expect him to know any more than he knew about Lewis guns in a tank. "Did you see how he looked at my coat?" Quainton asked me gleefully as we saluted and took our leave.

As the days went by new faces appeared. Robinson, a small, dapper, alert ex-infantryman; Cartwright, a tallish, pale-complexioned, newly commissioned officer without war experience or, it sometimes seemed to me, any other. Both these were posted to my section and when I was promoted Captain to command it Cartwright took over my crew—O'Toole, L/Cpl Forman, Driver Allen, Gunner Hayler, Gunner Allen.

Hauser, although in our battalion in England, was hardly known to me. He was promoted to section commander; from now on he played an increasing part in my life. He and his crew seemed to live on terms of mutual exasperation. At Ypres, before we went into action, he and his crew were one day on more than usually bad terms. In sudden exasperation he put his driver out of the tank saying, "Here, give me the controls", and drove it straight into a large water-filled shell-hole. Getting out he addressed them. *"Now you've got something to grouse about! Fix the unditching beam, get it out of that mess, and come and tell me when you've cleaned it up."*

We were none of us surprised to hear one of the men mutter behind his stocky retreating figure, "I'll shoot that bloody little German bastard first time we get into action, you see if I don't." They never did. They came near to worshipping him, and if it were possible to make an idol out of a short-sighted, crop-headed, dark-haired, irascible little man they would have done it. I tried to find out from him how he had managed, with a name like that, to be accepted by the army, but never succeeded. It was the only subject which made him look as if he was feeling amused by the recollection. "I told them I came over from the Hanseatic League and was meaning to work my passage back to Germany." He wrinkled up his nose with a characteristic cross between a sniff and a snuffle. It was difficult to tell whether he was amused or irritated.

We both knew we were in the running to be promoted to section commanders. More highly favoured than either was Quainton who was popular with most, but hated by Clifford, Homfray, Broome and others who considered him, like me, to be one of the smug, pious crowd. Homfray was a Carthusian who affected superior, lackadaisical ignorance of anything so vulgar as soldiering. The affectation concealed a genuine and profound unfitness for his job. I now think it was a by-product of the cover-up system of the public schools' unfitness for training the leaders of a great nation.

Looking back it seems to me we never allowed ourselves to realize that the 5th Battalion, to which we had become so attached in England, had ceased to exist. A new battalion was taking shape under our eyes.

Bagshaw had gone, no one knew why. He was probably useless when he came to us as a section commander and was certainly useless afterwards. Our Major had gone and his place had been taken by Gatehouse. Clifford—'tape worm', he was tall and thin—Homfray, and Captain Cook, promoted to second in command, were our senior officers. A swarthy, greasy-faced young man called Green completed our company officer strength. Drafts of twenty or thirty new men came in from day to day. Their names had to be learned and our lists of crews amended as they were allocated.

The Colonel sent for me. I was to return to Harrincourt Wood with two tank crews chosen from the men in the battalion who had not been in action. There were three tanks in working order there; these I was to take over from Corps Workshops who expected us. Our job?

The front was now stabilized, but the gunners wanted our help. To the right of Gouzeancourt there were some half dozen 9.2 howitzers. The gunners would tell us where they were; they were stranded between British and German lines. It was imperative that we should get them back and not let them fall into German hands. The gunners thought—and, said the Colonel, he quite agreed with them—it would be easy for a tank to go up to them at night, shackle tow lines to them and pull them out of non-man's land to safety behind our lines.

It was dangerous of course. Nobody could be such a fool as to suppose that one could clank enormous cables and towing chains about no-man's land at dead of night in the neighbourhood of valuable big guns without setting off retaliatory fire. The Germans had now become sensitive to the presence of tanks. Indeed, they learned then a lesson which became useful to them in 1939.

The orders might have been less unwelcome had I thought the Colonel had any idea of the nature of the hazard to which we were committed. But I doubted it. I had achieved a state of mind in which I felt aggrieved that I had to fight. Romance, such as sustained me before Ypres, had gone; yet I could not say what was the matter.

I unburdened myself to Quainton. His contribution must have impressed me for I have never forgotten it. On a slip of paper he wrote, "Above all do not forget you are in good hands", and slipped it into my pocket. 'God's hands' he meant of course. It soothed me. But there was something wrong with me—or religion. For one thing the words had an ephemeral value, short-lived like the military music of the massed bands of the 51st Division before action, or a tot of rum after it. I felt self-conscious as I had when I knelt publicly to say my prayers in the marquee.

The journey was interminable, but I was relieved to be out of the camp. Preparations had already started for the Christmas celebrations—casks of beer, great joints of meat, meaningless decorations in the mess hut. I do not remember 'Peace on earth, good will towards men', but it would not even have seemed incongruous had it been there. On the great day itself they would be canned to a man: that I did know.

179

One advantage of army travel was that one became a postal packet, someone else's responsibility. When I arrived at rail-head I was turned out into the darkness and pouring rain by the RTO. He had to see that an officer got off that train at that rail-head. Having done so he could go back to the shelter of the warm, dimly-lit fug of his office. Someone saluted; it was the driver of the car to take me to Brigade HQ. My men I would meet the next day where they had gone to take over the tanks.

The car stopped, I got out and a guide took me along a communication trench to Brigade HQ. The Very lights along the front floated up into the darkness, burned white for a while and flickered away. It was a silent, rhythmical display.

I suggested I should look at the first of the guns we were to tow out. The guide was uncommunicative; I was in the way, a bloody nuisance who had spoiled a potentially quiet evening. We came to a spot where I had to leave the trench and crawl. A monstrous shape rose out of the ground; it was the first of the howitzers. I could make nothing of it till a Very light flared up and showed the silhouette. Someone had painted on it in large white letters, 'Crack O'Doom'. The enemy gunners had registered on it with such accuracy that it was a total wreck. It could not possibly have been towed anywhere. I stumbled and a burst of machine-gun fire warned me to mend my ways. There was nothing to be done; I collected enough detail to report and crawled back to the trench. The guide was waiting.

At HQ I made my report. No one was interested; I gathered that the HQ staff were against the project from the first. The next day I was ordered to take my men back to the battalion; the scheme had been cancelled.

18

CHRISTMAS Eve. Now for the jollifications.

The camp was dilapidated. When snow fell that night there was not a hut into which it had not driven, covering the sleeping men with an inch of freezing slush by morning. I was not surprised that I saw the first drunks by 9.30. An A Company sergeant arrested them and put them in the Guard room.

It was customary for the officers to wait on the men at Christmas dinner. Surprisingly this was not an occasion for settling scores; in spite of the opportunity it offered it passed off in good humour and friendly expressions. By the time it had become alcoholic the officers had withdrawn. I was disconcerted to find that the men were not known to us. I was fortunate in having four of my original crew present, but Hauser, Quainton and Broome had none, and men of other crews were still not more than faces to us.

After our own dinner the three of us, with Cartwright, Green and Robinson, sat on in the hut that served as our company mess. We must all have been oppressed by the lack of familiar faces. The new officers were surprised that we knew as little of the men as they did. When we talked of this and explained why, the conversation rapidly petered out. Either we knew little of our job as officers or else...

It was clear that something terrible must have happened at Cambrai. Robinson, who had been wounded during previous service with the infantry, asked if the battalion had been "unlucky". No; it had not occurred to us that the battalion had been unlucky.

"On the contrary"—it was Hauser speaking—"we've been damned lucky. The 51st Division had never had so few casualties—not even in trench warfare. They told us that in an advance of over five miles they had had only six men wounded."

Quainton said, and Robinson agreed with alacrity, that these figures were miraculous.

"But", said Cartwright, "how did *you* have so many casualties?"

The conversation languished. *Had* we been unlucky? It hadn't occurred to any of us. How many casualties amount to 'unlucky'?

Our company had lost almost two thirds of our officers and men, killed, in the one and a half hours from zero. Certainly that sounded unlucky. Or perhaps it was just bad luck that the German gunner major had not run away with his men? The rest of the battalion had not lost any men that day. On the other hand, at the end of ten days they also had lost all but three tanks and a corresponding number of killed. Come to think of it, we had never been in action, according to Battalion HQ, without losing at least one third of the fighting crews.

Who had been killed? This reminded Quainton—"I see that we are not to have a battalion mess. It's company messes from now on, Gull says. It's jolly awkward because you can never get any news." It was most peculiar; there *was* no news.

Green: killed in action. Despard: killed in action. Bayliss: died of wounds. Cohen: wounded. Crankleton: missing, believed killed—very likely indeed when you consider that one of his men was there when he was blown to bits. Ball: very much alive, but... He was such a nice fellow, good company, witty, the perfect foil to his friend Green—till that day he got under the tank.

'Their name liveth for evermore.' In the hearts and minds of the survivors it did, till they also died. But what had happened to the 5th Battalion, that fine-looking crowd who sang 'Should auld acquaintance be forgot' that beautiful morning at Wool Station? The illusion that there was a 5th Battalion was more powerful than fact; we were swallowed up amongst so many new boys that we hardly existed. The future, the traditions of the battalion, lay in our hands—Hauser, Quainton, Broome, Green, Cartwright, Robinson and myself. *And* Homfray—representing the Greater Public Schools. *And* Clifford?

A few days after November 30th Hauser and I, with about a dozen men, had been collected together hastily with our Lewis guns and put in to hold a piece of trench under the command of Clifford. Nothing happened, but it was uncomfortable because it was very cold. We knew nothing about infantry work and we lived on iron rations. These consisted of one tin of bully and two captain biscuits each every day. We were not allowed fires so we could not have tea. The water tasted of petrol because it came up in cans from which the petrol could not be eliminated. When Quainton joined us a day late he made great play of imitating the Major, rolling the drink round his palate, pronoucing on its bouquet and assessing the year of its vintage. He did it well; there was no difficulty in recognizing the character portrayed.

Clifford's contribution to the spirit of his troops was to arrive in the small hours of one morning, shouting "They're coming! The Boche are attacking! Stand to arms! Pass it on!" We did.

It was peculiar; there was not a sound. "They must be coming on tip-toe." After some tense moments I said I thought I could hear them taking off their boots. "Better not stand down though—they might start throwing them at us", said Hauser.

Eventually we did make them stand down. Clifford, who had gone off blubbing and shouting his 'orders', never explained. He was shame-faced but in no way apologetic, and soon recovered what, for want of a better word, one must call his equanimity.

The incident was trivial, but Clifford and Homfray were not an impressive pair on whom to pin our hopes for the future. Nor could I honestly feel superior—only different. That accursed VC still dangling over my head felt more like a sentence of death than an authoritative guarantee that I was a one hundred percent brave man. I knew I was not and I hated feeling I knew nothing of infantry fighting either.

The lack of knowledge of the basic elements of war became more oppressive with the rumours, always active, now louder and more insistent, that Tanks were to be abolished. Haig was said to have turned against them since Cambrai. "Good God, why?" we asked. "What have we done wrong?"

The story was that a tank had crashed through a bridge and fallen into the water below. The whole advance had therefore been held up for two or three vital hours.

"Where were the RE's? Where were the Guards with their bloody pontoons they always cart around?" (It was popularly supposed that the Guards kept them for crossing the Rhine if they could only get rid of the rest of the British Army hanging around interfering with their progress.) We were very indignant; the rumours had a brassy insistence which we were not able to dismiss. Less personal, deeper and more sinister was what was going to happen when the German army, free from the Russian entanglement, turned to the Western Front.

Homfray, who was alleged to leave the running of his section to his batman, was as disturbing as Clifford. The armour of irresponsibility was proof against any contact with reality. Broome and Clifford indulged their trembling forebodings.

"Mark my words...", and "I wouldn't be in the Staff's shoes..."

"No danger of *that*—yet", said Quainton.

Combined with Homfray's studied fatuity the whole made an

orchestra of monstrous background anxiety. It formed a counterpart to our ignorance of the past. Perhaps this had something to do with Quainton's asking, and my agreeing, that I should go with him to religious service.

The evening found the two of us trudging through rain and mud to the chapel hut at the bottom of the camp. Our battalion padre was away or we would not have gone. He was cheerful and smooth, not a muscular Christian; it took time to savour the brand of his Church. We did not know the substitute but Quainton with easy optimism insisted that he couldn't be worse than ours.

The hut was so badly lit that it seemed rather to accentuate than modify the darkness outside. It could have held perhaps two hundred men; there were three men and ourselves. Despite the encircling gloom we could see that the padre was of spare build, his features being cadaverous rather than ascetic.

The dark and cold seemed to become more penetrating as if directly related to the progress of the service. My mind wandered. I remembered that our parson at home had told a sentimentally disposed congregation that the communion service to which they had subscribed for use at the Front was in regular demand just behind the front line and within range of the guns. My parents were present when he read the letter from the priest. Had I come across it? It might remind me of home. They realized, of course, that over such an enormous front line it was unlikely, but I might keep a look out for it. It was always there—a place called Etaples. I promised to do so, but did not mention that we would be very unlikely ever to be so far from the front line as Etaples.

The padre had started on his homily. It was hard to believe that he was advising us that it was important to look on the bright side of things. He spoke of a soldier who remained undismayed when his leg had been shot off by a shell. "After all", he had said philosophically, "I only have one boot to clean now." Perhaps the other three members of the congregation were permanent office staff, I thought, but even so it was a hoary chestnut to choose as an anecdote of personal experience for inspiring us that day.

We drifted out. It was still cold and raining, but at least the air was fresh. When we got back Clifford and Homfray were in the mess; Clifford gave us a would-be insolent stare. He did not bother to lower his voice too much when he muttered, "Here comes the pious brigade."

19

THE disappearance of the Colonel and Gull was unemphatic. In England the splendour of the Battalion Headquarters was such that the two persons of the Colonel and the Adjutant seemed of themselves to be the source of an effulgence, a fountain of uncreated light. Shorn of battalion parades, an orderly room, any discernible function, they ceased to emit enough glow to be distinguishable from ordinary worms. Lacking any evidence whatever I must fall back on my imagination to supply the deficiency. I suppose, accordingly, that Gull and the Colonel without their orderly room, with a battalion mess to act as a suitable setting for their brightest jewel, the Prince of Wales, with the threat—the very vulgar threat—of a horse-whipping and no horse to share it, had to look round for some means of filling time to prevent its being filled by something worse. In this quandary I imagine they fell back on precedent, and in their search they discovered efficiency, ruthlessness, unpardonable failure. All that was required then was to find a failure. What could be a more glaring example of failure than the disaster to B Company? It was, my imagination tells me, only the work of a moment to draw up a convincing and suitably damning report requesting the immediate recall and dismissal of B Company commander.

They could hardly have been more unfortunate in their choice of a scapegoat. Dear, kindly old sweetheart that he was, our Major was formidably well-connected. He also had a most unforgiving disposition and a keen and aristocratic dislike for bounders; what is more, he was liable to regard people who boasted of their princely friends as bounders.

Of course, it was all a most unfortunate misunderstanding, but... well, 'Gully' and the Colonel went—without even a farewell address to their troops.

Quainton went on leave just after this and wrote me the letter from which I learnt of his meeting with the cycling captain who was all that was left of staff car and colonel and adjutant of happier days. He had more news.

'When you go on leave don't go to see Cohen. I went—it was dreadful. He has lost both eyes, his right arm and both legs. He didn't know who I was though the nurse told him. He's simply—just has a silly grin. The nurse told me afterwards that every now and then he becomes terrified, cowers down in a corner of the room and sucks his thumb. Once he told his doctor that at these times he could see a patch of lawn open up, his mother rise out of her grave and walk slowly towards him. Otherwise he told no one—just went into a corner, scuttling on his stumps with astonishing speed, stuffed his left thumb into his mouth and waited trembling. When the fit was over he would go back to his silly giggling.'

'For though the body dies the soul shall live for ever'. I hope not; with all my heart I hope not.

Two days later there was another letter from Quainton, but this time it was to Clifford of all people.

"Look", he shouted to us, "look at this! Can you believe it?"

I read it and I could certainly understand his astonishment. 'Such a lark!' it said, 'You'll hardly believe it! I was just driving the car along the road when suddenly, there I was—in the ditch! Nothing whatever the matter of course, but the next thing I knew I was shoved into this looney bin and labelled 'shell-shock'!' That was all but for the usual opening and closing greetings.

He did not like Clifford; he knew Clifford liked none of us. Why then Clifford? As I read I could feel his eyes fixed on me. I read it slowly and carefully, wondering what to say, determined not to give anything away.

I handed it back. He was jubilant. 'What do you make of that? He's working his ticket. Why, he admits it himself! He's just fooling them. He's got wind-up! He knows very well what's coming to us as soon as the fine days come—the whole of the bloody German army from the Russian front. He's shrewd, he is."

I knew Quainton was not a fraud—he was worth two dozen Cliffords. As soon as I could I tackled Hauser. He sniggered and snuffled. He certainly did not believe Clifford, but he had nothing to suggest. He clearly did not regard it as an advertisement for the 'pious brigade'. Nor did I.

Why, oh why, write to Clifford? When I spoke to Carter he had nothing to say, but his attitude suggested, without words, "Well, what else do you expect? Why get mixed up with that snivelling crowd?"

The dark and gloomy days were made worse by the realization

that the 5th Battalion had gone. Stokes, Bayliss, Cohen, Despard, our Major, the Adjutant, the Colonel—where were they? Now Quainton, snuffed out with a snigger. Hauser, Carter and I were the only ones left. Hauser I did now know; Carter was too old. Homfray, Clifford and Broome: what confidence could one place in them—or in us? However mystified I felt I could not stifle the feeling that Quainton was a damned fool. And if Quainton was a fool, what kind of fool was I?

The winter was horrible. Without the glitter, the veneer to disguise the sordidness of our winter predicament, depression grew. No talk of the advantages of losing a limb—twice as 'lucky' in Cohen's case—quite covered the growing menace of the Russian defection. Something, however bogus, had been lost and there was nothing to replace it. Carter spoke of the merits of the Bhagavad-Gita. I could not have understood even if Carter had been the man to explain.

Time crawled by. January—nothing. February... nothing. March... a move to a forward position, that is, to within seven miles of the front—nothing. It began to be said, as our spirits rose with the lengthening days, that the enemy had 'missed the boat'. This immortal phrase, to which Neville Chamberlain was to add fresh lustre when Hitler missed it on his way to Norway, did not seem out of place when glorious campaigning weather, day after day of warm sunshine, went by. *We* would not have missed it like that! *We* would have caught the boat as we had done at Ypres in August. Unfortunately there had been no boat to catch—and we needed boats, not tanks. At Cambrai there had not even been a pontoon to catch.

Someone marked out trench positions, sited on reverse slopes with white tape, and told us that our men must dig them and revet them properly. It was not serious of course, but in war—you never knew—we might have to fall back and then it would be a good thing if the infantry had prepared positions to fall back on.

Rumours grew; they became weighty; even *Comic Cuts* seemed to know the date of the German offensive, and the date of the postponement, as if the writer at least believed.

Just before we were going to start digging I was ordered home on leave to attend at Buckingham Palace for the investiture, for I had been awarded the DSO. The first intimation was a letter which had been forwarded to me on which some wag had pencilled 'DSO' and an exclamation mark.

I was pleased; proud and pleased. I could hardly believe it. For a while I didn't give a damn whether I deserved it or not; I knew I didn't anyway. But '2nd Lieut. W. R. Bion, DSO' looked good and it felt good. Second Lieutenants with DSO's were rare birds anyway.

But by March the glow had begun to fade in the more ominous light of the threatening offensive. If only 'they' had supplied me with a dollop of courage to go with the medal—how nice it would have been!

At Le Havre I was made OC Boat; this particular position was *not* coveted. It was imposed on the most junior officer on the boat and necessitated certain tiresome but important chores. It led, however, to a moment of glory when at the end of the trip the major responsible for landing me with the duty caught sight of my ribbon and made a most handsome apology for imposing such a job on someone so distinguished.

20

THERE were about sixty officers and men present in a large room which turned out to be an ante-room to the Hall in which the investiture was to take place. A private, who had been awarded a DCM, and I were the youngest there. I was by far the youngest officer to be up for the DSO so a large, fierce and extremely important colonel addressed me personally.

"Now, mind what you are at. March up to him and stand to attention facing him. You've got your ribbon on? Well that's something at any rate", he said with the tone of one who must be thankful for any mercy however small. He continued, "His Majesty will put the medal on you so keep your hands out of it. For God's sake don't try to help; just stand to attention. Don't move and above all *do not try to engage in chat* with His Majesty. When he's done, step back and march out. Remember—no chat!"

I couldn't possibly have engaged in chat with anyone, let alone 'His Majesty'. The only thing I could have thought of saying was, "For God's sake get me out of this hole."

At last the ghastly moment came. There were few DSO's and before I could tell how, I was in front of the King with what looked like a picture hook stuck into my ribbon. On this he hung the DSO. As I was about to back out *he* started to chat.

"You were at Cambrai? That was a very fine action. You lost your tank I believe? Did you get it back?"

"No sir, but the infantry did."

"Ah! Excellent."

I could almost feel the colonel breathing fire down my neck; why had he not told His Majesty "and above all—don't chat!" Why pick on *me*?

As I was going out a large hand whipped off my DSO and slapped it into a box. Before I could defend it or myself he was handing me the box. I didn't dare to see if the medal was there or if he had just substituted the box and stuck to the medal.

Outside the Palace gates was a small knot of press photographers and civilians. Through the lane they formed I escaped to the end of the queue where my mother waited for me. It seemed a shame that she had not been allowed in to see and share the glorious moment which was in fact so much hers and so little mine.

I could not have explained to anyone why it weighed so heavily upon me. But at least I could understand why a VC was virtually a sentence of death; why men said that winners of the VC either broke down and found a soft job in England, or were killed subsequently trying to deserve the honour they had won.

I have little memory of that leave other than fierce unhappiness. Seared into my mind was one silly, trivial occasion, and one stupendous and numbing.

My mother, defeated and helpless in the face of my taciturn moroseness, asked if I knew the riddle of the miser's most hated flower. "It's the anemone", she said, "because it reminds him of someone asking 'Any money? Any money?'" My response was a stony silence which was so hostile that it frightened me. After a moment I felt stealing over me such pity for what I was sure was her utter misery that I looked at her, caught her eye and the fleeting trembling of her lips. The tension was released. "Damn silly things, medals", I said, "but very nice to look at don't you think?" She wiped away her tears, relieved at being able to weep openly.

The second event followed almost immediately—voices in the distance, calling urgently, coming nearer, newsboys. I did not need to be told; I felt that the news was so old, so very old that I read it mechanically, with tired eyes. The banner headlines read 'Great German Attack Opens'. I read on: Blah... blah... blah, said my mind. I could have made it up in my sleep. Daylight had caught up with my nightmares. 'Dense fog...' Quite. I suppose their troops, like ours, must have had luck... What? '... holding the enemy in our battle positions... Tincourt'. Our battle positions? There could be no doubting it. We were holding them in our battle positions— 'Tincourt' being the battle positions mentioned!

I remembered the climax of a funny story about a man trapped in a blazing house who was urged to jump from the roof-top into a tarpaulin below. 'And at last old Bill 'e jumped. And we couldn't 'elp larfin' because there weren't no tarpaulin there!' Well, I *could* help laughing; because there weren't no battle positions there! The lying jades! The lying bloody twisters!

"How's the news dear?", said my mother in her calm, matter-of-fact little tones. "Good?"

I pretended to be absorbed in the news while I tried to think of a suitable lie. '... enemy's overwhelming forces. They attacked in a

strength of three troops to every one of ours'. Let me see now...
When *we* were attacking we considered that the attack had no
hope at all if it was not *at least* in a strength of three to every one
defencer. 'Thick fog'—fatal to the attacking troops. 'Three to one'—
barely margin enough for starting an attack. Who then was
overwhelmed? And why?

"Yes", I said at last. "Pretty good they seem to think. Sounds all
right." I folded up the paper. "Lucky I am at the end of my leave or
I would have had to be recalled." I was due to return at six thirty
from Waterloo Station the next morning. The lying bastards, I
thought. If only the trenches had been marked out in *red* tape even
the Germans might have been held up!

We walked slowly along Green Park to our hotel. It was hopeless
to pretend; my mother was no fool. It was simply a matter of
compelling our face muscles to do their drill.

By eight that evening I felt neither of us could stand any more.
Pleading the excuse of an early morning and a long day I suggested
we should go to bed. She agreed—like an automaton.

As I entered my bedroom and closed the door I felt I had entered
Hell. I have entered it since, not often, but too often. To others
who have to do the same I can say: it's not so bad if you stick it out.
After the first three or four times it's not so bad, but don't do it till
after twenty-one—nineteen is too early.

The next morning when I saw my mother's white powdered face I
recognized misery. We did not talk; we had withdrawn. We said
good-bye in the hotel and a taxi took me to Waterloo.

'Everybody suddenly burst out singing'—I did not; not even after
the war. Never, never again. I was not unhappy—indeed I often
felt I was much happier than most. But no more singing; never.

There was singing at Waterloo; alcoholic singing, but
surprisingly little. The platforms were a mass of khaki—'recalled
from leave', 'all leave cancelled'. We took whatever coaches were in
front of us and in due course the train pulled out.

No more cares, no more thinking; no worries and nothing to do
but remain a parcel of BEF. until one reached one's destination.
Where was that? If you were a gunner, 'Ubique'. 'Quo fata vocant.
Quo fas et gloria ducunt'. But what if you were a 2nd Lieutenant of
Tanks with a DSO? Where the hell did one go from there?

In fact it turned out to be Le Havre. I stuck it for three days.
Then, following the example of other impatient souls, confident
that in the chaos we should not be found out, we 'deserted' towards
the Line. It was coming towards us anyhow.

21

THE technique of travel was simple—thumbing lifts. At the end of the first day I found myself at Etaples—where the communion service was said to be right behind the front line under gun-fire. Well, perhaps it *was* a bit exaggerated, but the news from the front seemed likely to make the lie approximate more closely to the truth by bringing the gun-fire up to the communion service.

A gunner captain with whom I travelled for about twenty miles said, "I see the wicked Germans have been bombing one of our hospitals." He pointed to a newspaper paragraph and winked heavily. "Clearly marked with the Red Cross too. I know the ruddy place—there are ammunition dumps for at least five miles along the railway. They've got the hospital right in the middle of it. No wonder they marked it clearly with a Red Cross. I nearly had kittens every hour I was there—wound in my leg; couldn't run", he explained.

I had been directed to bed down at a small hospital just outside Etaples. It appeared to be a peaceful spot. I found a friendly RAMC doctor who showed me where I could lie up for the night and as it was a lovely afternoon I unpacked my safety razor to mark the spot as mine, and decided to stroll round and move on after a night's rest.

"How is it you are so slack?" I asked him. "I would have thought you would be chock-a-block with wounded."

"Efficiency, my lad. The moment this shemozzle started they sent all wounded that the Boche didn't or couldn't capture straight to England. Result—the first decent holiday we've had for years. We've got one poor devil in that hut over there, that's all—he's dying anyway."

I was worn out. I lay down under some pines and went to sleep. When I woke the sun was beginning to set. For a time I was aware of voices mingling with dozing dreams.

"Aren't I *awful!*" It was a girl's voice. "You *don't* think I'm awful do you?" The man muttered something. The girl spoke again. "It *would* happen on my half day—and me going out with you."

Again the man's voice. "All right", she replied, "you stay here; I won't be long."

I felt, as I had felt my last night in England, that my nerve must have gone. I was petrified with fear at an ordinary lovers' lane conversation such as one might hear any night in England. I could not make up my mind to move. Before I had made up my mind to stay she was back.

"OK. He's snuffed it." The two walked off. Lucky he had died in time, but what on earth was the matter with me? Not shell-shock pray God. Not... ridiculous!

The next morning I felt quite rested. Before going off I said goodbye to the RAMC man and thanked him for putting me up. He had found out that orders had come into the RTO's office that all Tank Corps were to report at Le Tréport, the Tank Corps Depot camp. I checked up with him to find out where it was.

"I hear your officer patient died."

"Yes; he shouldn't have, but he kept on starting up and trying to get out of bed. Thought the Boche were after him. Last time he was so terrified—he thought the nurse was trying to murder him—he leapt out of bed, ruptured his wound. Well, so long. Good luck. What? Oh yes, she's a charmer." He winked. "But you haven't a chance old boy—half the thugs in the town are after her."

Le Tréport was a magnificent camp, but I saw little of it. At HQ I asked the Adjutant for news. "Blangy: I'll give you a warrant, but I would get on anything on wheels if you can—the 5th Battalion are refitting there. So long—and good luck." He saw the ribbon. "That's very nice. Had it long? Congratulations—should get you anywhere—without a warrant!"

A lorry was going out of camp. I jumped on next to the driver to get a lift to the rail-head. Then I found he was going to Blangy. Hardly believing my good luck I asked him to put me down at Battalion HQ when we got there. He had to concentrate on his driving, leaving me free with my thoughts.

So; the officer had died of wounds—or was it shell-shock? Shell-shock was obviously complicated—from Quainton who, according to Clifford, was working his ticket, to the officer who did not bother about his wounds but thought that everyone from the Boche to his nurse was trying to murder him; all apparently had shell-shock. War was also complicated. My experience of it so far should have added up to something, but from it all I learnt nothing—presumably because at nineteen I had become too set in my ways. Now I suspect that I was aware of a lack of discipline either of the kind that is a part of spontaneous maturation, or of that which depends on endless mechanical repetition such as military drill. This last I had seen when the Coldstream Guards took Gouzeancourt; I could therefore imagine a feat of arms which could *not* be conveyed by words however eloquent. For lack of any such training I had my childhood and schoolboy culture. It gave me something, but neither the discipline of repetitive command, nor the 'heaven' of middle class England, nor an exo-skeleton taking the place of a skeleton for an endo-skeletonous animal, can serve; still less in the domain of the mind.

At last we arrived and I reported to HQ. To the voluble inquiries of the Colonel I made the appropriate conversational replies. I had, of course, had a good leave. No, I had not been besieged by bevies of admiring females. I quickly escaped to rejoin my company.

My first impression was that the battalion had not altered. I had met O'Kelly and Fitzwilliam at HQ and here were the old Gang. Both adjutant and colonel had come to us before March, but the Adjutant I had met only when he told me I was to go on leave. Here were all the old familiar faces—Homfray, Clifford, Carter, Hauser, Cook. Aitches was a newcomer from A Company where he had been a section commander in the original battalion. He was likeable, but timid. As I know now, and suspected then, A Company would not have transferred him unless they wanted to get rid of him by kicking him upstairs. He was with us to be promoted.

Broome, rosy and youthful as ever, had no horror stories. "It was pretty thick I can tell you", was his contribution to the saga of March 21st.

Where were the others?

"What others? Oh yes, you met Cartwright and Robinson didn't you?—I had forgotten. Bridges? We don't really know, but Robinson was killed. In fact all the men in tanks were done in I think. Cartwright may have been captured after escaping from his tank." That was as far as I went with Broome's story.

As I had missed all the fighting I was first choice to take a party with Lewis guns up to the front at once. It was the Adjutant himself who had come round to our mess to give me the message in person. Written orders were being typed out and would be sent round soon.

He drew me into a corner out of hearing of anyone else. "Things are pretty damn serious I can tell you. We have no tanks and I'm certain the rest of us won't be long after you. I'm sorry it is so soon after your leave. You are really the only officer..."

I was furious. Why? I cannot have realized that I was supposed to fight. I was dominated by a romantic idea that my business was to be a hero, decorated, and to spend the rest of life basking in the warmth of approval. Fitzwilliam was guilty too; had I known it his apologies only showed that he also was an amateur soldier. I felt it was good of me to have 'won' the DSO—I think I must already have begun to believe this. I hope it didn't show; fortunately the light in our corner was not good. I dredged up some commonsense from somewhere while he talked.

"Of course you realize we are shot to bits—only senior non-tank crew officers left—we useless non-combatants. The Boche have torn another gap in our line; we have to help stop it. I'm expecting orders to come in any time. We are to 'stand to' for immediate movement to the Line—supposing there is one".

"Not like Cambrai?"

"Oh God, worse, far worse. As far as I can make out it's as bad as March 21st. Only this is to the Channel ports—if they get across the sea. No retreat and no surrender."

Ah, my cup of tea after all—heroism. But I knew it was not. This was not an agreeable option for 'public school men of suitable character'. It sounded a simple, straightforward order like laying out kit, just so, for inspection; or 'all officers must return salutes in a soldierly manner' and not as if they were acknowledging a well-deserved tribute to their superior merits; or 'the Guards Division will retake Gouzeancourt'.

22

I HAD not counted on getting back to the battalion to be hustled off straightway as if I had been having a nice time while they were fighting. Except for the 'nice time', which was my responsibility, this was no inaccurate summary.

O'Toole was there, and Hayler; Gunner Allen was shut in, uncommanding. Of the rest, about a dozen, I knew one or two faces including a Corporal Smith, cheerful and stolid. To my great relief Hauser was added to the party thus giving me company and a second in command.

After a deal of eager but curiously ineffectual bustle we loaded ourselves into two lorries. Our morale was not bad; it was not good. It was replaced by representations of morale remembered from earlier pre-Cambrai models. We jolted to a stop—Arras. Gunner Allen made a rare emergence to speak to me.

"They say this place is honeycombed with passages and tunnels under the whole of Arras. Wouldn't mind staying here for a bit." He relapsed into silence. From what I had heard from O'Toole it was the communication, not the silence, which was remarkable.

The pause was long enough to let the men get tea. Then Hauser and I clambered onto the seat next to the driver. Orders were to proceed to a point behind the Messines Ridge. The jolt, rattle and roar of the lorry would have made conversation difficult had we wished to talk. For my part I was glad to be left to my own thoughts.

I was more relieved than I would have thought possible to have Hauser as my supporting officer. I had not lost my affection for Quainton, and I had friendly memories of the South African, Stokes. I was dis-illusioned by Quainton and dis-enchanted by the background from which we came. The rhythmical rise and fall of the cold brilliance of the Very lights pierced the velvety blackness. We were travelling parallel with, about five miles from, the Front Line. What the devil were we up to now? I felt ignorant in detail of my task, of my place in any larger design. We had no rifles; Hauser, O'Toole, Smith and I had revolvers; six Lewis guns were

196

manned by four men each. I did not like Lewis guns; I thought them unreliable and unsuitable for any job we had to do inside or outside tanks. They sounded 'tinny' when they were firing. Our job?—to reinforce infantry. Training?—purely technical and applicable only to the machinery, guns, engines which we had to use. Of fighting we knew nothing and we were supposed to engage one of the world's greatest professional armies. Could the nation possibly be in such dire straits that we twenty men could really be required to reinforce the Front? We were, had we known it, GHQ Reserve—no less.

Foch had decided that in no circumstances were the reserves he had accumulated to be committed to the battle. He gambled on the line holding till the great enemy attacks of March and April had exhausted themselves. This we did not know. What I and thousands of others like me were to learn over the next few months was desolation, loneliness, defeat.

Cook turned up the next time we left our lorries. "These trenches here are where Carter and I will be. They are advanced Company HQ. I'm OC Company. We shall call ourselves B Company. One mile in front is the Infantry Brigade; they are down to the strength of one company, spread out over a mile. You must spread out your six Lewis guns over that same mile. There are no supports so no support trenches—unless of course time lies heavy on your hands and you like to dig some." He gave a cold, acid smile. "I don't think time will lie heavy on your hands—we have been told the enemy has to break through at no matter what cost. There's only you lot and this bunch of infantry between him and the sea thirty or forty miles behind. There are no orders for retreat because there is no retreat arranged. You hold on—unless of course you are dead. Any questions? Of course not—there aren't any. Well, good-bye. Don't forget—one mile, Divide 1760 yards by six Lewis guns."

I divided the party into six and we advanced in open order of sections; three infantry guides were there to show us the way. I said I would be with the third section from the right if wanted.

Dawn broke about half an hour after we reached our position. I could see then that our trench lay at the corner of a hutted camp. It stank because it was full of dead horses. An infantry officer told me the enemy trenches were fifty yards in front and that they liked infiltrating through the huts to throw a grenade or two into our line and then disappear. It did not happen while we were there, but his report cost us many an anxious hour; perhaps it was well for our vigilance.

I posted the Lewis gun nearest me with a field of fire down a lane formed by the huts. Doing something physical was a great relief and I planned to walk the length of our mile to post the other five guns. As I was nearer the right flank I decided to work towards it first.

I had not gone ten yards when I found the trench had been obliterated; nor could I see where the trench continued on the far side of the burst. I set out to crawl the gap but found I was at once observed and fired on by a machine-gun. I had already fallen so much under the influence of this eerie place that I felt relief at this evidence of a human being's existence. Still, bullets are bullets and I didn't want my brains spattering out of the back... I began to pull myself back by my toes. This led to another burst of fire. I did not want to stay there all day. I dared not try to get up and run for it. After some minutes I tried again; same result. If this chap gets annoyed, I thought, I shan't be surprised if he takes more careful aim. I felt better when I buried my head into the mud.

After what I thought was a decent interval I again began to pull myself out by my toes. This time the response was immediate, but it was aimed rifle fire—not machine-gun. This felt personal and intimate. Throwing caution away I scrambled back as fast as I could to the remnant of trench. I was pouring with sweat and trembling.

It was queer. I had no idea where my marksman was, but for the first time, and only once again in the war, I felt engaged directly with a person who was trying to kill me personally. The fact that the encounter was entirely one sided gave it an added peculiarity of being animal—the hunted animal. I was having an unusual view of 'sport'.

I waited for a moment or two to recover a more usual frame of mind. Then I walked back to my men. I told them the way was blocked and said they had better be careful at places where the trench was blown 'in case' such spots were covered by machine-guns or snipers. I said I was going to try the left flank.

A few yards to the left I found another destroyed patch of trench. Heeding my own advice this time I picked up an abandoned rifle and crawling on my belly raised the butt slowly and cautiously till I thought it might show. At once a burst of machine-gun fire knocked it out of my grasp as if it had been struck by a sledge hammer.

I went back to my men. This time I would wait till dark before further experiments.

After a while I relieved the sentry. I told two to keep by the gun ready to fire, and the other two to start digging the trench deeper, throwing the earth so as to seal off the ends of the trench to give us some defence from enfilade fire as well as the existing protection from front and rear.

Before long Gunner Sears called out that they had reached soft mud. He took my place whilst I had a look. As I watched I could see water welling up from below; it was obvious that we could dig no deeper. I felt unable to think, at the end of my resources.

It seemed important to keep the men occupied, so for that reason more than for any other I told Sears and his mate to hollow out two upright shallow depressions in the front wall of the trench so that they could just recline in them, and if possible sleep in them as they stood. Taking over the sentry job I told them to make the depressions as strong and firm as patting with entrenching tools allowed.

23

THE remains of the camp gave very good cover for any sniper who wanted to approach our line. As I was not a soldier it did not occur to me that the same might be true in the opposite direction. Had I been a soldier I might have wanted to go in the opposite direction, but as I was only a public school boy dressed up as a soldier, complete with decoration, I had not the necessary resources. I felt, secretly, that my morale was bad.

Nowadays I would not make such a simple diagnosis, but as it was I was impelled to prove my courage—the lack of it being, as I thought, my main defect. This erroneous idea was, and still is, generally held. Cromwell knew there was something wrong with his armies. He was opposed by a great man, Prince Rupert, who had courage and a high morale, but temperamentally was an amateur and could not see his problem in any terms other than those of the amateur outlook. Cromwell, who might appear to be even more of an amateur, was temperamentally a professional; his approach to his material, the 'decayed tapsters and serving men', was characteristically professional. He saw that, coming into a situation which he, like Rupert, had inherited, something had to be done to remedy the past and forestall the future. Rupert had a cause, the Royalist cause: Cromwell had a religion and a God. The god of the Royalist cause was a poor specimen of human being who, despite all his attempts and those of his later followers at sanctification, could only reform, too late, radically poor material which in fact remained the poor stuff it was. That was a bad start for Rupert's foundations. Patriotism, Edith Cavell discovered much later, was not enough. On this foundation Rupert failed to erect the necessary structure for an army at war.

Cromwell, a farmer, had learned in his contact with the real forces of nature that there is no substitute for discipline. He applied this discovery to what was, superficially, an entirely new situation. It was therefore second nature in him to realize that his soldiers, if they were to be soldiers, must have discipline as well as a cause. His God had to have qualities superior to those of a fallible and frail human being. With 'cause' and its attendant structure of discipline Cromwell had an immeasurably superior foundation on which to build. His cavalry improved: Rupert's did not. Both men had the same disadvantage, namely, coming into the story too late. The minimum conditions necessary for the work to be done cannot be improvised for they require generation of time for maturation. The seeds must be there but also the soil, the nation which allows them to germinate.

When I entered actively for the first time into the nation's affairs it was as a recruit destined as a matter of course to become an officer; I did not qualify for a vote in a general election till the fighting was over. Now, at Messines, I was re-entering a war which from my viewpoint had fundamentally altered. I could not say why I felt this; still less could I formulate the change of which I had become certain after Cambrai.

When I peered cautiously at the huts in front of me I was still untrained—not a professional, but certainly not an amateur. I was no longer obsessed with ambition to be brave; that I knew was beyond me, but I did not want to be disgraced. There was usually no danger of disgrace because there was nothing disgraceful to do—you cannot run away in company or, at least, it is relatively difficult. As a section commander I was to learn of problems associated with loneliness and isolation. As I peered into no-man's land I was to experience one of them almost at once.

A sheet of corrugated iron slithered from a roof and crashed to the ground. I was watching that spot at the time so I knew what caused the grinding metallic sound that preluded the crash. Then the silence which was absolute flowed back and enveloped first the camp and then our party in a hideous fear. I watched. I waited for the grenade thrower. Nothing. At last, to break this evil spell, I looked at my watch. It was twelve minutes past ten. I returned to stare at the camp. The sun was shining, the sky blue. The Lewis gun, flanked by the two intense gunners, glistened like a small sinister idol, the centre of a strange religion. There was no sound. I kept my gaze on the huts for any sign of movement.

At last, feeling it must by now be past noon, I looked at my watch again. It was not quite a quarter past ten. I looked at my watch incredulously; the second hand was moving and the sun confirmed the hour. Again I felt fear. Could I possibly last till evening? In desperation I stopped thinking about the past or future; I began taking compass bearings on every object within my limited view. To my relief my fear began to ebb away. It was an experience familiar to me in my childhood nightmares but not in waking life. It was to be repeated over and over again in this new horrid shape throughout the war till at last it began to lose its horror by force of repetition.

We took it in turns to do the simple jobs I had laid down. These changes afforded us all relief until I judged it had become dark enough for me to start my tour to the left flank.

Some dim recollection that troops always 'stood to arms' at dawn and again at dusk made me tell the men to 'stand to' regardless of the fact that they had done nothing but stand to arms all day. Experienced troops would know that no one would be likely to be prowling about a ruined camp at ten in the morning; an experienced officer would not have started to tour his section of trench at dusk. I was not experienced, not trained, not disciplined. Therefore—I set out. Having passed, on my belly, the part of ruined trench where I knew I would come under bursts of fire from the machine-gun I began my walk along the intact though ragged trench. As I did so I heard the moan of approaching shells. It was the start of the evening 'strafe'. I did not know this; to me it was all hell let loose. The entire trench system began to break loose and start skywards in great and little clods of earth. I was sure in my ignorance that the enemy had started a night attack—and in my ignorance I was quite correct.

Feeling I could hardly be in greater danger outside the trench than in it I walked, stumbled and ran along the top. So long as I remained alive and unwounded it was faster than trying to scramble along the trench and to some extent I could keep a direction. I fell down, threw myself down and was blown down every few yards, but eventually I was hailed by a voice from the trench. I stood on the top and shouted my inquiries, thus displaying my coolness under fire—I hoped. One of the men pulled me in; I may even have had enough sense to hope that someone would.

The crew had made themselves relatively comfortable and were encouraged by the presence of an infantry officer. I went into the dug-out where there were three officers. Ordinarily they would have been in candle-light but as the candles were extinguished at once by concussion from the shell-bursts they were relying on a torch, the battery of which must have been exhausted.

I was excited and under the impression that I was engaged in repelling an enemy attack, whereas they were under the impression that they were undergoing a sordid ritual—so-and-so wounded, so-and-so killed; 'shuffle the cards old man, and pass the whisky'. I cannot believe my intervention and the subsequent conversation meant much more than a shrug of the shoulders and the assumption that I was a 'case'.

I ventured that our gunners did not seem to be answering the enemy barrage. A sardonic face turned an angry look on me.

"What makes you think we have any gunners? We've had no artillery support, no air cover since we came."

Apparently he saw 'the ribbon'. Anyhow his look softened and he began to smoulder rather than to flame.

"How long have you been here?" I asked.

"Three weeks", he replied. I knew they were a West Riding regiment because I overheard one of my men ask one of theirs as we passed in a communication trench when we moved in, "Who are you chum?"

"West Ridings—who are you?"

"The fucking Tanks—walking."

I excused myself as I had to get to our left flank. I probably made some remark intended to convey good will or a desire to help. If so I cannot imagine what impression other than one of stark idiocy it created on them.

24

I STARTED off in the trench till I was out of sight of my gun crew and then continued as before. It might be daft to expose myself like that but at least I had some idea where I was going. It might be daft to leave the shelter of the dug-out. But how, in war, does one decide what is daft? The answer is that one does not, if one can help it, decide these things in war. They are decided in peace, formulated in training manuals, enforced by orders. Such is the perversity of the human animal that these prudent dispositions intended to protect against irresponsibility and uniformed improvisation are then erected into rigid barriers as a defence against thought.

Thus, after Cambrai when Quainton and others of us who began to have doubt about our wisdom in taking up arms came to the point of decision, we fell back on inertia because we had decided to fight supposedly when in a godly, righteous and sober frame of mind. The solitary exception to this convention was a scruffy, red-faced, unshaven scoundrel who, being asked by our then apoplectic colonel—appropriately named Bulk—what had caused him to enlist, swivelled his blood-shot eye on the display of patriotic ribbon before him and said, "Booze". When we learn, like the child walking, to act automatically without expenditure of thought we also learn how to avoid pain by economizing thought.

Again a shout; I jumped into the trench where Hauser and his crew were. Hauser said he had been to see the left flank gun under Sergeant O'Toole and found them in good form. Then there wasn't much point in going on to them? He agreed. He also agreed that the enemy was going to attack.

The barrage increased in intensity, but as we had no Very lights there was no way in which we could see if his infantry had left their trenches. Then to our right I thought I saw figures. I drew my Colt and began to drop ammunition into the chamber. It gave me relief to be doing something. I heard through the din the chattering tinny fire of Lewis guns and hoped that they were ours. There was a Vickers firing about twenty yards to our right.

"Must be one of the battalion guns."

"I didn't see any when I came."

"I should have thought you would hardly be able to see anything at all. It's not a German gun anyhow", said Hauser.

As I was loading my revolver I felt it was the end, the last straw. I decided if the enemy came to grips I would empty my revolver into any German I could and then surrender 'hände hoch'. It did not occur to me that the Germans would not be idle while I was firing or that I would still be in a dangerous place liable to be killed at any time after surrender. I felt it would all be over.

I finished loading carefully and methodically. Hauser told me, a long time after, how funny my stolid method seemed and how immensely reassuring. Out of the corner of my eye I saw the attack to our right peter out—or so I thought. In fact I could not possibly have distinguished; I must have realized this for Hauser told me I had warned our gunners to expect enemy in front and also coming along our trench from the right.

The rest of that night was made up of fitful gunfire, shells blowing in our trench, machine-guns—but apparently no response from us. The dispiriting effect was profound and only became clear when we could compare our lot with something better.

We were in that position for three weeks. I have no clear memory of this period except one day when the monotony of helplessness was broken by a display in strength by the Royal Flying Corps. Suddenly a formation of bombers and fighters appeared above our lines and swept the skies clear of enemy planes. The demonstration lasted for half an hour. For us who had seen no British planes for three weeks it was a revelation of power almost unbelievable in its majesty. Though the enemy dribbled back in his ones and twos after our planes had left we never again quite lost the sense of pride and assurance.

A similar sense of mastery was communicated by the French just before our relief. One day we were told that from nightfall we should be supported by the French artillery who were relieving ours. Our gunners were firing with worn barrels—when indeed they were able to fire at all. The result was premature bursts so that instead of shelling the enemy we had the mortification of being peppered by shell-bursts from our own guns at the back of our necks. There was a celebrated story of a warrant officer who had fallen in his men under a flag of truce, marched the small party back to the supporting gunners of the 7th Division and offered to surrender to them. The 7th Division were proud men and did not like this bitter comment on their worn guns, honourably worn; our times did not lend themselves to such humours. We did not pretend to relish the advent of French gunners who we assumed would be even worse than our own.

The night proved restless. The French, said to be the famous Nancy Division, the 11th, the Corps de Fer, had moved in to support behind our right. The enemy, presumably having wind of the relief, were unusually active. The French responded, not with a few Very lights, but with a pyrotechnic display of rockets, 'flaming onions'—so named after their appearance in the night sky—star shells, and a peculiar noise which first resembled a beating of many biscuit tins and then became the characteristic bark of what was then the most famous artillery gun in the world, the French 75. Instead of passively enduring what we could not cure we found a screen of fire put down between us and the enemy positions.

Starved of hope as we were we could hardly bear the relief which these friendly and efficient gunners gave us that night; since the previous evening we had had to withstand six attacks on our position. I will not say we had beaten them off. We had countered them; we had fired on them. Why they had persisted and why finally they had stopped I do not know. Perhaps their nightmares were worse because hope was mixed in with them, while ours were untroubled by anything so unnerving. That night was like a refreshing rain.

The terrible disasters which have befallen the French, starting with the mutinies of 1917, have laid many brave men of a brave nation open to the imputation of degeneracy. But April and August that year gave me a short, profound insight into the French fighting man which threw a glaring and unwelcome light on the frivolity that marked some of our attitudes.

When the French infantry relieved us they were complimentary about our efforts; they were astonished at our extended line and the insignificant numbers with which we had held it. They were gay; they seemed in no way anxious to disguise their arrival from the enemy. When they were alarmed they advertised it by the truly beautiful firework display. When the enemy put down their barrage there was nothing half-hearted about the answering 75's. And as one of our men, hardly able to credit his eyes, reported, "Sir! They're all standing on the top of the trench peeing into it before they get in!" I looked back and sure enough that was exactly what they seemed to be doing.

A couple of hours later we were in billets, two or three farm buildings in good repair. Hot water, shaves, more or less clean clothes, conspired to give an evening meal of bully beef stew a sense of luxury. Cook, Carter, Hauser and I were with fifteen men left out of twenty. Never had we known so few casualties.

An orderly brought in a message. Cook read it and when we had finished our meal, but before we had completely relaxed, he said quietly, "Sorry you chaps. Pack up—back we go. The Boche have broken through. We must man the line—quick—at Chinese Wall, before they get there. Lorries are waiting."

How cold the night had become, how dark. No brilliant white of our barrage illuminating the distant line—only the sombre spurt and immediately dying glow of bursting enemy shells to show how much closer the line had come.

This time I had four gun teams and a new officer, Osprey, under me. Cook again was in command at Advanced Company HQ with Carter as his second in command—though in theory he was the Reconnaissance Officer and marked to go back to that job if we ever had tanks again. I was to establish my Section HQ somewhere between Company HQ and our gun positions. By the time we reached our position there was not a sign of any disturbance, let alone battle and breakthrough. Thank God! Thank God! Could it be a false alarm? I devoutly hoped so. But it was not; the breakthrough was to our right.

The silence and lack of activity was soon obtrusive as even more unnerving than the chaos of shell-fire we had just been relieved of by the French. I didn't know what was happening, or what had happened. The war had become a terrifying game of chess in which we had to participate. It was difficult to find an adjustment to the fact that one had become a metaphor with which one was familiar as a debased cliché. We were mere pawns. By God—so we were!

25

W E were to fill a gap on the left of the Lowland Division. I spaced
out my four guns with Osprey at the second post from the left. It
might as well have been the tenth post from the middle for all the
difference it could make. I have put this down precisely because it is
the kind of precise nonsense we used, to give substance to a figment
of the imagination. It was the New Religion. There was a warfare
on earth in which our four Lewis guns were enrolled in the forces of
Light and Truth against the Powers of Darkness—The Devil's Own
maybe? But that was only a joke—this was not a joke.

The bold contours cutting the sky-line, Messines Ridge, the great
crater of the old battle—perhaps one ought to patrol round it to see
if any enemy were there. Sweating with fear I set out. Then I
became aware of figures on the crest; an enemy patrol. I had no
grenades. But I had a revolver, blast it. I could fight. No, I
couldn't—I was outnumbered. I was scared to death. I did not
know where the enemy were, where our lines.

They saw me and then mercifully turned on their tracks and went
back the way they had come. More Angels of Mons, or just devils
from Hell, or shell-shock, or simple ordinary wind-up? I scrambled
back to the trench, said good-bye to the second gun crew from the
right and set out while it was dark enough not to be seen, to report
to Advanced Company HQ. On my way I passed a curved
corrugated iron sheet which formed the roof for an ideal little hut
for my section HQ. If only I could locate it by map reference I
could tell Cook and Carter *just* where it was. It is such a relief to
know *exactly* where everyone is. When you have no idea whatever
where you are yourself it is, as I discovered, an admirable
substitute.

"Yes", I said nonchalantly, "I saw some Boche. No, they weren't
doing anything. Going home I should think."

"Did they see *you*?" said Carter.

"I think so."

"Did they fire at you? You're sure?"

Surely, I wondered, he's not working up for another decoration;

it was hellish enough to be trying to earn one I had already. But Cook was paying no attention. The covered bit of trench, in which Cook and Carter were, looked cosy I thought.

"All right Bion. Let us know when anything happens."

I found the tin hut again and crawled into it. I was glad to lie down. Above my head a small piece of mud was suspended, held to the roof by a dried grass stem. It quivered now and then with distant explosions.

I think I dozed. At any rate it seemed that the bit of mud was swaying, slowly, smoothly like a pendulum, like the pit and the pendulum of Poe's story. How my head ached, though I could not have banged it. But the guns *were* banging and the grass now was dancing, not swaying. Dancing! Jigging up and down like a corpse on barbed wire when a storm of machine-gun bullets made a breeze.

I got up and quickly crawled out of the hut. I felt it would drive me mad if I stayed there another minute. It is peculiar that so many people feel they will go mad—in another minute!—if the baby won't stop yelling, the dog barking, the telephone bell ringing—and now if the damned guns won't stop banging. No good telling them I would go mad if they didn't stop. I felt I couldn't stay there another minute!

Shells were falling close around. Perhaps the enemy had found the map reference of that blasted hut. I hadn't given it to Carter; they would never be able to find me. They wouldn't look for me anyway. Who was looking for Cohen? Or Stokes? Or Bayliss? I wasn't. I felt like a cornered rat. There was nowhere to go. 'They' were trying to club me to death. Clumsy brutes! Like trying to smash an egg in the angle between wall and floor—with a hoop. So simple really. But no; they were too clumsy to finish me off, couldn't solve the problem of how to club me to death. And I couldn't even sit up on my hind quarters and put my little paws together and pray the damned swine to let me off—just once! Just this little once! Oh God! I will never be naughty again—never! The guns were fewer! Well, maybe *once* more. Damn it, they've started again! Oh God! I *swear* I won't. Please, *please* just this once!

I got out. Sulky, frightened, resentful—God be damned for making a cringing rat of me!

At number two post (from the left flank you remember—not that I give a damn if you don't) I could not find Osprey. I bawled his name; I became angry and yelled.

There was a slab of concrete which had been blown by a shellburst so that it covered a hollow, probably part of an old trench. From under this crawled Osprey. Pale, watery-eyed, unshaven, he was 'like things you find under a stone', but he *was* a thing under a stone!

"Osprey!" I pulled myself together. "Osprey! What the hell's the matter with you?"

"Nothing", he said weakly with a voice like his pale watery eyes. "Nothing. Why?"

Well, at least he could talk. I began to swear and as I swore I realized how relieved I felt.

"Look, you must shave! You really must! You look simply terrible. And you must make your men shave."

He began to laugh. "*You* don't look too well-shaven", he said.

Of course I had not. I had forgotten that. "I know", I lied, "that's what reminded me. I'm just going to, so I thought I would tell you as well."

He seemed satisfied. Anyhow he did not go on laughing and he didn't seem to feel I should set an example to my men. Then I remembered; no tanks, no water, let alone hot water such as we used to boil on the exhausts. I got my razor out of my knapsack and had a dry shave. Another time, I vowed, I would not be so thoughtlessly efficient. It brought the blood to our cheeks—if not quite as we would wish.

Osprey had frightened me. If I really looked as he did when he crawled out from under that stone, what would our men be like? I took him with me to each gun post in turn. To my relief the men looked much better than their officers. Osprey agreed readily enough not to take shelter in that way again; so readily in fact that I was sure he was afraid of what that rat-like life had done to him.

For two more days nothing happened to break the monotony of constant, vigilant staring at no-man's land—the crater edge, the slow rise to the crest of the ridge, the grey mud so similar in all but colour to Hill 40, inspired a state which was not nightmare, not waking, not sleep. It was an animal existence in which the eyes held sway. One did not think; one did not look; one stared. What we felt reminds me of a young child who had been sexually assaulted by the Germans in their last days of power in a village near Lille. She had been cutting some meat off a dead mule by the roadside when we came upon her. She looked up, stared and silently slid away leaving the meat as a cat might abandon its prey. While she disappeared down steps to a cellar we waited and then realized she was watching us from behind a door.

The grey scene later formed an amalgam with the scene at the Steenbeck and became the backcloth of a dream I had at Oxford—'when the war was over'. Night after night I found myself on my belly clinging by my toes and fingers to a glistening slope at the bottom of which was a raging torrent—the dirty trickle of the Steenbeck. Towards this I slithered. If I tried to arrest my progress by sticking in my toes or fingers it accelerated the descent; if I desisted, it again accelerated my descent. I did not make a sound. I just woke up bathed in sweat.

I had reached this mindless state when word came through from Cook that we were to be withdrawn. It upset my equilibrium but it was further upset that evening because it was clear that the enemy shelling of our position was becoming protracted beyond its usual limits. I had reported to the infantry battalion commander that we were being withdrawn. He was a nice man, a regular soldier of about forty, a Colonel Stewart. He said he was glad for our sakes but would miss us and our guns. He asked me to stay near and talk.

"Let's talk about something reasonable. Let's forget this damned war which is hotting up again. I think he's going to attack." He peered out over the parapet with his binoculars, but it was already too dark to see. "Do you know the de Coverley essays?"

He was delighted when I said I did. "They really give you an impression of a world worth living in." It was almost impossible to talk because the shell bursts were too continuous; you can't shout about gentle and civilized manners. He went on talking but did not bother to try to make me hear. His face seemed in the light from the gunflashes to have lost some of its lined, careworn pallor.

26

I BROUGHT our gun crews together ready to leave though now I was sure our relief would be cancelled. Most of the fighting seemed to be over to our right by Mont Kemmel. That was where the star shells and 'Brock's Benefit' were concentrated, and that is what saved our relief—it was obvious we were not the main object of the enemy's attention.

Our orders came. Although I felt sure we should be recalled, perhaps enveloped by the attack if it spread to our sector which it was sure to do if it were successful, I was glad to go—or I would have been if I could have rid myself of the shame at leaving the infantry.

It is impossible to feel anything but amazement at what the infantry suffered in that war, and impossible to think anyone will convey it. They say that the Spanish infantry never recovered after Rocroi in 1643. When I read about it at school the phrases sank into my mind; now I can believe that what I witnessed was a disaster of that order—nothing less than murder of the spirit of incomparable men. For me the disaster was to have survived and to undergo the mortification of being watched leaving the battle by men condemned to stay.

Loaded as we were it seemed easier and more practicable to ignore the shelling. The whole back area, every path and crossroad, was under fire and to try to proceed by short rushes between flattening out on the ground would only mean that the danger was prolonged.

Carter and Cook met us. "All right?" "Yes, except the fire I told you about." We had lost no men since early that evening. A small lorry took the whole party, guns and all, racketing and jolting down the remains of the road. Cook said we had been reinforced and the new men would be waiting for us at our camp. We didn't need more men; if they could have reinforced our spirits that would have been something; more men was nothing.

That night Mont Kemmel fell. No one knew why it was not retaken. "Our chaps did retake it", an infantry officer told me. "We got off to a good start and got right round behind it to our final objectives. Just what the doctor ordered. The French were supposed to be attacking on the other flank. But the bloody bastards didn't even leave their trenches! If they had done their bit *we* would be sitting on top of that place now with a decent packet of Boches in our cages!"

We were not ordered back. Though we did not know it at the time our infantry experience was over. When our detachment was withdrawn we had to pass through St Omer, the HQ of the Second Army. General Plumer happened to be there and not at his Advanced HQ. He stood at the side of the road and took the salute as the brigade of which we were part marched past. He looked, we said, like an old walrus with his white moustaches. There were mutterings of "Good old Plumer!", for we had heard that he always said "Thank you" to troops as they left his Army. Perhaps that is why troops knew they were in his Army. There was no need for him to issue orders about 'backs to the wall'.

One famous General was to review our battalion, when we were still a battalion, at Ypres. We paraded at eight in the morning. Before the great event, which was to take place at half past eight, we inspected and reviewed our every button till at eight thirty the rain came down. We had to stay on parade as 'he' would arrive at any moment. By eleven thirty we were soaked but though we had lost our shine we were still far from bedraggled. Our scouts warned us—'he' was coming! A fine shiny car approached, slowed up. There was an impressive figure in it—the General? He leant forward so we could all see him and saluted with his swagger stick. The car gathered speed again. And was gone. "'Struth!" said a man in the back rank of our company. "Blimey! I'm wet!"

He must have been a good general to be famous; he must have had an enormous amount of work to do. Later when he fell into disgrace I do not doubt that an episode such as I have recounted would mean that he had many fewer advocates than he might have had. Had Plumer fallen into disgrace I do not doubt that many would have remembered how he had wasted time at the roadside instead of getting on with his work. 'An old fuddy-duddy'. But he was reputed to have a good chief-of-staff named Harrington who did his thinking for him, so perhaps that saved him from disgrace. It may be, however, that generals who watch their troops march by choose good chiefs-of-staff; or even good quartermasters who do not earn fame for their army as the worst fed of all—as they did for the Third. I was only a part of the skin on a boxer's knuckles and

213

could not know what lay hid in the mighty brain of the bruiser behind.

We were back in comfortable billets in one of the villages in the neighbourhood of the Central Workshops. As I was now a lieutenant and the senior of my rank I had a bed and clean sheets in a room to myself. I had a new uniform and new underclothes from army ordinance. The uniform was of good material and fitted me in several places. Above all, I revelled in being without lice for the first time for almost eight weeks. This meant that I did not have to make the agonizing choice between being warm and itching, or being free of bites and blue with cold. The itching of the new uniform gave me some anxious moments but as it adjusted to some of my more prominent and obstinate bulges that anxiety diminished too.

The comfort of clean clothes and a civilian bed played a big part in my mind; I often longed during later stages in the war for a repetition of that wonderful experience. The reconstitution of our company mess, regular parade hours, the routines of assimilating new officers and men, the training in infantry tactics as far as we had learnt them—I worked hard on this with my section as did Hauser who had now become commander of his section—all filled time and helped to repair appearances, but it never felt quite right.

Captain Robinson came to us as a reinforcement. He was older than the officers contemporary with me who had been the original tank commanders of the battalion in England. He seemed somewhat foreign because he was an American. Yet we did not think of him as a man of different nationality so much as of the same nationality with peculiarities which, when we did notice them, were very peculiar peculiarities. For example, he did not seem to understand our jokes. He also had jokes which were different from ours even when verbally almost identical.

One day Robinson asked Hauser and me what we thought of a German automatic pistol he had. It certainly looked a beautiful little thing. I said I wished we had things like that instead of the clumsy great .45 Colts. Hauser said the German pistol could never stop a man dead—like a Colt.

"Stop him dead! Ha! That's a good one!" laughed Robinson.

"What's so funny about that?" asked Hauser. "When you are at close quarters you don't just want to kill him; you want to stop him as well—so he doesn't rush into you and kill you before he passes out."

"Oh yes, of course, I see. You mean you stop him 'dead'. Very good."

He showed us his watch. "Where did I get that? Same place of course. I told the Boche officer to hand over his pistol and then his watch too. He seemed a bit fed up but he forked out all right. It's a beauty isn't it?"

We agreed; it was. Then Hauser said, "Isn't that what you call looting?"

Robinson said yes, he supposed you could call it that, but then it was a bit ridiculous to call it that when after all he was only a bloody German. For his part he thought it jolly well served him right.

Carter, who had come up and heard the latter part of the conversation, joined in. "Do you think then that you'd only 'loot' English soldiers?"

Robinson was becoming puzzled and rather resentful at a conversation which he felt was carrying fussiness a bit far—beyond a joke in fact.

A day or two later I bumped into Carter and Robinson again. This time Robinson wore no Sam Browne belt, and Carter though walking close to him was not talking. Carter *was* wearing his Sam Browne.

"Good Lord!" I said, "You look as if you were escorting an officer under arrest."

Carter looked angry and uncomfortable. Robinson said, "I am".

I was about to put my foot further and more firmly into the mess I had started to make when Carter caught my eye. He seemed to be begging me to refrain from making a bigger bloody fool of myself than I absolutely had to.

Later Hauser and I tackled Carter about it and under secrecy he told us the following facts. I was puzzled and indignant; I liked Robinson. Hauser was indifferent, but then he did *not* like Robinson.

Robinson *had* captured the officer; or at least the officer had surrendered to Robinson. All this was a bit vague. The officer was wearing a fur coat; Robinson asked him for it—whether with or without threats was not clear—and after some argument he handed it over. "The rest you have heard from Robinson", said Carter.

A man called Colefax came and listened to all this open-mouthed. "Bloody ridiculous, I call it", he said. Hauser was inclined to agree but changed his mind.

"After all, it is loot—by military law. Thank God no one ever surrendered to me or I might have done the same", I said. But I didn't believe that; I feel sure it would not have occurred to me. It seemed a bit mean—like hitting a man when he was down. I turned to Carter. "Did *you* arrest him?"

Carter who was unusually ill at ease said of course he had not. "I was ordered to be escort. Thank God it's someone else's job now—1st Battalion's. Personally I thought he was boasting and had invented the whole story to show how gallant he was."

"I thought he was a liar", said Hauser. "That's why I said I thought it was looting—to scare him. I was sure he had just bought the things from a prisoner and then decided to tell the tale about it."

Carter said it looked like being an expensive story. I returned to my problem. "But who do you think told on him? Who ordered his arrest?"

"What on earth makes you think anyone 'told on him'?" said Carter becoming exasperated. "You heard him yourself. He goes all over the place shouting out what a fine looter he is and you say 'Who told on him?' He probably went and boasted about it to the Brigadier himself. Anyhow, the order to arrest him came from Brigade."

Robinson was not unpopular and as the news of his arrest spread the debate became a source of embarrassment and uneasy questioning. One story was that the German officer himself complained to Brigade. This gained credence; it could even have been true. 'All's fair in love and war': such were the proverbial phrases with which one was familiar. They are spread like a carpet covering the human mind, usually dormant and dark, but becoming active and luminous in accordance with the movements of the forces concealed below.

Robinson disappeared. I am still haunted by the expression on his face—incredulous, unbelieving. "Surely", he seemed to be saying, "this can't be happening to me? You can't do this to me?" Yet warfare between civilized states should be governed by a code of law. Who says they are civilized? Was our Colonel civilized? Or our Company Commander? 'They tame but one another still'.

At about this time a letter was handed to me by the corporal of our company office. It had been sent to the Battalion HQ by the mother of one of our men who had been killed in action. Did I know who wrote it? If not, could I find out and let the company officer know?

The letter said, 'Dear Madam, By the time this reaches you, you will have heard that your son, Gunner X, has been killed in action and how brave and universally loved he was. I want you to know that he was the biggest rat and meanest coward I have ever met. He was not killed in action. He was a skunk and he died of fright before he got near danger. If you have any more lily-livered curs like him in the litter keep them out of it. We don't want them endangering the lives of good tank men.' It was not signed.

Robinson and this letter floated up to the surface of my mind as part of my Oxford education. The city of 'dreaming spires' was not what it might once have been. Even in sleep the dreams had an inappropriate quality.

27

W H A T had happened to A and C Companies after the Grand Ravine? The A Company commander survived, but I did not meet him till chance threw me into his company at Oxford, and by then he could not remember, or remembered something which made me feel we were talking of different people.

"Do you remember what happened to Green?"

"Green; oh yes. I remember him *very* well. That fat fellow with rather piggy eyes?"

"I always thought him one of the wittiest and most cheerful people I ever met."

"Yes", rather vaguely. "Yes, wasn't he! I remember him *very* well."

"Do you remember what happened to him?"

"Yes, very well. He got killed. It was at Cambrai, or it may have been just before; Vlamertinghe perhaps. No, it *was* Cambrai, because I remember there was some question of his kit. He was a chartered accountant."

"No, barrister."

"Something like that—one of the learned professions; awfully good chap I thought."

What had happened to them? Stokes? Yes, I know, killed at Cambrai, but—is that all? He had gone to South Africa as a farmer and was nearly ruined, lost all his capital through five years of drought in a row. Then the rain came and all was saved—more than all. "It's all a matter of luck; if you have five years drought straight off you're for it. Still, I mustn't grumble. It taught me to be jolly careful when my luck turned. I saved something; then *this* business! So back I came." He was always cheerful in a sober way; always modest and unassuming.

Despard? I knew what happened to him of course. But I knew nothing of him before I saw him lying there, sweating, with a deathly pallor on his face. "I'm done for; I know it. That mag-pie... all up."

What, for that matter, had happened to me? Something queer—

and this is how it happened. Some time during those eight weeks with the infantry my section and I had to go and hold a village at all costs. The place was alive with shell-splinters and bullets that flicked by like wasps. The sapper officer in command told me where he wanted the section. I got them into position and set them to dig a trench. I then reported to him again, telling him that I had left Second Lieutenant Bridges in command because I had to go back to Company HQ to report. He was too harrassed to pay much attention but told me to come to him on my way back. I gave Cook and Carter my position, showing them on the map, by which time two billycans of soup, hot beef stew, were packed into hay boxes to take to the section. I felt very grateful for Tipledy's old-womanly efficiency but had no time to find him to tell him so. I was in a hurry; I had to hurry my orderlies too, with their slip-slopping loads in the hay boxes. We must have gone a hundred yards, nearly to the village, when it became clear that something was wrong. The village was being shelled. So what? Boche machine-guns, on *our* side of the village! This *was* wrong. Our infantry came falling of the boundary of the village—on our side. The blasted place, to be held 'at all costs', had fallen.

The infantry fell into already prepared trenches—real, not tape this time—and there they stayed. No one had heard of my men; my section had simply disappeared. Captured? What did 'captured' mean? I was never able to discover. Not until after the war did I hear they had been taken prisoner.

Chinese Wall, Messines, Wytschaete, Mont Kemmel: all those eight weeks were spent with men I did not know—just remnants of a battalion. Had they just held up their hands? The question haunted me. In my deepest heart I felt and still feel that that is what I would do. Amazingly it did not happen; the circumstances were never quite right. Either I was not there, or the enemy was not where I was.

The next day, as there were no men, we were cleared out. I came out of it with a horrible load of guilt. Every explanation was specious, whether of guilt or of innocence. There was no relief. I was a more efficient soldier, but I was not the soldier I had been. I tried once or twice to discuss it with Hauser, with Carter. They seemed to understand the feeling but they had nothing to say. I learned that when no one has anything to say the time has come to be silent.

The debate with myself did not cease. *That* was not so easily dealt with then or since. Sooner or later one is faced with the fact that there must be something which is greater, more important than one's own death. However great a coward one is one cannot on that or any other ground claim exemption. The obvious answer is ready to hand: life is more important and death only an unimportant terminal event. But for the coward this is not true. In the period of rest I had experiences—like a bed and clean sheets—which I long remembered. There was the green grass in which I tried to carry out section exercises in fighting; there were blue skies. But the comfort had oozed out of the sheets; the green did not remind me of the far-off hills where it was greener; the blue skies no longer reminded me of the lark-song with which they were filled in a certain field in Hertfordshire, but only that they 'sing so out of tune'.

The state of mind which I experienced bore some resemblance to states spoken of by religious people. The resemblance was close enough to stir a revulsion against and rejection of any religious idea known to me. In so far as I had changed since Cambrai, and of that I had no doubt whatever, I had become closer to, and more sympathetic with, the views of those who regarded the pious as canting humbugs—myself very much included. Quainton had not been killed; he had become the shadow of a shadow. Cohen when I saw him was an ugly joke; so was the story of the advantages of having one boot less to clean. Still, that story was not a part of Holy Writ, not even of the apocryph to the Apocrypha; it was rather a piece of dirt clinging, as it were, to the religious boot. More to the point perhaps was the story attached to Corporal Smith's burial.

When I had finished my walk through the shell-fire by being pulled into the trench, I started shouting instructions to Smith. I remember being impressed and comforted by his sturdy, cheerful demeanour. While I was facing him he seemed to stop paying attention; his face became flabby and lifeless. It was peculiar to discover that the lifelessness of his expression was due to his being lifeless; he toppled forward onto me and slithered into the trench. So the bombardment, like the bullet which had shattered Captain Edwards' brain, *was* dangerous. Of course he had not been wearing one of those bullet-proof Bibles or prayer books, but no more was I. There was the 'whole armour of Faith'; Cohen certainly had worn that; as a Jew converted Christian he had paid a high price for it—Quainton told me so, having been on such terms with him that he could discuss those things. God knows what had hit Cohen; somehow it managed not to kill his body, but killed *him*. Perhaps he was one of those whose graves are known only to God.

Smith—or had he now qualified to be called only It?—was an infernal nuisance. In the middle of this clearly dangerous bombardment, while we expected the enemy infantry at any moment, we had to bury him (It?) While I took over the main duty of watching at the parapet the others dug. Of course it was ridiculous; anyone, any soldier would know that Smith (It) could wait. "No hurry at all", he might have said with a cheerful grin. But It (late Smith) left it all to us. Rigor set in very fast. He seemed to have arms everywhere, stiff and unaccommodating.

"Smith-y? Smithy?" For a moment I thought that his friend Grayson had gone mad and was trying to get him to co-operate. He said afterwards he was making sure he was dead.

Into this shallow scraping we finally forced him. It was too shallow and this was what finally caused trouble. He would have to be re-buried properly. Four or five of his friends, when they came to hear of what had happened, wanted to go back to the line as soon as we had been relieved and re-bury him—with a religious service.

I referred the matter to Cook because I said I thought it was risking the lives of the men unnecessarily. Cook reluctantly agreed to let them go if it were practicable. Unfortunately it was. A temporary hush had settled on the front. They went to collect the padre. It would only take an hour, they said—and that indeed was one of Cook's conditions. The padre refused—there was no shortage of good reasons and I thought Cook was quite wrong to agree anyway.

The men knew of a private, not of Smith's persuasion, Church of England, but a baptist, who agreed (since he was by profession a minister of religion) to go with them and conduct the service.

They went; Smith was properly, that is to say, deeply (and of course religiously) buried and there were no casualties. There the matter might have rested but for two facts: Smith was popular; the padre was not. There followed a rambling and rumbling debate of which snatches would from time to time float up to my ears. After a week or so I was finally able to put the bits together.

The Captain played cards 'a damn sight too much'. This I had heard before; he was usually the main organizer of the Battalion HQ bridge fours. He never did anything; what he was expected to do was not stated, but the refusal or failure to bury Smith was clearly a point on which the charges could be hung. 'The Divisional RC padre was not like that: he jolly well *had* to go.' The comparison did not suggest that the RC Chaplain was a nice man—in fact he was unpopular—but that he was under orders and had to obey them. If Gunner Smallman could bury Smith why couldn't the C. of E.? Again, it was not suggested that Smallman was a nice man; he was somewhat unprepossessing, censorious and smug, but for the time being he was almost popular. This debate continued sporadically and now and then bubbled to the surface until the participants themselves faded away.

28

ONE day on a route march we were approaching the crest of a hill which was decorated by the unusual sight of two horsemen. Even from a distance they seemed to be spectacularly smart; one of them was carrying a lance from which a pennant fluttered. As the head of our column, now a company almost at full strength, neared the crest a commotion of orders broke out—clearly 'some ruddy general'. For the life of me I couldn't think whose army we were supposed to be in. We were all marching at attention and just before it was my turn to give the order, "Eyes right", I saw that the officer we were saluting was General Haig.

I suppose we were all glad, for once, that the order gave an opportunity for a long, hard, legitimate stare. The tramp of marching boots and the faint rustling patter of the lancer pennant in the breeze—that was all. As we marched away we heard the clatter of the horses' hooves and Haig and his escort were gone.

Amongst tank men it was held against Haig that he blamed the hold-up of the advance at Cambrai on the tank which destroyed a bridge by crashing through it. He was not 'good old Haig' as Plumer was 'good old Plumer'. He was too soldierly for one thing. He was suspect, like the rest of the Staff, but not as suspect as the politicians; no one would have said 'good old Lloyd George'.

Nor for that matter would it have occurred to anyone to think, let alone say, 'good old God' or to have any ideas about His Staff. A padre had to be pretty bad to excite any interest whatever. Corporal Smith's 'funeral' soon became one man's obsession and then faded out—just another unfinished story.

Our last Church parade in England was addressed by the Chaplain General to the Forces. His sermon had as its text 'Soldiers be content with your wages'. "Some of you", he said, "may think this a queer thing for me to talk about when you are about to leave for the Front." Well, yes, we did a bit; I almost began to think the closing hymn would be 'Goodbye Dolly I must leave you, for I'm off to face the foe'.

May drifted into June; June into July. Then, at full strength in men, we drew our full company strength in tanks—twelve. We were once more doing tank training.

The training did not last—no one had any ideas on the subject. What was clear was that in battle tanks drew fire. That we *did* know, but how did one train for that? How were Hauser, Carter and I to discuss training before action?

A special angel committee might say, "One of you had better go into training. Who's for getting killed? Well, no good discussing that; we had better leave it to the luck of the draw. No good bothering about the etceteras."

"Etceteras be damned. You forget the people with the etceteras go on living."

"Well then, odd man out:

Heart ache, belly ache, shell-shock, death,
Head wound, leg off, blinded, death,
Rich man, beggar-man, hero, thief... OK?

All got your parts? Now, what about the training? Fall out on the right all those for death. Parade at the padre's tent at 11.30 for Holy Communion and short course in letters to the bereaved. The others will attend the last part for writing to the family of the deceased *after* the action."

"Oughtn't those for life to go to the padre too?"

"Life? Let me see now"—the committee anxiously study the pamphlet of instructions—"Ah, here we are now. Life... Life Everlasting..."

The officers in unanimous horror, "Oh no! Not that..."

Certainly Hauser, Carter and I scouted such an idea though I felt some residual belief adhering rather as egg-shell adheres to the newly hatched chick. Carter had just been awarded the Military Cross. No one had the least idea what for, though no one had the slightest doubt that he deserved it. Hauser had been recommended for the MC 'as usual', and as usual he had not been awarded it. All three of us were now really exempt from the heavy odds of the tank crew stakes because we were now all section commanders and went into action on foot, outside the tank. In a way this solved our problem for we had all learned to walk and there appeared to be no other qualification. As I discovered later, map-reading remained useful to meet the requirements of the fiction that we were going somewhere.

Where we were going, when we were going and what for, was beginning to be asked just as the need for secrecy had become apparent to all except, according to the army, the Silent Service.

The immediate destination was not secret and all the officers knew it was a devastated village, Berle-aux-Bois, in which by some accident the 'Bois' retained its leaves. The entire battalion moved together for the last time. We knew no one in other companies; we travelled at dusk, detrained at ten-thirty and drove our tanks some three miles from rail-head to Berle-aux-Bois. There we concealed our tanks under some trees and spent the time in polishing them—which was as good a way of preparing to 'draw fire' as any.

A Guards regiment was somewhere near. The sentry over our petrol dump challenged a marauder, was not answered and fired. Our Company Commander, Aitches, who had just been appointed was rightly furious.

"Don't you realize, you damned fool, that you might have set the petrol dump on fire?"

"Well sir, my orders were to keep watch and challenge anyone. If they didn't reply I was to shoot."

Of course he was quite right. We had forgotten all that peacetime nonsense. No one had fired a rifle since we had first gone into action; no one had considered them as anything but a part of the ritual of going into battle.

"Did you hit anyone? My God, I hope you didn't. You're jolly lucky to have missed hitting the dump."

Sergeant-Major Cannon replied for our now terrified sentry. "Yes sir; he wounded Guardsman X in the leg."

"Did you do it on purpose?" asked Aitches with ashy lips.

"Yes sir", replied the sentry, "as near as I could aim at where I heard the man. I thought it might be an enemy."

The naïvety of the man created a stir; we had not yet reached the stage of connecting war with sentry duties and enemies—but we *did* know something about 'drawing fire'. There was nothing for it but to pass the ghastly news to the Guards Battalion. And though we were now fearful of the consequences there did seem to be some sense, in an old-fashioned way, about the sentry's behaviour.

"Yes, but this chap wasn't an enemy. It's a damn serious thing to shoot one of our privates."

"For that matter", said Carter, "it's a damn serious thing to steal Tank Corps petrol."

So it was; and ultimately that view prevailed. The Guards had much less reverence for guardsmen than we had. They tried him and in addition to his flesh wound he received a stiff sentence— they probably managed to get him for a 'self-inflicted wound'.

29

A LESS easily assimilated experience of a Guard's battalion was my visit to co-ordinate operations with them in case of attack either by us or the enemy.

I was shown into the dug-out which was their headquarters in the part of the line they held. The Colonel, Adjutant and various orderlies were present and busy. A junior officer asked me my business and I told him briefly, but from Colonel and Adjutant I could get no attention though I had come at the time appointed for my appearance. As time passed I began to feel neglected, then nettled. I whispered to the junior officer who broke into the conversation between Colonel and Adjutant to say I was going. Both bade me good-morning in the politest possible indication of utter indifference. I was alarmed, thinking they did not know why I was there.

I expostulated, "But sir, I haven't co-ordinated tank plans with yours."

"My good man", said the Colonel with astringent kindliness, "We shall take and hold *any* position, tanks or no tanks. Good morning."

'Good morning', I had to understand, was an order. Exasperated, intimidated and humiliated all at once, I cleared out. As I proceeded back up a dried mud track I became aware that howitzer shells, five-nines, were bursting along the track; then that they were suspiciously close. I was still annoyed with the Guards. What made it more annoying was that the Colonel's remark was almost certainly a statement of the obvious. I had seen them sweep up at Cambrai, like a very efficient housemaid tidying up warring children and putting them back, like their toys, into their proper boxes. I knew, and had even seen a little on our way up to Messines, what happened when they, with both flanks exposed, stood for three days before Hazebrouck and resisted any attempt by the enemy to tidy *them* up. It was no good being indignant; they were magnificent, blast them!

In the meantime it looked as if *I* would soon be tidied up. If I had not had any attention at the Guards Battalion HQ I was having it in full measure now. Someone, probably yawning his head off with boredom, was passing away the idle hour by sniping me with his howitzer. The previous 'bracket' should have given him the exact range as I was about equidistant between the bursts, so at any moment now I could expect the packet right on target—me. I scurried into a scrap of disused trench and flattened out as I heard them coming—three shells together. This was personal attention with a vengeance.

It was a good shot; chunks of the trench fell on me. If only I had had field glasses I might have been able to pick out the observation post responsible. I was sure he would be watching his shooting through *his* field glasses so I got out sweating—it was a very hot day and flattening out and getting up is a hot occupation. I wondered if the Boche gunner had a cool beer by his side. Turning towards the line I stood up and, hoping he was watching, cocked a snook at him. But if he was using his glasses he would also see that I was sweating with fear—I felt he wouldn't even need glasses to see that so... I got a move on. I was *not* going to run. I had only another hundred yards to go before the path reached the wood which would shelter me from sight. On the other hand the intersection of path and wood gave him a perfect map reference on which to register his guns as I approached. I could not run in any case; there was nowhere to run to. It was the cornered rat being clubbed to death all over again. Nothing happened. At the edge I stopped and before diving into the wood I pulled out my handkerchief and waved it; perhaps he could see my good-bye.

Shaken and very ruffled I went in to Aitches. Cook and Carter were there. "Well, what have you arranged?" We poured over the map together.

"Well", I said, "this is their position." I traced it with a shaky finger.

"Yes, we know that."

"They are going to hold it."

"Yes. Where are our tanks to be?"

I traced a wavy line behind the Guards position. "Alternatively", I drew another wavy line, "we can if we prefer it, line up here in front of their position."

"In front?" said Aitches in astonishment. "Where are the Guards going to be?"

"Same place as before—they are going to hold it." Carter was grinning.

"Now", said Aitches, "if the Guards attack the sugar factory here", he pointed with his thumb, "that's supposed to be the direction of the divisional advance, where do they want us?" I pointed to our village. "Don't be a fool!" he said, "that is where we are now."

"I know; that is where they want us. Or somewhere a damn sight warmer."

"And what about the sugar factory?"

"They will take it."

"Is that what they said?"

"Not quite", I admitted, "but that was the gist of it."

"That's no good at all Bion—you'll have to go back and fix it up properly."

"You try fixing things up properly with the Guards. They don't like tanks mucking about on their battlefields—nobody's."

I was spared further argument the next day because I had to go to a Court of Inquiry into the accidental death of a civilian. By that time the discussion with the Guards had been referred to the Brigade where as far as I know it died out.

I reported to the President of the Board, Lord Wachett. "I really shouldn't be the President. There must be some mistake— according to these papers it is my accident." He saw my ribbon. "That's very nice", he said, indicating the DSO. "Where d'ye get it?" I told him. He wagged his finger at me. "You be careful my lad. Once you get one of those things they collect others. As I always tell my son John, if you ever meet a man with more than two rows of ribbons you can be tolerably sure he's a waster." This was a novel view to me especially as it came from a regular soldier whose family had always been military. I said I thought it was unlikely I should run the risk of one row, let alone two. "Don't you believe it. Look at me."

I did. The first ribbon was a dark red affair. And it was in the right place. "When I got the first I thought I was safe, but if I get another I shall have joined the rogues' gallery myself."

He turned to the other officer who with me composed the Court. "This is damn silly. I can tell you just what happened. I was in the back of the car when Jenks, my driver, was crawling through this village—not a yard more than five miles an hour—when I saw this old crone standing on the kerb. As we came up to her she stepped smartly off the kerb to cross the road to the undertaker's opposite. I suppose she was going to have her coffin tried on and may have been a bit preoccupied. Anyhow, she fell down and broke her hip.

When she died about a week later it turned out that she was worth millions of francs, the sole financial support of her son and grandsons, and now great-grandsons who aren't a day older than thirty and therefore depend on her. So they want compensation so they can all carry on till they get over their teething troubles and start earning for themselves. Let's go and get a drink. They'll have to reconvene the Court. I can't think what they are up to."

It was a beautiful day and a pleasant change from polishing tanks. Lord Wachett followed up his views about decorations and their dangers with comments on the 'hardships' of the Navy who hadn't any fighting to do and had to invent their exploits. "Not that they are a bad lot. I always liked their Grace—bang on the table and say, 'Thank God!'—except when the padre's there; then of course it has to be a long-winded affair. Why do they always think God perfers long-windedness? Or even Latin? Or both? What's wrong with 'Thank God'?"

Back with my section I found that two eminent war artists had been painting the tanks as they appeared concealed beneath the foliage of the trees. They were indeed so eminent that they assumed a proprietary dictatorial right over the task.

"Now mind young fella, if you move those tanks you must put them back in exactly the same position—*exactly* mind you!"

It was refreshing to find that getting the war into perspective meant for these two eminences the getting of perspective precisely into their pictures. "I don't think I care for your composition" was countered by "Well, I don't see why you think *your* composition is an improvement". They did not talk much to each other, and not at all to us beyond impressing upon me the vital need for tanks to be at the proper place at the proper time—to get painted.

The next night we moved, never to return. "I hope it didn't spoil the picture", said one of the gunners. Everything was of tremendous importance: I felt I had this impressed on me so incessantly that it would be impossible ever to forget it. "Mind you put those tanks back—if you *must* move them—exactly in the same place."

"Mind", said Carter, "*absolute* secrecy. Tonight at rail-head at ten fifteen. What arrangements have you made about disguising the tank tracks so they cannot possibly show in air photos?"

I knew the answer to this; I had thought of it at Cambrai. "We have a large harrow affair towed by the last tank. On it we have all our kit to weigh it down. This will destroy all the tracks made by the whole section."

"My God, that's a good idea! Do you mind if I pass it on to Aitches? It should be passed on to Battalion."

"It's a battalion show then? Whole of one Corps?"

"It's a damn sight more than that—I can tell you *that* now. But absolute secrecy!"

"Tell Battalion; or Tank Corps HQ for all I care. But get a decoration for it."

"Decorations are not for the likes of reconnaissance officers. I shouldn't be too keen on winning your DSO either if I were you."

30

THE scheme of track obliteration worked well. Reconnaissance planes reported next day that no tracks were visible. Our crews were not worn out by wearisome and inefficient spade work through hours of darkness.

'Taisez-vous! Mefiez-vous! Les oreilles ennemies vous écoutent!' The legend on the platform at Etaples was the French injunction to their civilian population—absolute secrecy! But absolute!... The din of the silence seemed to swell into a row. Who the hell cared anyway? We had heard it all before. The sky was cloudy and overcast. Enemy planes must have seen it—whatever *it* was.

No, only one plane had been over and that had been shot down. Our planes had orders to shoot down any enemy plane—without fail. Absolutely without fail.

So they got it? No, it was fetched down by AA fire.

It was too tiring even to bother to call the man who told us that a liar.

It was August; since it was a Great British Offensive it seemed reasonable to suppose it would rain like hell. So it was not altogether implausible that the cloud screen was so thick that air observation was difficult. But, only one enemy plane over! And that shot down by the gunners! If it weren't so bloody silly one might even laugh.

We could see we were at a very big marshalling yard. AMIENS it said. It was the morning of August 6th. "Tell one of your officers to get your tanks off; you are to take cover at once. The guides are there. We" —it was Cook speaking— "must go to Brigade HQ at once for the conference."

It was a large tent, full of officers; they were all Tank Corps. Whatever kind of show required the whole Tank Corps in support? "They must be arranging to end the war", said Hauser sarcastically.

Silence fell on us. The General was speaking. "On your left, extending as far as Villers Bretonneux will be the Australian Corps."

Christ! Those bastards! We did not love the Australians. There had been a local attack, which was a failure, in which tanks had taken an even worse beating than usual because the Australians had gone too far and too fast without mopping up. Uncleared-up anti-tank guns had therefore arisen behind them and destroyed the tanks.

"Those bloody tanks", said the Australians. "Too slow, too damned cowardly to keep up. We had broken right through! Where were the tanks? Nowhere—as usual!"

As I say, we did not love each other. For us their magnificent indiscipline was just indiscipline, paid for in blood—Tank Corps blood.

The General continued: "Extending from the right flank of the Australian Corps to the Amiens-Roye Road will be the 10th Southland Division and the Canadian Corps. The Southland Division will leap-frog through the Canadians. The 5th Tank Battalion will have its right flank over the Amiens-Roye Road and will be there supporting the Nancy Division, the 11th."

Australians, Canadians and the Corps de Fer: it sounded as if somebody meant business.

"The 5th Battalion will continue to advance"—just like Cambrai, German gunners permitting?—"and will then support the Canadian Corps for the rest of the advance."

The 'lecture' went on; it was not interesting, not novel. The tent was hot, but we listened. The river Luce ran across and parallel to the 5th Battalion front; there was not much water in it. In fact it was not an obstacle; 5th Battalion would find out if it was swampy. In any case there was a brick bridge across it and the 5th would cross by that. The bridge of course was not standing—it had been blown to bits when our line was stabilized at the end of the March 31st show. Still, the rubble might stiffen it up a bit. It would be much safer than anywhere else. Though of course the enemy would shell it... and so forth. He droned on.

"The 1st Battalion will..." I could relax, go to sleep even? Better not. "At Villers Bretonneux... 1st, 4th 5th, 7th..." Obviously a big show. At last. "Any questions? Right. Now company and section commanders will be briefed. Carry on."

We broke into small groups. The river Luce... that is what I wanted to know about. The ground was like Cambrai—beautiful except for the river Luce.

"Any resemblance to the Steenbeck?" I asked. It looked like it on the map; it squiggled about a bit.

"God no!" said the briefing officer. "It's hardly a trickle."

"That is exactly like the Steenbeck."

"My dear chap, this place is as dry as a bone. Not even a Grand Ravine to have nightmares about. Forget it! Anyhow, the Steenbeck's at Ypres."

"So long as they keep it there I don't mind", said Carter. "I hope they will keep an eye on it."

"Somebody must go and reconnoitre it", said the Staff officer. "I shall be going. What about you?" He turned to me and I agreed. I would as soon know the worst and know it myself as depend on someone else. "There's no time to spare. Will you be ready at 12.15? Right. Meet here."

We finished our company and section briefings and map scrutinies. We could think of nothing to say—but still I said it to Carter.

"My God, I hate this. It puts the wind up me."

He turned to me angrily. "Why the hell do you keep on talking about it then?"

"I don't. And aren't you?"

"Of course. I'm scared out of my wits. I'm not daft—you'd have to be daft or a nit-wit *not* to be scared. But why talk?"

I was angry and felt no better for feeling he was right. I went off in a huff and discovered that the officer with whom I was going to reconnoitre was a man well known to almost any regular soldier for his war exploits.

He had been trained from his boyhood days in a German public school to serve in the British Secret Service. His endowment of hatred had been carefully but unwittingly nourished by his school mates. He spoke German so faultlessly that he was reputed to have commanded a German regiment in the Line for a week before he 'deserted' back to the British lines. He was said to have been dropped behind the German lines by British planes when such a feat was unheard of—except on the occasions when it was linked with his name. As I have already said, I was not feeling brave although for the moment I had a meritricious courage through being cross.

We looked at the Luce; it seemed dry. We poked it with a stick; it seemed damp. I fell between some large stones; my feet had become wet. "Let's lie out here for a bit and see if we can find out anything." It was a beautiful, clear and hot afternoon. But I was shivering—only partly through fatigue. I did not feel aware of fear, but I was excited.

I started to take compass bearings as my way of keeping fear at bay and giving myself something to do; I hoped it looked military.

I took bearings of the bridge in relation to the mud track by which we were to approach. I took bearings from the point ten yards beyond the Luce bridge where we were to swing left and take up our battle positions. My companion was very patient. I was grateful to him for not asking why I was engaged on so idiotic a procedure. When I began to take bearings for the rest of the battalion whose right hand company was A Company on our left, he drew the line at further topological enthusiasm.

We crawled out between two British outpost positions. It was quiet, hot and very peaceful. My companion kept using his binoculars. I tried to think of ways of dissuading him from crawling further. At last he thought he had found out enough.

We started back. "You must have got the position of the river Luce mapped out with an exactitude never before achieved." He didn't seem to be trying out his sarcasm on me. Suddenly remembering how glad I had been to know the direction of our front line trench at Chinese Wall I said, lying, "I often find it useful to know some bearings."

31

ON my return the company, to my surprise, were very busy. I reported to Aitches; he said a message had come through that zero was the next morning, 8 o'clock, August 8th.

I was met by Asser, a spectacled, cheerful lad who had joined us a week earlier. I suppose he reminded me of what I and my friends had been like in England. He was about a year younger than I. I had told him to act as second in command to me and to take over if I was killed.

It was a stupid appointment. The most senior of my tank commanders who should have had the job by automatic succession was Corkran. He was pasty-faced, rather like Osprey in appearance, but with even less stamina. I had put O'Toole in his tank because I thought the crew needed a good man to strengthen it to make up for its officer.

After him came Robins, an ex-infantryman with a Military Medal. I thought he, though a very nice fellow and much superior to Corkran, was curiously dependent. Had I been more experienced I would have given the job to Greene; he lacked action experience, but was tough; he looked robust. He was not liked by any of the officers and men, but I think he, and not Asser, should have had the job. They were the same age. Greene came from a tough background and showed it. He was 'what the army is coming to', and those who didn't like what the army was coming to would not like him.

Asser was, despite his studious appearance, fiery. If it had not been out of date by that time to be aware of patriotism one would have said it burned in him with a pure flame. A brother, whom he adored, and a father who was an even greater though more romantically shadowy figure, had both been killed in action, his father in late 1914.

He was bubbling with cheerful excitement. He told me the whole section was ready, ammunition all sized, engines and guns tuned up to perfection. He was proud and happy. Had I ever felt like it? I couldn't believe it. Greene I might have resembled, but Asser—never!

I congratulated him and advised him to go and get some sleep if he could. I was sure he would not be able to sleep, but I did not want him near when I went to see Corkran and his crew. Corkran was glum and sore at having been passed over; it was partly because I felt he was that kind of man that I did not want him. Osprey and Corkran had been alike in this; they did not seem able to feel with their men and yet retain their awareness that although they were men like their men, they were paid to be gods, very minor gods perhaps, but gods.

Osprey had faded away; there was a path leading away from the battlefield which was well-worn but soon became lost as streams are lost in dry land. Osprey had been sent back to administer the remains of the company, the 'administrative details', a job for which an officer was necessary, but for which an officer could not be spared. My driver Allen found the same facility available for the non-commissioned ranks; he had had to go on light duty after Cambrai. From that point of vantage he made himself useful as a tank driving instructor to a school for 'refresher' courses in driving. With great difficulty we got him back to the battalion. But back with us his driving capacity seemed to deteriorate. He was too slow, too conscientious, too careful; at the same time the driving school did not hesitate to deplore the loss of a man who was too good to be wasted on fighting tanks. His instruction was too good and his manner too amiable to be lost from a job in which some tact, especially with senior officers, was a *sine qua non*. The last point was decisive; I had to admit that tact was lost on the Germans. Bagshaw, our original section commander, was the first of the officers I knew intimately to seep away in this discreet and tactful way. They were not robust enough to get shell-shock; they got nothing at all.

After Messines a vacancy had occurred for a Company Sergeant-Major. O'Toole and a Sergeant Cannon from A Company were candidates for the post. Cannon was a smart—to my mind too smart— little man. O'Toole with his red face, hideous flapping ears and ungainly physique had everything but his looks to commend him. He was a disciplinarian of whom they made fun—to his knowledge—but they did not dare to disobey. He had compassion too as he showed when he had to deal with my gunner Allen. "I don't know what's come over him since Cambrai sir. He has a silly grin. Sometimes I think I'll run him in for 'dumb insolence', but it isn't really that sir. I told him to report sick but he isn't sick." I saw Allen; it was as O'Toole said. He did not talk but every so often a private smirk would flicker across his pasty pudding face. He had never made a lively impact but this was new; he was out of this world.

Cannon, to my sorrow and annoyance, got the job. I had told O'Toole I was sorry but could say no more without compromising Cannon, now our Company Sergeant-Major. I knew he was bitterly hurt by his rejection. I went to find him.

"Well Sergeant, how is the crew? You have still got Gunner Hayler of our original crew I see. Have they shaken down well now do you think?"

He was ill at ease and so was I. He made conventional replies and then said, "Do you mind if I say something privately sir?"

"Go ahead", but I had come to see him because I thought he wanted to say something privately, although I could not have guessed what.

"Sir, I don't want anything more. I don't mean I want to be invalided out—no shell-shock for me. But this time sir, I feel I want six feet of earth and nothing else. I know it's got to happen; I feel it in my bones sir. Will you write to my people sir?"

I told him that of course I would but I did not think there was any need to think of that. I am amazed now that even allowing for my not yet being twenty-one I could say anything so silly. Both of us had had far more than our ration of escapes; both knew it.

"I'm still very sorry you didn't get the CSM job. After this show I'll ask the Colonel if *he* can't get you transferred."

"It's not that sir. I don't want a transfer. But I mustn't keep you now sir. Thank you very much for letting me talk to you sir." He saluted and went off.

He was a kind man, however uncouth his exterior. His defiant assertions—"I'm an orphan!"—were flung out, at least when he was new to the battalion, as if they were a private banner.

I went off to lie on the ground and get some sleep. The ground was hard, but I was tired. So I slept and I had a terrible dream. I awoke just as I was about to go into battle; it was unnerving to find that I was.

The dream was grey, shapeless; horror and dread gripped me. I could not cry out, just as now, many years later, I can find no words. Then I had no words to find; I was awake to the relatively benign terrors of real war. Yet for a moment I wished it was only a dream. In the dream I must have wished it was only a war.

I had to hurry for I had two jobs to do. One was to 'repair' the bridge, but before that I had to visit the HQ of the First French

Division and have a word with some officers on the staff of the Nancy Division who were going to meet me there after the close of their conference at Army HQ. I told Sergeant Noyes to meet me at the bridge over the Luce with six men, picks and shovels and full battle order at 5.30 when I judged there would still be ample light for the job but not so much as to make our presence conspicuous to the enemy observers.

Our position was on a high plateau, well wooded so the tanks had ample cover. From this there sloped down the mud track leading to the Luce crossing. The full distance was a couple of miles but I could point out almost the whole journey to Noyes from where we stood. I told Hauser I was off and hurried, hurried with the dread of the dream chasing me, sometimes walking by my side in the way figures at Ypres hurried along the duckboards beyond the canal.

32

FRENCH HQ was busy. The conference had finished and I found my officers discussing it in informal groups. They looked worn and anxious but showed no trace of the defeatism which many have professed to have seen since the news of the mutinies of 1918 became common knowledge. A junior officer came up to ask my business though it was clear he had been forewarned and guessed why I was there. I replied in dregs of sixth-form French. He spoke to his Major, a few hurried phrases. The Major kept looking in my direction; he did not look pleased. When I approached him it was evident that he had been led to expect a French-speaking officer; he satisfied himself at once that that was not what he had got. He was angry but polite, terminated his interview and went back to business.

I stood alone amongst these tense men. I noticed that one of them was wearing the Medaille Militaire and was without his right arm. As I waited, at a loss to know what to do, it began to occur to me that I had been sent on the strength of my name. This I found to be the case when a French Intelligence Officer came to speak to me. Clearly he did not want to blame me for what I could not help, but it was evident that he thought French was taught in our schools and that the army staff would not send a 'French-speaking officer' without first finding out if he could speak French.

By this time I too felt that I might have been asked; I did not like being the evidence for one more example of the incurable frivolity of the English. With aid of pencil and paper I made clear to him and a French infantryman what my section, the right of the British line as far as Tanks were concerned, were meaning to do and the precise hours at which we meant to do it. This I knew by heart; it was the bare bones of the operation orders covering the interval between zero hour and our rejoining the Fourth British Army—the Canadian Corps.

My impossible, ever-so-funny 'parlez-vous' sixth-form French meeting his, presumably, 'baccalaureat' English, was not a suitably reassuring back-cloth for a serious dialogue. I did not feel frivolous; I felt in every possible way incompetent. We declared ourselves satisfied with the result of our laborious stammering match, saluted each other and parted.

At the river Luce I met my men. I told them what to do to fill in the bed of the stream with rubble and fascines so the tanks would not sink. They had to work hard and fast because the entire battalion of tanks had to cross the Luce at this point without fail to reach their starting points. If they got bogged down in a swamp where the enemy gunners would have them helpless, concentrated like dinosaurs in a prehistoric catastrophe, the infantry of two whole army corps, one French, one British, would be left without armour.

I sat conspicuously on the mound of bricks that marked the spot where the parapet of the bridge had once been. The men sweated and worked in the bed below. I did this because I knew that the enemy were said to shell this crossing every day and it would not do to leave my men there while I took up a safe position elsewhere. I sat motionless, but "Hurry, hurry, hurry..." I screamed noiselessly, tense and sweating within myself. Sometimes I tried to get relief by jumping into the rubble below to help with some unusually recalcitrant chunk of masonry. My watch hand had crept to six. This was the time the gunners were reported to open fire on the bridge each day; I knew that they were creatures of habit. I walked a few yards from the bridge. If only they would start while I was away! I came and sat down again and lit my pipe.

It was a beautiful evening, calm and glowing. The trees on the plateau above us were untroubled, the great clusters of leaves drooped heavily on the branches.

The men's picks, the scraping of shovels, my breathing seemed to be all. One large lump of masonry on which my tanks might have been wrecked remained. I put the whole party onto trying to roll this away. Together we were shifting it. As I sweated and strained with them—one of my intervals of relief—I listened intently for the sound of a distant gun and the following rushing crescendo of the first shell of the evening 'strafe'. The rock rolled over slightly. Once more—"one good shove"—and it toppled out of harm's way. "Fine", I said as calmly as I could, "knock off."

"And for Christ's sake hurry up", I added as I realized that they were not showing any urgency.

It was 9.30—when the enemy usually terminated their nightly strafe. I did not let the men have a rest till we were at least half a mile away. There they could fall out for a break and a smoke.

As I say, it was a fine evening. Even the heavy clouds which for three days had screened our army's preparations, had cleared away. It was like the Norfolk Broads when the wind drops at evening after a day of fine sailing.

Carter came down the mud track and joined me. "OK?" he asked. "OK", I replied. I sent Sergeant Noyes and the men to rejoin their sections. "And you can take off your battle order as far as I am concerned. You've done a fine job."

Left to ourselves Carter and I went to look at the bridge. "No shelling?" "Not a whisper." Still, there was no point in sitting on a spot which could erupt at any moment. We moved back to the mud track and waited.

At 9.50 Handley Page bombers were to start flying along the front; the noise of their engines was to cloak the roar of tank engines so the enemy would not become suspicious. Soon we heard the characteristic pulsating drone.

"Not bad. If you had never heard a tank engine and were a bit hard of hearing you might, if you were a bit drunk, just possibly think a tank engine was a Handley Page bomber." I agreed. Just then from two miles away we heard the roar of the first tank engine starting up.

"On second thoughts", I said, "nobody could possibly mistake that row for anything at all. It's just a 174 h.p. Ricardo Tank engine." "So it is", said Carter bitterly.

The tanks, after the first one, helped to screen each other. As each engine started, the driver throttled down to slow speed so that the roar soon became a diffuse murmur, and the murmur became an undifferentiated noise like traffic on the roads; it was just possible to believe that the enemy could be deceived.

Perhaps this is what some German officer reported—"There seemed a very considerable increase in road traffic behind the enemy lines."

Carter, to pass the time, spread out his map. "There on your left will be the Amiens-Roye road stretching dead straight, unmistakably, for mile after mile. It is lined with poplars so you can see its direction and check your own by it." I had seen it myself even when I was lying on the ground taking a worm's eye view of the front. "Amiens-Roye road—I suppose there are poplars lining it still?"

"You just said so! Do get it out of your head that all battlefields are the same as Ypres!"

"What has happened to those ruddy tanks? They should have

been here years ago". Carter looked at his watch. I hadn't seen him so jittery before. "Oh well, I suppose not. They don't seem to be making such a terrible row as they were. Still, it's about time they showed up."

So it was; and so they did. The first of the huge shapes came out of the blackness, in low gear, hardly moving, so that the idling engines could easily propel the tank forward without strain. They were exactly to time. The intense relief... Something made us both look back to the bridge over the Luce. It had gone; utterly and absolutely vanished behind a dense wall of fog.

33

No one had mentioned fog. There could not be a fog; the river, the banks, the low ground, all were as dry as a bone. I myself had seen it. Why, oh why, had I not reported back from the reconnaisance that there was danger of fog? I had cursed the fools who acted as if forty tons of steel could float on Ypres mud. Yet here was I...

I could see the report: 'An experienced Tank Corps officer had been sent forward to examine and report on the suitability of the terrain for tanks. Unfortunately he thought of absolutely everything and even noticed that there was no water in the river bed, but still failed to see the obvious point that since the water had abandoned the river it must have taken to the air.' There it was—thick, solid, impenetrable.

"Now what?" said Carter. I heard my own voice talking. "Let's go and have a look." We walked down and came to the wall. The next step and we were trying to see our hands. At arm's length they were out of sight.

The first tank had stopped with engine throbbing. There was the whine of a shell and the burst—a five-nine. Then more. I knew it was all up; they must have known all the time. Scared out of my wits I pulled out my lucky charm, the cabalistic figures, supposedly compass bearings, actually a record of my early afternoon fear. A torch made them just readable. I would pretend they were compass bearings, seriously taken for the express purpose of leading tanks.

Carter had some white tape. Why had I not put it down in the afternoon? Of course, I had forgotten, we could not show tapes the enemy might discover and use to make his own conjecture.

Back with the first tank I told him to stay halted and lend me three men. Carter had gone to Brigade to report the bad news at once. Another tank arrived; the 'pile-up' had started. I could have murdered the commander when he said in a fatuous, carefree voice, "What's up?"

With the aid of the three men I translated the figures into a taped pattern on the ground. It led across the rubble that had been the bridge. It turned sharp left; it led straight, parallel to the Divisional

243

front, at right angles to our line of advance. Then 'parallel with the Amiens-Roye road, lined with poplars, straight as a die, as far as the eye could see'.

I told the first tank to come on. Of course the tape would be chewed to bits. What would the second tank do? I did not know. I did not care. "Follow-my-leader", I said.

When our company was in position I went back to my section. I checked our company position by compass. Lumps of steel, each weighing forty tons, were disposed in a line with the correct distance in yards between them in accordance with the scheme laid down in battle orders so that the whole infantry attack was supported with tanks in correct proportion to infantry. The only problem was what the figures of compass bearing had to do with direction on the ground. I did not know what the magnetic lumps of steel had to do with the compass bearings.

Cook came up. "Ah, *there* you are". "Yes, where are you?" I asked. "It *is* thick", he said. "You are sure you've got it correct?" he added as if a possible danger had just occurred to him.

Aitches arrived. "Well, so long. I must be getting to Advanced Company HQ. It's nearly time." He walked off—or was he running? It must have been the mist that had swallowed him so fast. It was half a mile to Advanced HQ. According to me he had four hours in which to get there. Of course, it *was* foggy.

A Company appeared and took their position from us. No one had taken compass bearings. I wondered how I had got into such a mess. Had I been ordered to reconnoitre the position? The tanks for one army corps were now relying for position and direction on... God knows what. I had not dreamed that my compass bearings would be taken seriously by me, let alone by Corps troops.

I found Hauser. On one of his tanks was a dixie fixed to the exhaust so that boiling water was available for his shave. He was now scraping away.

"Do you *always* shave before action?"

He looked at me in surprise. "Of course. Why not?"

"Oh", I said, "I don't know why not; only it just hadn't occurred to me."

"Hadn't occurred to you? Why, what do you suppose all these parades, kit inspections and stuff have been about then? I always have boiling water kept ready."

I told him how worried I was about the fog; he agreed that it was very thick. I said I thought we might lose direction; he agreed that

244

he thought it very likely. I said I was afraid we might end u;) finding ourselves in the river Luce. "Anyway, it won't matter if we do. Didn't you say it had no water in it?"

I felt it was time I got back to my section. A thought suddenly occurred to Hauser. He shouted it after my disappearance. "By the way, what bloody fool led us into these positions?"

"Don't know; we just came I suppose." I did not feel up to discussing the matter just then.

The fog was worse then ever. It came in great billowing masses that swirled around one's face and bandaged one's eyes and choked one's lungs. Here and there men were coughing and trying to stifle their coughs. The silence was uncanny. Could these coughs come from German sentries? I propped myself up against Corkran's tank. At least I did not have to be inside the cursed thing.

The brigade Intelligence Officer had said there were no less than four heavy guns—9.2's—in the corner of the wood opposite us. Such guns were useless when fired by us; they made colossal craters where the high explosive shell plunged into the ground. Then the enemy put barbed wire round the top and a couple of machine-guns inside, and the British advance would be held up for days by this ready-made fortress presented by our gunners to our foes. But now? We were going to use six 12inch howitzers to concentrate on that small patch. An infantryman had told me, "The joke about an artillery duel is that they don't fire at each other—they fire at *us*." This time apparently these monsters were to fire at each other.

The infantry were to give the wood a wide berth because of this bombardment which was to destroy not the big guns, but small anti-tank guns which in turn were believed to be there to protect the machine-guns. It was the job of two of my tanks, Asser's, and Corkran's against which I was leaning, to enter that wood at zero plus twenty minutes, by which time our guns would have ceased fire and all enemy guns would have been silenced. To deal with the machine-guns was thus the function of these two tanks. But why would not the smallest, least significant guns have been silenced by all this concentration of fire? The dinosaurs of the artillery would have destroyed themselves—the 9 inch because they were not so powerful as the monstrous 12 inch howitzers; the 12 inch howitzers because their own enormity and power destroyed them, made them immobile and useless. The machine-guns survived because the soft and feeble slaves serving them contained something even softer and feebler, the human brain, which was liable to ooze out of the back of the skull if that skull were deliberately perforated by yet another gun held by an even more vulnerable and feeble animal who had had enough soft human brain to imitate his ancestors and climb up a tree. So the machine-gunners, having had the wit to emulate their ancestors and live in holes in the ground, would emerge from these holes, dug deeper and yet deeper, when the gunners had done their dinosaur-like worst, and shoot the infantry.

Other machine-gunners, drawing on their brains, particularly the simian, tool-making and using qualities, evolved a machine-gun with a tougher skull—a tank. What happened then I—as I leant against the one containing Corkran, Hayler, O'Toole and Forman—could not imagine, then or for many years afterwards, because I was interrupted by fear, fear which became suddenly acute as the engine roared into life and at once settled into a gentle purr.

34

SOONER or later my parents would be bound to have the telegram announcing my death; the war had only to go on long enough. Already I had exhausted my quota of chances of survival. My mother and father, particularly my mother... There was no time and this was no place in which to pursue such thoughts. The soft, caressing mist, the great pall of blackness which had now begun to grey with the approaching dawn, was matched by the silence turning to the pulsating throb of the engines along the front. I watched the minute hand motionless, creeping, rushing headlong to zero hour.

The two men who were to be with me as runners, the Sweeting brothers, and I lifted our eyes from our hatches to where behind us were the heights of the plateau from which we had descended to the Luce. The great wall of fog was suddenly illuminated and given shape by the stabbing white flashes of our guns. For a time it was soundless like summer lightning; then the shrill, demented screaming air above and the roar of the barrage. We turned to our front; the tanks had gone and we were three men alone.

We hurried, the fast, loping Ypres walk, but on firm ground, not duckboards. It was almost a run, as if we were going somewhere. We were not; were were only getting away, as far as we could and as fast, from the ground on which we stood. I had an idea that we could somehow escape the zone of the enemy's counter-barrage. What a time he took! What had happened to him?

Then it came. It was exhilarating, like my walk along the trench top at Messines. Two of us went on. "My brother!" he screamed above the din. "Come on!" What the hell had happened to him? Lost in the fog? Stopped to do up his bootlaces? His disappearance was complete.

We couldn't 'come on'. There was a shell-hole apparently deep enough to hold both and into this we stumbled and fell, keeping our heads down as close to the earth as we could. There I tried to think. I had two hours in which to reach the rallying point where I was to meet Asser and Corkran. A quarter of an hour later I was to meet the other two tanks commanded by Greene and Robertson.

This place seemed to afford immediate shelter—for all I knew as good a place as any other in which to spend my time till I was due at the rallying point.

In this supposition I was entirely wrong; it was based on the experience of Ypres where any shell-hole could be regarded as good as any other. As Carter had said, this was not Ypres and my lack of experience and sheer terror of moving once I had got into the shell-hole led to the most dangerous solution I could have chosen. The shell-fire was intense; lying there in the dark I supposed it to be universal as it would have been in any of the battles I had so far experienced.

Gradually I tried to get my head up enough to form some idea of where I was. On one of these occasions the fog and shell-fire momentarily cleared sufficiently to see away in the distance what I thought were the poplars of the Amiens-Roye road—running straight as a die into the distance. I could scarcely have believed that the sight of the road would bring so much relief. It was almost immediately destroyed; the road, now completely hidden from sight, was in an entirely wrong direction.

I could not understand it; I was too dazed by the shell-fire. Worse still, every lucid moment offered me only one explanation, and that one too terrible to entertain. With my head jammed to the earth I gradually worried it out.

The trees showed that Sweeting and I were walking parallel to the front, not towards the enemy. I tried to loosen my compass. As far as I could tell we had kept the same direction as the tanks. But the tanks, our whole battalion, had taken direction from this same compass.

Sweeting was trying to say something. He looked horribly anxious, almost ill. "What?" I shouted, putting my ear to his mouth to catch his reply.

"Sir! Sir, why can't I cough?"

What a question! What a time... I looked at his chest. His tunic was torn. No, it was not his tunic; the left side of his chest was missing. He tried to look. I stopped him. I found his field dressing and pretended to fix it across the gap. And then he saw, under his left arm... He sank back as if relieved, then started on a new tack.

"Mother, Mother, Mother..." Well, thank God for his damned mother. Now at least I could have some peace and pay attention to the shell-fire. I pressed myself as low into the shell-hole as I could.

If the Amiens-Roye road was behind us the tanks would be enfilading the French advance, and the Canadian Corps would be without armoured support—that is assuming that tanks were any damned good anyway.

Sweeting was trying to sit up. "For Christ's sake... try not to be a damned fool man! Lie down blast you!" My anger must have impressed him even if he couldn't hear. I couldn't hear either but I could see his lips moving.

"Mother... Mother... Mother..." Then he saw me looking. "Why can't I cough sir?"

I could not stand it. Those tanks—perhaps they were enfilading the Canadian Corps?—the French First Army without support looking for that joke Englishman who understood French? I began to whimper.

"Sweeting, *please* Sweeting... please, please *shut up*." He shut up. I knew he would start again. I caught a glimpse of the poplars, waving. There must be a strong wind. Why did it not blow the fog away?

"Why can't I cough sir?"

Why can't you cough it away? Why can't... I began to vomit but I had nothing to vomit.

"Mother... Mother... Mother", he was muttering. How then could I hear him? I looked up. The shelling had stopped. The sun was shining. The fog, the night, had gone.

The Amiens-Roye road had resumed its proper place on our left. We were in a shell hole at the edge of a cart track and the track was edged on the other side by tall grasses, not the poplars of the Amiens-Roye road.

I was not relieved. "God damn it God! That was *not* funny." Utterly exhausted, I said "Sweeting, I'm very sorry. There will be some bearers shortly. They will take you to the casualty clearing station. You've got a Blighty."

He was too far gone to call me a liar. His eyes were glazed over. Enough life flickered into them at my words for him to say, "You will write to my mother? You *will* write sir, won't you?" He was alive now and urgent. "Sir! You will write to my mother? Won't you?"

"Yes, of course."

"Her address is..."

"Don't. I have it. We have it in the office."

And then I think he died. Or perhaps it was only me. I handed him over to some infantry. "Sweeting, I *have* to go now—to the other tanks...". Thank God he was paying no attention to my drivel. Two men, one on either side, draped his arms over their

249

shoulders and stumbled along with him to the casualty clearing station. Sweeting. Gunner. Tank Corps. Died of Wounds. That, for him, was the end.

35

IT was a glorious afternoon. Marvellous—just the day for a battle. And now, let me see. Yes, I could get on with my job. The ground too was perfect; no mud, just right like Cambrai for tanks. In fact there was one just ahead of me—burning, burning fiercely. Every so often it seemed to be hiccoughing with indigestion as a fresh packet of shells exploded. 'It was not possible to get near it'.

In fact it was quite possible; I could have got in at the door which was open on the far side and finished it all. Out of the door hung three blackened bodies like disembowelled entrails. I knew it was Corkran's tank. So—that was the last of those of my original crew who had remained with the battalion; the last of Sergeant O'Toole.

On my right I could see the French Foreign Legion sitting in an extended line. I found an officer and asked why they were not getting on. Was it lack of one of my tanks? He could speak better lycée English than I could speak French. "Yes, we are held up. There is a machine-gun in that village there." He pointed to a village in front. "When we have had our lunch we shall not be 'held up'. We shall get him."

I waved him good luck and good-bye and set off to look for Asser. The Canadians on the left of the Roye road had swept on far in advance, apparently unobstructed either by machine-guns or lunch.

A short figure, made to look even shorter by his trying to run with his arms above his head, waddled towards me with surprising speed. He fell on his knees in front of me and tried to clasp my legs. "Kamarad kaput! Kamarad kaput!" What was the matter with me I do not know. Although I was late for my rendezvous I allowed this crazy fool to drag me by my tunic to a dug-out about twenty yards away; it was not much more than a scooped out improvisation with a tin roof on which some turves had been planted. He invited me to go in. I pulled out my Colt. I was not so mad as to walk into a booby trap; I pushed him in first. Inside he fell on his knees again by the side of another German who was lying with his body on the floor, his head jammed against the side of the dug-out, his left leg bent sharply from the hip joint and his left boot above and behind his head. He was dead; he couldn't possibly be more dead. The kneeling German wanted me to bend down and feel his heart. I was frightened. "No—nein, nein... tod", I said. He burst into tears and again tried to hold me. Cursing myself for a fool I tore myself free and left him to blubber by himself. I was shaken. Obviously I was not fit to be a soldier, let alone an officer—decorated at that.

I found Cook at the rendezvous. "What the hell have you been up to? You're twenty minutes late." I told him I had been held up by the barrage; that Corkran's tank had had a direct hit; that the French had been held up but were just resuming their advance. Put like that it sounded as if I had had quite a busy day. At least Cook appeared to be satisfied. In the next war they would not dress up people like me as soldiers.

All our objectives had been taken and the infantry, gunners, engineers and signals were in pursuit. For the first time Greene, Robertson and Asser, our surviving tanks commanders, could meet as a victorious unit with less than one out of three killed. Unlike Cambrai there was no point on our front where we had been checked. The army was far beyond its day's objectives.

Cook, Carter, Robertson, Aitches and I stood beneath a tree, Greene and Asser not having rejoined us yet. "Look there!" said Carter pointing back down the road to Amiens, "Reserves!"

We had not seen reserves before. The road was a mass of troops stretching mile after mile down to the valley of the Luce. Here and there transport and guns had left the road to press on faster than the infantry. It was a clear, sunny afternoon. On the hard ground the gunners, the horse limbers, had nothing to prevent them from travelling fast on the wide open spaces. I had not seen troops marching in column since Le Havre. It was a marvellous sight—but too late. We watched in silence, all dejected.

Aitches referred to Cook. "We've got to keep up haven't we?" Yes, those were our orders. Grease up, fill up with petrol, keep in close touch with the advancing infantry for action when we were needed.

The night the sky in front was lit up by fires, not ours but the enemy's as the retreating troops set fire to their dumps; for once it did not signify disaster. It might earlier have been a sign for rejoicing, but now it was only a sign for 'what next?'

Asser's crew were sleeping under the tank. I pulled one out and told him to wake the crew. I found Asser under the overhanging snout.

"You have to go up the road and support the French on the right and the 42nd Division on the left."

I realized he was not awake. He was stiff with pain from lying on the hard, cold ground; they had all fallen asleep before having had time to put anything under them. "Do you hear me?" He assured me he did. I repeated the orders.

His crew were all asleep. I was furious and propped the first man against the tank. Now, I thought, he will hurt himself if he falls asleep again. I told Asser to help me rouse his crew. By the time we had them all standing Asser seemed to have become permanently awake. I therefore repeated the orders—this time in detail.

"You are on your own. I shall be with Greene and Robertson and two tanks from C Company to make up the section. Don't bother about the 42nd Division—you support the French. They attack at dawn. The crazy loons in command of the 42nd Div., in spite of what I had told them, will not attack till ten-thirty—without smoke—so as to make sure our tanks will be smashed before they get to the starting point. But you", it was four-thirty and still dark—"can start now. Make the crew walk and don't let them into the tank till the last moment. That may wake them up a bit. Try to...". I changed my mind and said no more. I was horribly afraid that the moment the crew went into the warmth of the tank they would fall asleep. Asser was now his cheerful self, amused and excited; I did not want to tell him my horrible fears. What was he to try to do? The crew were not fit to fight.

For two days we had followed the Canadian Corps with no fighting but endless hard work to keep up and maintain the tanks in fighting trim. As I had told Asser, it had been resolved to make up my section with the two C Company tanks. Hauser's section had had one day's fighting since August 8th; Homfray's and Carter's had also fought on the 10th. Direct hits and mechanical failures left them now with three tanks between them. The proportion of killed to living remained one in three.

Clifford, mercifully, had at last been transferred to a new company to be formed in England. It was likely that Greene would be given his section when it was re-formed. Carter, Hauser and I were the only originals left.

I found my four tanks, collected together the tank commanders and went over the orders. They were not orders; they were sentences of death. Cook and Aitches had tried the previous evening to insist to the divisional command that zero would have to be at dawn. When the mind will not receive the obvious there is nothing to be done.

The tanks were hidden, each under a small clump of trees very conveniently placed, separated by an average interval of fifty yards from each other. At 10.25 they emerged and drove to cross the front line of the division at 10.30. There was no gunfire, no machine-gun fire. As the tanks crossed the line the enemy machine-guns opened up. I walked behind Greene's tank hoping, by being as close as possible, to escape the machine-gun fire.

The infantry did not leave their trenches. Terrified at what would happen to the tanks without infantry support to keep enemy gunners immobilized—a very slender hope at the best of times—I doubled back to the trench, tumbled in and begged the first officer I could find to open immediate fire. Nothing except the advance of the infantry could have saved us, that I knew, but if their machine-guns opened up... They couldn't; they were ready to advance. They did not fire and they did not advance.

Hauser, who had gone into action sitting on the back of one of the two tanks under his immediate command, had also run back to see what had happened. It was uncanny; nothing had happened—that's what had happened. But he was unmistakably terrified; we both were—and both perfectly safe in the trench. The troops might have been sleep-walking.

We looked at the tanks; they had nothing wrong with them. They were quietly purring their way forward and were already too far away to catch up with them even if we had wanted to do so. As there was no method of communication, wireless or otherwise, we could only stand and watch, the Colonel almost demented, Hauser and I ghost-ridden.

The tanks rolled up a gentle grassy slope. There was a soft muffled explosion. Robertson's tank opened as a flower in a nature film might unfold. Another thud; then two, almost simultaneous, followed. The whole four had flowered. Hard, bright flames, as if cut out of tinfoil, flickered and died, extinguished by the bright sun. One tank, crewless, went on to claw at the back of one in front as if preparatory to love-making; then stopped as if exhausted.

We stared, fascinated. Then we went to the Colonel, saluted and asked formally for permission to withdraw. He was in no fit state to know what we were talking about, but he nodded agreement. Two of his men gaped at us open-mouthed.

We never heard of that infantry battalion or that division again. Perhaps they had had long experience of the qualities of their General and his staff.

Like a boy learning a task set for detention I repeated mentally, "I must remember these four officers and all their men are dead." I do not remember the slightest suspicion of mourning or regret. It was as if my only concern was to avoid a social blunder by speaking as if I were not aware that 'their name liveth for evermore'. Greene, Robertson and... who were those two poor sods from C Company? Or was it A Company? I'm damned if I knew.

Aitches was silly and made me feel he was on the verge of giggling. Cook was tight-lipped, his eyes bright and hard. "Right. Give me a written report—now. And make it snappy. *And* short."

Hauser, Carter, Cook, Aitches and I—it suddenly seemed as if we had an enormous number of officers. There was Asser too of course. That would be more still unless something had happened to him.

It was only about 11.30. Time for another battle before lunch, especially if we 'made it snappy' like the last one.

"I'll see if I can find out what's happened to Asser", said Cook.

I volunteered to keep to the French zone while Cook kept to the border between the two.

"I thought I told you to write me a report." Cook's tone was icy.

God damn your bloody eyes, I thought. But I kept my mouth shut.

36

I WROTE the report. Hauser read it. How could one spin it out enough to make it short? From that day to this I have had no other experience which was so utterly devoid of mystery yet totally incomprehensible. Troops can mutiny; these merely failed to leave the trench. Staff can be hesitant; this divisional staff was adamant. Generals can be stupid; this one impressed my hidden reserves of intelligence. There were night attacks, dawn attacks, feint attacks; but not a 10.30 attack—surely not 10.30?

What happened after I had no idea. If I had sat for an examination in which I was called upon to read the account and the complete the story I could not have done it.

Greene was dead; I did not like Greene. He was too ruthless, to pushing, out for himself too much and too often. Should I say this in my letter of condolence to his mother? 'Fine officer... a great loss to all his comrades... his Colonel remarked to me the other day that he would go far...' So he would have, but someone had put a stop to all *that.*

Robertson? Such a nice fellow, quiet, modest, reserved...

Cook was back and drew me aside. "We found a bullet through his heart." I stared at him; he looked serious. I nearly said "Liar!"—what I meant was "Don't be a melodramatic ass!" What I said was "Oh". Then I burst into tears, wiped them off my face. "Sorry", I said, "I'm tired." Cook looked at me curiously. I hoped he wasn't going to suggest I had 'shell-shock'.

"I'd better go and write to the relatives", I said quickly and cleared off.

With some wads of paper, ammunition box for a table and petrol can for a chair I started off at a great pace. 'Always cheerful and a perpetual source of...' of what?

I suddenly remembered Sweeting. I had not written—of course I had not promised to. "Sir, you will write to my mother won't you?" I wiped the sweat off his brow with my sleeve. "Mother, Mother, Mother..." His mind was wandering, thank God.

And to whom am I supposed to be writing? Must be rather a nice woman, I thought. Yes, but suppose she was that fat old trollope who had turned her angry eyes on my moonface and said, "What the bloody hell!" that day in Woburn Place, years and years ago...

"Finished?" It was Cook again. "Good God, what *have* you been up to?" I told him I wouldn't be long and scribbled furiously.

'Hero and strumpet voluntary—One of the best' (Mother, Mother, Mother) 'Always could be relied upon' (Mother, Mother, Mother) 'We shall miss him'. Chorus: (all letters) 'Luckily he died instantly and could not have experienced pain.'

Fortunately someone on the staff, foreseeing the danger that a tank commander would surrender his tank to the enemy—"You know what these tank commanders are"—had provided that each tank carried a charge of high explosive. That explained that fascinating opening of the tanks like blossoms greeting the sun.

'Dear Madam, I am sorry I have not been able to write to you before about the death of your son. He was a good lad and you must have been a very good mother to him. I was with him at the end when he knew he was dying. You were the person who was in his mind in those last hours and it was your name that was on his lips. I hope you will feel proud that he loved you so much. I am, dear Madam, his officer that day...'

Cook heard a rumour; the battalion was to be withdrawn from the line. It seemed likely to be true of B Company since half a dozen officers and no men did not at once suggest itself as obviously useful. The next day the news became official. We could not rejoice but we were relieved. I supposed it would mean withdrawal for some days, perhaps even a week or so, to one of the villages near Regimental Workshops. Packing up was always a dismal business for me but this time I had to pack up the effects of officers from whom I did not wish to be parted. Even Greene's death was difficult to tolerate; he had at least been reliable and tough.

The Colonel was reputed to be the only officer sad to go. He was accused of having worked very hard to win a DSO by offering our tanks as ready for action however few remained and however worn. If so, he should have been offered half a dozen DSO's for intelligent anticipation and support of the needs of the Commander-in-Chief. Haig was perhaps the only man, soldier or civilian, who knew the war could be finished that year. Had he not held this view and forced it, it is impossible to know what price might have had to be paid by failure to catch the tide now running in our favour. What could not be grasped by high government officials, even when explained by Haig himself, could certainly not be grasped by junior officers—especially junior officers in my state of mind. I was unable to grasp anything; for once I could even feel free from fear. The loss of the four tanks was almost a physical blow, so difficult it had been to believe the sight as it unfolded before my eyes. The death of Asser was different but had the same quality of being blunt, unable to penetrate the most superficial layer of one's mind. It was in this state that I obeyed a summons to see the Colonel.

Redfaced, garrulous, healthy and smart in his yeomanry amateur way, he talked of this and that. Then I heard him saying, "Bad show what? That affair with the tanks—must have been terrible for you."

"Yes sir", I agreed. It had not in fact been in the least terrible for me but I thought it as well to keep this to myself. It was no more terrible for me than it was for him except that it went on in front of me while my eyes were open wide.

"We have now", he went on, "only four tanks left in the whole battalion. On August 8th we started with", he looked at his papers, "thirty-six."

I began to feel suspicious; what was the old fool talking about? It was most unlikely that he wanted to talk statistics to a junior section commander. Then it came.

"We have a bit of a tough nut to crack. The army commander especially wants four tanks to help with a job at Méaulte—you remember that place? The Christmas camp?"

Did I not! That's where I heard about the chap who was lucky enough to have lost his leg.

"This place is just near there—Happy Valley—you probably know it." I certainly knew it by repute.

"But sir", I said, "I haven't any tanks left. All my section and the crews have gone."

His voice was smooth, almost sympathetic, rather like the Major, I thought, only he had not been so coarse—silkier, as befits a genuine gentleman as opposed to the 'officer and gentleman' type. "Yes I know. But we want a reliable man." (That bloody DSO again?) "Winsop has all his four tanks available." (I breathed again.) "But he is not really the man I would choose for this kind of job." (I felt my breathing had been premature.)

"He has a Military Cross though sir." This Military Cross had created a mild scandal. Winsop was regarded by all the officers I had known as 'no damn good at all'. He was a military version of the 'dumb blonde' of strip cartoon fame.

The Colonel became confidential. "Bion, that MC was not my recommendation. He had it before I came here." He went on, strained, staring at me, "He is in my opinion no good. I can't help it—I'm very sorry, but there is no one I know on whom I can rely as I can on you."

Pure cajolery, I thought bitterly. In fact he doesn't know me from Adam. I had hardly seen enough of him to know more than his reputation for Irish blarney. In any case, what the hell was I belly-aching about? It was not so long since I had been complaining about being left out of an action at Ypres. Oh, for the Guards Division! Soldiers, real soldiers and above all, Orders!—not blarney. Not, "Will you be so kind as to oblige me by fighting for your country?" This was what it came to, the glorious voluntary system. It was a failure to understand that there is nothing voluntary about being attacked by a powerful, well-armed army.

"I don't think the Military Cross should be awarded to officers who are no good sir."

The Colonel still had his eyes fixed on me. Perhaps he had begun to wonder if the same rule should not apply to people who had been awarded the DSO. After all, it was a higher decoration than the MC. I saluted and went out before, as far as I knew, the thought had occurred to him. When a young man is granted a decoration perhaps he should also be given a permit entitling him to go and win it at any time in the next six months.

I took over the four tanks and set out for Happy Valley.

37

WE passed by Villers Bretonneux, through the Australian Corps and on. I remember little except feeling ill and tired. There was a beautiful lake near Villers Bretonneux; sometime later, the next day, there was woodland and I felt eased by the green grass and firm ground on which we travelled smoothly. There was much engine and tank track trouble; the tanks were nearing the end of their mechanical life so we all knew we must have mechanical failure.

I was vomiting badly; I did not know till the day before the attack that I had contracted the influenza which had appeared as an unknown pandemic inflicting all armies. I was at divisional HQ trying to absorb my orders when a medical officer saw me looking ill and diagnosed the infection. He advised me to take a couple of bottles of champagne into action—"Your runner can carry it." "And if it makes me drunk?" "Then he can carry *you*."

Luckily the orders were simple—drive from our starting point towards the enemy and go on from there; then stop. At least, that was what I thought they were as I contemplated my trembling hands; not fear this time—fever.

It was a hot day. The rolling devastated region of Méaulte shimmered in the heat. I sweated and trembled and staggered about till I found myself back with the camouflaged tanks.

This time the action was to start at 'dawn'. It always did, unless it was obtained by the divisional commander of the 42nd Division. '*Never, never* say "dawn". Be exact', said the manuals. Orders had to be '04.20' or '06.30' so that all watches were precisely synchronized. We all—tanks, gunners, infantry, the whole division—attacked at the same moment. Or I assume we did because I have never heard anything to the contrary. The Germans were not co-operating, and as I myself seemed to be present only very fitfully my account is even more incoherent than is usual with sophisticated versions of chaos.

The first thing of which I have any recollection is sitting in an infantry trench, pausing before making an advance. The sun was hot. The camouflaged tanks at which I had arrived the previous evening were somewhere in the battle. I could not see them. My two runners had one bottle of champagne for which they showed some solicitude though they seemed more concerned for me.

A man with his chest and belly exposed was lying on the trench floor. His face showed a deadly pallor but he was breathing and sweating. Some flies were settling and crawling on his belly trying to reach a neat puncture in the lower half on the right side. The flies were periodically disturbed by one of two privates who stared dully with unspeculating eyes at their wounded mate. I pulled myself together.

"Shouldn't the stretcher bearers get him back?"

"Him? No sir—he's a gonner." I gave up.

Someone was blowing a whistle. We all scrambled out of the trench, my two runners shoving and pulling at me.

Time to advance. I felt extremely fit; it seemed queer but unmistakable that the battle was doing me a lot of good. There were a number of wounded, ours, not German; I thought it strange that they were in grotesque positions.

There was in fact nothing mysterious about it for the enemy had gone, retired, leaving the position to be held by a small rearguard with high velocity guns whose shells had the same unpleasant quality as those near the Steenbeck—the whizzes arriving after the bangs. So one could not duck as one heard the shell approaching. This explained why the infantry lay about in grotesque attitudes and groaned.

At last I saw one of the tanks. It had stopped; the petrol feed had broken down.

"Come on!"

"Where to sir?"

"Where to? In, of course. We'll ride the rest of the way." They probably thought I was drunk. I told the tank commander to carry on as before when he had got it started again. Just then it *did* start, so suddenly that he was hurled against the sharp edge of the ammunition racks. The blow was on his temple and he lay there unconscious. I took over command of the tank; or perhaps it was the alcohol.

The scene was yellowish; not summer landscape, not autumn, not anything, but warm, and the tank was hot and stank of petrol. Nobody was about, certainly no enemy. Even the lack of mud gave a nightmare quality to the drive, for in real battles one did not travel fast and easily across rolling downland unopposed. Nor did one go for rides in tanks if one felt ill and bright-eyed.

I turned to shout to the driver. "Lots of sausage balloons up." I pointed to the long array of dark shapes looming almost overhead. Funny the way German observation balloons always looked so dark compared with our silvery shapes—obviously the Devil's Own.

I tried being jocular. "Do you know", I shouted, "I get the feeling we are being fired at!"

The driver looked tense and pale. He must be tired, I thought.

"It's those balloons sir."

Of course—it had not occurred to me! We were under direct observation; they must be concentrating on us. But in that case why were there no shells bursting round us?

"Get out!" I shouted. "All of you! Walk close behind." They tumbled out. I took over driving the tank, meaning to drive a zig-zag course with the escape hatch over me open. Then I realized that with no crew I could not steer the tank and could not drive anywhere but straight ahead. I had no sense of fear. I opened the throttle so that the tank was at full speed.

Before I knew what I was doing I had left the driver's seat and joined the crew behind. It was difficult to keep up with the fast-moving driverless tank. Then, only then, panic overwhelmed me. Suppose they were *not* firing at us? Suppose they did not hit us? A fully equipped tank in complete working order would have been handed over to the enemy, abandoned on my orders by its crew.

I could not catch up with it; as I stumbled and tried to run to the door I fell. Then mercifully the shell hit, pierced and burst. The tank stopped, flames spurting everywhere. In a moment it was a total wreck.

I felt bemused, unable to grasp what had happened. I only knew that I had failed in my desperate resolve to get back to the tank. Had I succeeded I could not possibly have survived. Every course I had initiated had almost immediately seemed to be an irretrievable blunder. It was not a repetition, it was not a reminiscence, but again I had the sense of being a cornered rat which a giant was nonchalantly aiming to club to death. Even as a rat I was incompetent—like a mouse I had once seen sit up on its haunches in what looked like an attitude of prayer to Lord Cat Almighty who at that moment was luxuriously licking his paws and washing himself. I had escaped—apparently. Who knew what Lord Cat Almighty was up to during this short respite? 'Remember also the humble beasts...'

We worked our way back through the high velocity area,

through the zone of shelled men, back to... And then I remembered I had on me my leave pass which the Colonel had caused to be dated as valid from 4.30 that day. I was to be picked up by a box-body car at the cross-roads of the village from which our attack had started. Of course such a point, well marked, easy to refer to by map reference co-ordinates, would be the focus of attention by enemy gunners. At that cross-roads I was to remain till picked up—alive or dead?—by the box-body.

The sun was still high. I leant against the warm brickwork and waited. The shelling was not heavy but it was accurate and monotonous. It blasted the houses of that cross-roads; they were rhythmically blotted out. I did not want to miss the box-body. I sat down on a chunk of masonry. It was like watching the ruined camp at Messines when time ceased to flow.

The gun—I decided that it must be a single one alone—was firing at extreme range or I would not have been able to hear its shells coming. I decided to lie down to save myself the bother of throwing myself flat each time. How boring it all was. I thought I heard the box-body coming. The driver was driving like hell. I also heard the shell coming—like hell. I thought it would be a dead heat.

As the smoke and rubble dust cleared I saw the box-body, stationary, with racing engine. I scrambled into the back. "Home John!" I bawled. By the time the next shell arrived we were clear of the cross-roads and a hundred yards away on the road to Boulogne.

38

I MUST have been fortunate in the timing of the journey for by 4.30 the next afternoon I was in the terminal stages of a turkish bath near Russell Square. It was quiet and two old fellows were discussing an item in the evening paper.

"I see", said one mellow voice to the other, "we've been over the top again." There was a note of complacency, of pride in his voice.

How nonplussed he would have been if he had known that one of 'us' was listening hot, indignant. 'We' indeed! Who the hell was *he* to say 'we'? Now I can understand the genuine note of sadness for the comradeship that had passed him by, though it surprises me that I think of 'comradeship' in this context at all. I have no memory of thinking of the men of my crews in that action. I must have told them to report back to Company HQ. I remember joining with another crew who were going out of action with their tank—the only one, as it turned out, to survive the action—because I had to refuse a terribly mangled infantry soldier a lift. He was grotesque, like the German's 'kamerad'. He should have made me laugh if only I had retained my prep school sense of humour about physical deformity. "Hullo, fig-ear", we said—if we were big enough to be safe from retaliation—to a boy whose ears bore a striking resemblance to that fruit. Or, "Look sharp Hobson!", to a boy whose features were so distorted that he was known as 'hatchet face'. What fun, what wit! If only one could have seen the funny side of a grown man with his trousers full of faeces because his leg had been blown past his ear! Of course all that had been at 4.30 *yesterday*. At 4.30 *today* I was very comfortable in my turkish bath.

"Mother, Mother... You will write to my mother sir, won't you?"

"No, blast you, I shan't! Shut up! Can't you see I don't want to be disturbed?" These old ghosts, they never die. They don't even fade away; they preserve their youth wonderfully. Why, you can even see the beads of sweat, still fresh, still distinct, against the pallor of their brows. How is it done? Like the dewdrops on the petals of Rédoutés roses. Marvellous isn't it? So, so... death-like, isn't it? But of course it's just a trick—he's not *really* dead, you know. Please, *please* shut up. I will write, I really will. To Mother England—that old whore!

The turkish bath was very refreshing; I felt so clean. It's not *real*, you know; just a kind of trick. Really, of course, one stinks. They have a way of making people look so life-like, but really we are dead. I? Oh yes, I died—on August 8th 1918. We all had a good laugh about it at the Club where the rats—there was one old chap, bald, bloated, corpse-fed, who sat on my chest one night—it made me laugh because his whiskers tickled my face...

"Are you all right?" I awoke with a jolt, sense of humour all gone, to find the bath attendant peering into my face. "Excuse me sir, but I think you must have been dreaming." I hurried. I had not left much time to catch my train to Cheltenham where my mother was staying to be near my sister at school.

Cheltenham was very beautiful. The weather was good too. The shops were very nice. I liked the school too; that, I thought, was very nice when I went to hear a school concert. I often said so when people asked me. I think they wanted me to be enjoying my leave, not to be dwelling too much on what I suppose they thought were the horrors of the war. In fact I was not dwelling on the horrors of anything. Yes, I certainly thought Cheltenham was *very* nice. I stressed how 'very' nice it was. But although I did my best I seemed unable to convey a convincing degree of appreciation. Once only I felt I had established an emotional contact and that with a maiden lady, Miss Collar, with whom I had stayed on my holidays from school when my parents were not in England.

Miss Collar was a stout lady who wore pince-nez which were always highly polished and added brilliance to the professional jollity—she was joint owner of a boarding house for missionaries—of her welcome to her patrons. I did not think she liked me, an impression which was deepened when I once heard her, in tragic tones, describing how I had helped her by scrubbing out one of the baths in the establishment. I had, I remembered, done it very thoroughly by actually scrambling about inside the bath the better to reach the less accessible parts. I think—but I am not sure—that I had removed my boots before getting in. "And do you know", she was saying in an awe-struck whisper, "he actually used up one whole tin of Vim!" I realized she was talking about me; I slunk off thinking perhaps I may not have washed all the Vim out when I had finished. But when I saw her next she had recaptured her usual sparkle. I, however, never achieved the equanimity which I felt was expected of me.

On this occasion at Cheltenham she seemed less formidable though remaining physically undiminished, perhaps because her vegetarian diet had saved her from the worst rigours of rationing. She was ill at ease when she drew me aside to make a special and private request. After one or two cursory conventional questions about what it was like to be in action with tanks, she came to the point that was really exercising her.

"What was it like", she asked, "when you drove your tank over people?"

To this I had to give some thought. Certainly I had been very afraid, when I was leading a tank from in front, outside, by signalling to the driver through his front flap. But I had never driven over anyone; I had to admit that the experience had so far escaped me. I thought she seemed disappointed when we rejoined the banalities of more general conversation.

Relations with anyone I respected were intolerable, notably with my mother; I wanted nothing except to get back to the Front just to get away from England and from her. I can only hope she had a similar wish to be rid of me.

At last I had said good-bye and was leaning out of the train window. "Mind the door", I warned her, "it's filthy." "Everything", she said, near to tears, "is dreadful... I mean nothing is really cleaned up nowadays." And so we parted.

She died some months before it was certain that the war was to be fought again in 1939. Then her eyes rested on a vase of spring flowers and she was already confused. "The heads of the flowers are drooping. I can hold them up no longer. Will you hold them up for me?" She lost consciousness and died soon after.

39

THE battalion was again at Blangy when I rejoined it. It had changed out of recognition. Aitches had been reported by Carter to the Brigadier for having failed to be at his correct place in our last action. Since this was indistinguishable from the arrest of a senior officer by a junior, the Brigadier had strongly advised Carter to abandon his intention and Carter had wisely but reluctantly agreed. The matter was thus forgotten and a seal set upon oblivion by the return of Aitches to England to aid in the formation of a new battalion. As few people believed he would ever be so indiscrete as to be sent to a fighting front again, it seemed to be wiser in everyone's interest if his long experience in action with tanks could be employed in high rank in a training battalion. He had engaging manners and being in this respect unhampered by the regular army polish it was felt that he would be just the man to co-operate with the new democratic people's army which was beginning to emerge.

Holden, now taking over from Aitches, was an intelligent ex-infantryman who had been heard to mutter, "Oh God our help in Aitches past" when Aitches' promotion had first been announced on parade. In fact poor Aitches died of influenza within two weeks of being posted back to England. I like to think that his war memorial would set out his military virtues in glowing terms of appropriate splendour. But I doubt it for there was something unloved and pathetic about him.

The fact that Carter, Hauser and I were the only three officers who remained of our original company served as a link, perhaps the only one, between us. Carter was set in his ways and preserved the nervous, bigoted patriotism of a colonial age; Hauser seemed to have no views but to retain a lively, irritable impatience for the incompetence which he associated with all things British; I retained the remains of a disintegrated moral system in which I had been brought up and to which I clung because I had nothing better to put in its place.

The war situation had altered profoundly since our last refit and reinforcement at Blangy. Victory instead of defeat stared us in the face, but it wore so strange a look that it was scarcely less frightening. There were rumours that we would shortly be in action again, probably not far from the Drocourt-Quéant Switch on which the Hindenburg defence system hinged.

Ultimately we moved by companies, not to be reunited again as a battalion in action, though right at the end we had orders to move just before the armistice came into effect. But of an armistice there were as yet not even rumours. In so far as the end of the war came into our calculations, it was dismissed as a very old joke from which the humour had long departed. Perhaps it would be more accurate to say that the battalion no longer had the outlook in which such jokes could thrive. Not enough time in which to absorb too many lessons inevitably led to the learning of one or two and the neglect of all others. It was evident that catch phrases such as 'the first seven years are the worst', 'remember the hundred years war', had no relevance in tank warfare, but no more appropriate form of wry humour had grown to take their place. Some tank commanders escaped being killed long enough to be promoted to command sections. As section commanders their expectation of life was greater; they might accordingly survive to reach to the command or second in command of companies. For non-commissioned ranks it was virtually impossible to reach safety by promotion—as Sergeant O'Toole had shown. Slight wounds were so rare that the avenues of escape were restricted to chronic invalidism or forms of elaborate foot-dragging. After August 8th there were no senior officers with actual experience of tanks in action, and no junior officers who could reasonably suppose they had a chance of survival to higher rank. My interventions in action convinced me I was not doing my job as a section commander, but I was unable to imagine how I should do it. The prospect of action was one of loafing about on a battlefield in a highly vulnerable position both with regard to wounds—though this was no worse than for the infantry—and to reputation. The latter I had seen with dreadful clarity in the last action just before the tank was destroyed. It was to be brought home to me again before the end at Sequehart.

Looking back now it amazes me that I do not remember any occasion when it occurred to me or any of my friends to debate the military wisdom of our procedures. It is the more surprising that a critical attitude was common enough but never took a constructive form. It did not occur to me, or any tank commander of whom I heard, to report that Ypres was unsuitable for tank warfare.

Someone had to think of Cambrai and apply its lessons at Amiens on August 8th. The tank commanders who might have provided the initiative and knowledge were either killed in action or too stunned, stupefied, to contribute anything.

We complained. We complained of the Guards, of the Engineers for having no pontoons or bridges available when the bridge collapsed under the tank at Cambrai; we complained that there were no reserves when the enemy's feint attack succeeded in doing what his main attack could not do; we complained of the futility of the cavalry reserve, though I remembered thinking how impressive they looked as they went forward on the evening of November 20th; I remembered thinking how impressive they looked when I saw them lying dead in scores where they had been mown down by a solitary machine-gunner who had been presented by the Scots Greys with a target he had been unable to find in the open order advances of the infantry. I had been impressed by the 11th French Division who regarded their lunch as of more importance than a solitary machine-gunner who was whiling away the time by firing at nothing in particular; I had been impressed—so had we all—by the Commander of the 32nd Division who did not believe tank officers who thought their tanks required the protection of darkness, natural or artificial, against a resolute enemy gunner on August 12th, even after the German gunner officer at Cambrai had dropped a very broad hint by leaving his mark on our company. I was again impressed when I saw a photograph in *The Times* of post-war army manoeuvres; it showed a small number, three or four, of mounted cavalry men, the caption explaining that it was of a 'Cavalry patrol bringing in a captured machine-gunner'. It did not say what bait they had used and I was too busy wondering how I was going to earn a living to write a letter asking my betters for enlightenment. Besides, wasn't the war over? Had we not won? I was at Oxford then and no one had told me that in return for such privileges I was expected to contribute intelligence to the government of the country even if, as was certainly true, nobody would pay the slightest attention. I had not learned that any fool can engage in a successful action but that what was required, even in peace time, was the courage or brains to contribute one's quota in the face of defeat or probable defeat.

Haig had won his war, but his blunders—which he must have been intelligent enough to know—are now becoming increasingly clear to anyone who can be bothered to learn of them. Why a man with the defects common to all men became and remained

Commander-in-Chief is a question which can only be answered, if ever, when it is known why an ordinary man comes to be recognized as 'great' while all other ordinary men remain ordinary.

Blangy itself was familiar but a change was taking place, confusing and made additionally complex by occurring in an unfamiliar domain, the domain of the mind, the personality, the spirit. Even now it is difficult to formulate the shift of emphasis; although the thing itself has been known to exist for countless generations there is still no adequate vocabulary for its comprehension. I can say that while the battalion was at Blangy it was receiving new tanks; it was being reinforced with new men many of whom came from mining districts and whose whole youth had been devoted to learning the 'trade' of a miner; weapons and ammunition were readily available to refit. But I cannot so easily say why there was a belief that the army was near to achieving victory over the enemy.

40

CONJECTURE must now take the place of facts which I was too inexperienced to observe when they were there to observe. I did not have the ability to recognize that I was in a state of inner turmoil in an external world of emotional upheaval. There were two events which had a powerfully stimulating effect upon me.

The death of Aitches was talked about in our company mess chiefly in terms of incredulity, hatred and contempt. In the course of these talks I heard from older men something of the world from which he came. It was a world of great wealth in which the values I had always taken as established, unalterable, eternal, were regarded as a curious aberration particular to the poor, the vulgar, the contemptible and the weak. Aitches belonged to nothing. I could see he was as much an outsider in his father's world as I would be if I had had to associate with wealthy gaol birds, horse-racing addicts, the questionable type of journalism that thrived on the fringes of blackmail. Of this world I know more now, but only that part of it which strives, usually ineffectually, to escape from the thraldom which is felt but not apprehended. While I felt contempt for Aitches I was never sure that I was not the same kind of coward, separated only by the thinnest of thin partitions.

The second event was that news came through from a prisoner of war telling of the death of Asser. For some reason which was unclear, but I guessed to be the exhaustion of the crew, they were unable to continue fighting and Asser gave orders to evacuate. The enemy surrounded the tank calling on each man to surrender as he came out. They were helpless and put up their hands. Asser did not. To the call to surrender he replied, "I'm damned if I will." He was apparently still holding his revolver and no enemy could take risks if that was so. So he was shot and died instantly, being left where he was found later by Cook.

Though this story added nothing to what had already been guessed it was extremely disturbing to me. The first impression was one of utter waste; then a feeling that I could never in such circumstances do my duty knowing that there could not possibly be any other outcome. After Cambrai it was obvious to me, though even then not till a considerable time had passed, that I could have been killed a number of times over by the sniper in the tree-top. In the last attacks made before we were relieved by the French at Wytschaete I knew in my heart that if the enemy reached our trenches I could not go on fighting. I do not understand courage such as Asser's. I can easily understand all the *explanations* I have ever heard, but I cannot understand the thing itself. I have never heard of any instance of the hopeless war waged by individuals of any race or creed without feeling that in their position I could not be what they are. I cannot honestly say "With the grace of God there might I go also".

I do not know if Asser was sustained by any religious belief. In the short time I knew him he was always cheerful, modest, unassuming—how fast and how trippingly the clichés come tumbling out. The currency is so debased that the very language of love, like the word 'love' itself, can hardly be used in the presence of the thing itself. Aitches and Asser; both dead. They cannot really have been so different. 'And I, only, am left alone to tell thee'.

One or two regular army officers showed an instinctive fear of the future. One I knew was desperate to achieve a decoration which might serve as a life-belt in the stormy seas of peace looming ahead. The outcome for those who could guess at the future must have been black indeed. The prospects for the end of the war were, however, so extremely slight that I do not think that any of us seriously entertained conscious fears or hopes.

I had to take a section into action on a place called Tara Hill; the orders were based on a fiction that the hill was occupied by the enemy. I did not see any of our own or enemy troops, but it was evident that enemy gunners were still in action and had a good view of the hill which supposedly we were about to capture. After a time I decided, in view of the accuracy of the gunfire, that it was best to assume we had captured the position. This left me free to initiate an activity which I called 'patrolling the enemy position', and this in turn enabled me to shelter two tanks out of direct fire and make the third travel up and down without any crew. Since I was sure there were no infantry present I did not have the horrors of the Happy Valley action. The only danger lay in driving the tank till it was time to swing it round to go in the opposite direction. Luckily the gunners got it before anyone was hurt.

In due course the battle was deemed to be over and with one tank

less but all my men intact I was free to write my report. This I was
doing somewhat light-heartedly when I suddenly remembered Lord
Watchett's warning about 'two rows of ribbons' and restrained
myself. The regular officer who hoped himself to be decorated if he
could paint the warlike feats of his troops in sufficiently glowing
colours was still at large. The reality of the danger had been
brought home to me by my being awarded the Legion of Honour
for the action on August 8th. The citation had a curiously plausible
resemblance to the 'facts', yet I could not believe that the battle I
had experienced and the one cited were the same. I liked the
ribbon—bright red—and it went well with the DSO, but I found it
difficult to make an appropriate response to congratulations. The
first such occasion arose when our Brigadier, a distinguished
soldier and a very likeable man, wanting to congratulate me,
waggishly invited me to draw aside my trench coat and expose the
ribbon. As it was some weeks after the award had appeared in
Orders he was not pleased that I was not wearing the ribbon. He
must have felt, as I did, that this was a gratuitous display of mock
modesty. I had not in fact been able to obtain the ribbon but,
equally, I had not tried very hard.

My report on Tara Hill led to nothing worse than being detailed
for the job of OC Company in charge of base details while the other
officers had a turn at action. I had long ceased to mind being left
out of battle. I would not have liked to admit any deterioration
but I did not want to be reminded that once I had protested at Ypres
at being excluded. Nor did I want to stress too much that I would
hate to be wanted for the action on August 22nd. It was with
relief that I found myself turning in for a night's sleep with two
other officers sharing the tent, both juniors whom I did not know.
Hauser was 'up the line' to take his turn in command of his section
in action.

41

I MUST have gone to sleep at once for we all knew better now than to waste time awake if we had a chance of sleep—day or night. It was with sinking feelings that I was awoken by someone stumbling clumsily amidst our tent guide-ropes. I felt sure he was looking for the opening flap; I felt sure it would mean that he was looking for me. After a time he gave up looking and started to shout.

"Is Captain Bion here please?"

I pulled my blankets over my head and for a second or two pretended not to hear. Of course nobody wanted an officer in the middle of the night for any pleasant reason. Again he shouted, more urgently. At last I asked him what he wanted.

"You're wanted up the line sir, at once. It's urgent."

I pulled on my boots and staggered out into the bright cold night with my equipment. My three crews had been alerted and were waiting silently by their tanks. The messenger, whom I knew, was one on whom I could rely; checking the map reference to our destination I told him to get on and lead us there, the tanks following closely in line.

Even at that miserable hour it was very welcome to hear some infantry shout out as we passed, "Good old Tanks", and "Good luck". I was met by the second in command who told me the infantry were held up at a village called Sequehart. No great difficulty was expected but we must have the village.

The ground conditions were perfect as they had been since August 8th. The village dominated the far slope of a small valley. In the centre of it and easily visible was the church. Our infantry had penetrated the village but we did not know where the front line was. Therefore we must be careful not to open fire till we were really sure we were not firing on our own. I hardly needed to tell our men that, but it was bad news that we had to fight in such confused conditions. With the poor visibility from tanks, it made it particularly awkward if we had to exercise great care in selecting our targets. I arranged with our tank commanders as I went that I would try to be at various rallying points at particular times—if wanted. In fact I thought it nonsense because I would be far more likely to see that a tank was in trouble than they could spare anyone to come and look for me. Still, it sounded as if it provided a kind of programme.

The second in command gave us his blessing; I dismissed the tank commanders as it was time for them to shut themselves in and set off in low gear at their one mile an hour crawl to their starting points. These terms belonged, as did our tanks, to the rigid conditions of static trench warfare. We were engaged now in something so close to open warfare that neither training nor equipment was adequate; what was required was a capacity for improvisation and initiative. In my days of infantry training I thought I had both. Either I was mistaken or it had been beaten out of me by the sombre misery of Ypres and the sheer attrition of war on someone unsuited to fighting. I was too tired to think; I suffered a vague sense of grievance which was made worse by the feeling that I could think of nothing about which to have cause to be aggrieved. Sergeant O'Toole had had a grievance. I felt I shared it but I did not share the hideous foundation on which he had to build his structure of patriotism and discipline. I at least had some reason to believe that England represented a way of life for which one could be expected to fight.

It was past our supposed zero hour. I walked slowly in the direction in which the tanks had disappeared. As the sky grew pale I began to disinguish the church of Sequehart. At the time I thought its spire looked magnificent. I remembered having been told that spires were intended to remind men of the God who dwelt in the heavens above and watched over the affairs of men and women on earth. Then the sun rose blood red behind the church; soon the dramatic spectacle gave way to the light of day, the commonplace village, the machine-guns and the individual shots of rifle fire.

Those who were not fighting could and did say the enemy were defeated, the war won. This was not true or relevant for any of us there that morning.

In the valley, still shadowed by the ground rising gently up to Sequehart, was one of my tanks. As the light grew I realized it was not moving. It looked as if nothing was wrong. But when I came nearer I found it had had a direct hit. The shell had burst on the track, flung it back over the tail and effectively put it out of action as it could no longer move. But the fact of its hitting the track had saved the crew; no one was injured and Reid had formed the orthodox and useless strong point disposed in front and to the left.

It was then that I discovered another tank farther to the right and also immobile.

This had been knocked out by a direct hit from a gas shell. As the explosive charge was only enough to release the gas no one was hurt and the officer and one man had even escaped being gassed. I made them join Reid's strong point as there was nothing for them to do and no reason for withdrawing from action. Afterwards I felt I had been wrong. I do not remember making any decision in action which I did not soon regret, but this was peculiar in that my feeling of guilt about my last battle in the war grew steadily for many years after.

I was able to compare the full account that I wrote at the time with the impression I had years later when the details had disappeared from my memory; the feelings seemed to have remained and even grown in intensity. Thus, looking back I had an almost overwhelming sense of failure, in this wise:

There were four men all badly gassed. With help they could be made to walk. I felt it essential to get them away from the tank which I was sure would be hit again, this time with high explosive. The enemy were using three parts high explosive to one part poison gas in their bombardment. I laid out the men some ten yards or more away from and behind the tank. I then tried to get the men behind the track marked on the map, as was the track on August 8th, and therefore subject to fire. I managed the first two by making them walk while I bore their weight on my shoulders around which their arms were looped. As we went the enemy gunners opened concentrated fire on the track. At the latter stage we had to crawl, I doing most of the heavy dragging work. When I thought they were out of danger I told them to get back to casualty station while I returned for the last two.

They were much worse off and unable to help themselves. I saw our infantry retiring on the right of the village; I hesitated, not sure what to do. Two infantry men ran towards us shouting "Tanks!" They asked me to take the tank up to help beat back the enemy. I said I could not as the tank crew were out of action; they ran back with the message. Then I realized that if only I had not sent the officer and one man to join Reid we might have restarted the engine—I had forgotten that the three of us had in fact tried to start the engine. But perhaps because of the gas taken into the engine air intake we could not shift it with our combined strength; it was an inert mass of steel. Had they been there could we, with the aid of the two infantry, have restarted the tank and five of us have taken it into action?

Confused and exhausted I removed vital parts of the guns and, stuffing my equipment with these, managed to get the last two back to safety in two more journeys across the shelled road.

The crew were now all safe but I was left confused and a prey to guilt which was more intense when later that evening I tried to explain to our company commander how one of my tanks was reported as abandoned by the crew while still in full fighting order. The simple but unwelcome answer would be that the crew had had enough of it. Still more unwelcome was the idea that *I* had had enough of it and retained sufficient sense of reality to know that I had only to go on fighting and I would surely be killed—if the enemy went on fighting likewise.

The debate in my mind and the debate between the Company Commander and myself—if a few desultory questions could be described as a debate—were markedly bad tempered. I felt hostile, anxious and glad to pick a quarrel. I angered the Company Commander by calling him a bloody fool. I angered myself by immediately regretting it. I was startled and surprised when Carter told me quietly that if he had been the Company Commander he would have put me under arrest; I was disconcerted to find that I agreed with Carter. In fact it was surprising that though angered, the Company Commander had summoned up enough tolerance to pass over something which was extremely rude even if one did not consider the military impropriety. I felt tired, blast them! I was frightened too. There had been a time when I would not have dared to say "blast them"—not without apologizing at once. Wouldn't *dare*? What, a great big boy like you with a DSO?

How I hated these interior dialogues—still do. No, damn it, *no*; I don't want the DSO. I don't want to be a big boy. 'Oh my, I don't want to die! I want to go home.'

I remembered the matron at my prep school. "What? A great big boy like you putting your father to all that expense for an X-ray and nothing the matter with you? You ought to be ashamed of yourself!" I was. I had burned with shame when my father had taken me to a London clinic because my foot pained me and made me limp. It was X-rayed. Then the almoner spoke with my father while I stood by. I could not understand the conversation but I did catch some words of it.

"But", she said to my father who had been speaking low so I

could not hear properly, "your boy is wearing a college cap." That damned cap—I had forgotten it started so early. "If you can afford to send him to school you can surely afford to pay for an X-ray?"

My father seemed guilty. I think he blushed; I blushed for him. He was getting out a note case. It was awful. Never, never again would I have a painful foot. Still, I couldn't help limping. That fiendish matron—never, never again would I limp, pain or no pain.

But... I had not reckoned with cowardice. I still felt just as ridiculous. The DSO, the tank itself, were very inadequate protection. Even after Cambrai when my crew were told, I felt they looked at me as if to say, "What *you*? Recommended for a VC?" After Sequehart, as after Cambrai, I felt I might with equal relevance have been recommended for a Court Martial. It depended on the direction which one took when one ran away.

42

AFTER a month of rest and refitment the Colonel called together the senior officers. He and our Company Commander were both men I liked and respected—regular soldiers, efficient, quiet, unspectacular. I think we must have become veterans; Cambrai had finished off the enthusiastic amateurs.

The air was more wholesome for the disappearance of Aitches and Homfray. Of Aitches it could be said that the misfortune was a tragedy personal to him and to those under him who were expected by force of circumstances to invest him with an importance he did not have. The tragedy was repeated in the next war on a far larger scale when not only Chamberlain but the nation itself was called upon to bear an importance, loaded by history and the conditions of a present and a future, which it could not carry. Churchill himself added to the tragedy by seeming to embody the qualities which were required by the past, envied and outdated by the present, and insupportable and unsupported by the future.

In the insignificant physical and moral space occupied by myself in the First War even such trivial responsibilities as I had to carry were far beyond my capacity, my training and upbringing. To that extent I too shared the tragedy which was Aitches'. He, in so far as he can be distinguished from his environment, probably had not the personality required; the environment of great wealth, ruthless amorality, third-rate admiration, probably played its part in producing the feeble personality and would finally have destroyed it. Wealth, admiration, honour may mark already existing achievements but are poison when used as a substitute for the qualities which they are supposed to mark. They are similarly harmful when they are withheld until they mark nothing that is not already known. The individual who will not accept such marks of recognition, the society that will not extend them, is already in a bad way and becoming worse.

Homfray with his affectation of worthlessness was striving to disguise worthlessness which was the only genuine thing about him. He was the criminal pleading guilty to avoid investigation; he was a wolf in sheep's clothing. He was known as Tape, a name conferred on him on account of his long, slender appearance by Yates, an officer of the original 5th Battalion in England. But any name would be a disguise for yet another disguise. He was nothing disguised as an enigma disguised as a fascinating problem concealed as an ordinary person concealed as the excretion he was. He stank, but luckily for him he enjoyed the odour.

I have allowed myself in the exercise of this description the experience of a certain group of feelings; now I allow myself the further exercise of naming the group of feelings; I borrow from religion the term 'enthusiasm'. Indeed, I would think it legitimate to employ this term to the totality of the experience of writing this book. I do so because I want a term to summarize and identify an element of the total emotional experience described up to the participation in the battle at Ypres.

The characteristic that dominates the part of that experience of which I was aware—emotion and the dominant aspect of that emotion—is 'enthusiasm'. The change which took place in the battalion after action at Ypres, and between that date and the termination of the battle of Amiens, I would describe as decreasing 'enthusiasm'. The dates are arbitrary, an artificial boundary in time. Similarly the locale—in so far as I have attributed it to a particular group of people, the battalion or a section or sub-group of the battalion—is equally arbitrary. It is merely an attempt to simplify a problem, the problem of an individual, myself, and the reality of one individual's emotional life. For an approximation to the reality of the emotional experience of the battalion it would be necessary to have an account of that experience of which each participant was aware. Obviously, therefore, this account cannot be taken as bearing anything but a severely limited approximation to what it purports to describe. Its value lies in its contribution to a whole which does not and may never exist.

The Colonel explained that we were to go up to the Line. Where was it? Well, he was not yet sure. The line was moving now and he advised us not to think too much of The Line.

"If I were you I shouldn't even think too much of advancing or retreating either. I keep on having orders as if the whole British Army were moving forward in one piece. That means that if the Boches hold on, or try to disengage, or counter-attack, everyone always thinks their titchy bit of battle is the whole army falling back or defeated or winning. All I can tell you is—we are supposed to be going to Mons."

A rustle of papers amongst the officers as if a breeze passed over some tall grasses, or scabious flowers by a fresh country road, or a long meadow in far-off England...

"Isn't it Bion?"

Oh God, what's he saying? "Oh yes sir."

"I don't believe you are listening!" Still, he had a kindly expression.

"About Mons sir. We end up where we started."

"No, where the Expeditionary Force started."

"Yes sir. That's what I mean sir."

I entered our first village very cautiously. At the top of some cellar stairs stood a young slut of fourteen; she watched me, feral, eyes intense but empty of speculation. She watched me; watched. I felt I ought to say something—"It's a fine day"—or ask where everyone was. She felt, knew, I had spoken, was speaking, would speak. That instant, soundless, almost without action, she was gone, melted into the cellar below.

'Scuse me, said the Elephant's child most politely, can you tell me the way to have a baby?

Ask the cat.

'Scuse me asking, why the hell do you haunt my dreams you pasty faced little... little... school girl? Whore?

So? I was shocked. After four years of war, and two years of combatant service, mostly fighting, I could say, "Wot the bloody 'ell!", or perhaps it was only "What the bloody hell". But sex, pregnancy even, that took some getting over. It was true after all then; the Germans *were* wicked. I wondered if she had been raped. It came to my mind in a flash; I could see it all clearly like a neat Matania drawing—like 'The Royal What-nots kneeling in prayer at Holy Communion before Battle'. What shell-fire! You could almost smell the bursting of the shells! What did it feel like when your tank went over the body? Sorry ma'am, I forgot to notice, but it didn't dream well o'nights.

This little pregnant creature didn't look at all bad—really. She had gone past the civilized state, like the mobs chasing and taunting a mother with shaven head as she strode out angry and proud and defiant carrying her baby into shelter of a house in Rouen. There is a certain dignity about the wild animal to which this little child had come. Perhaps I should have taken off my tin hat and suddenly said "Shoo!". That would have sent her scuttling downstairs quick I bet! It would have been good for a laugh in the mess.

I was tired and it did not seem funny. I was relieved when other officers had as little sense of humour as I had. Yet should an officer, brought up in all the privilege and luxury of the governing class of what was then the most powerful nation in the world, be an immature innocent with a capacity for remaining so through four years of war? 'Stormed at by shot and shell, bravely they rode and well'. Still not an idea in hell, 'noble six hundred'.

In Marcoing the band played the Marseillaise to a silent, unresponsive crowd. It came to an end and they stopped. The band master, with a flash of genius, had an idea. "Play it again", he said. This time the crowd went mad. The street was suddenly filled with flags—Union Jacks, Tricolours, a few Stars and Stripes. Where had they come from? Where had they been hidden all these years?

The excitement died down as suddenly as it had arisen, like a sharp wind, a few heavy drops of rain and then a silence disturbed by the sound of distant storm.

43

ALTHOUGH I perfectly well knew the contents, I read the signal carefully when it reached me. It said that all troops would stand fast at the position they had reached at 11.00 hours on the 11th day of the 11th month. They were to cease fire but all the usual military precautions would be maintained. This I supposed was a way of saying the war was over.

For some weeks the command of the army had shown anxiety about what was called 'peace talk'. News of the German request for an armistice was known to everyone. We could certainly understand that if our army stopped fighting it might well be impossible to start it again. Although there was no danger, as far as I was in a position to observe, that the army would stop fighting, it was behaving like an ill-trained runner who keeps looking over his shoulder instead of pressing on till he has passed the winning tape. This was the more odd because there was no winning tape.

One of my men was walking beside his tank as it was travelling back to the camp; it was an undistinguished routine trek. The tank rode over an unexploded grenade which, being under the armoured track, burst harmlessly. But Mallard, the gunner in question, fell dead. It seemed so improbable that it took time to realize that one of the grenade fragments—it must have been the only one to escape from under the track—had penetrated his heart killing him instantly and leaving only a small puncture wound to show the point of entry.

'Dear Madam, I regret to inform you that your son...' was killed by accident when the war was over? Why make a fuss about it? What about his wife and children? Thank God he was too young and can't have had any. Oh yes he had though; and she was expecting a baby. 'Dear Madam, I regret to inform you that your husband...'. More fuss; about nothing.

Rations were bad; potatoes disappeared and the men grumbled. The company was paraded and I explained; the shortage would not last long as it was only due to the army having to give up part of its rations to feed the civilian population. The company heard me in silence. They did not believe it; they did not disbelieve it.

Six months earlier there had been a popular song with a refrain—'The war was over last July, It says so in 'John Bull''.

"You can't believe a word they say", a private said to me on reading some current example of official euphoria.

'We are holding the enemy in our battle positions at Tincourt'. I had read the lie out to my mother. Wonderful stuff, good old tape for holding enemies in their battle positions.

"Do you know", said an open-eyed incredulous young officer, "that where I was a chap rode out on a horse, right in front of our position, outed with his trumpet and sounded the Cease Fire. Then he rode back! Can you beat it?"

"Well! What did you expect him to do?" asked Carter drily.

"Where I was", said another, "the Boches spent the last five minutes blowing off every round they had. Of course our chaps let fly a proper barrage. It might have been the Somme again—wonder how many people lost their lives in that last little joke."

There were rumours: the Guards had refused to go on parade; the Guards had mutinied at their depot.

"Sir!" saluted Sergeant-Major Cannon, "Company refuses to come on parade."

"Tell them not to be so bloody silly." Off he went.

Here was a fine state of affairs. I had not the remotest idea what to do. All this stuff about the Guards—devilish awkward if it turned out to be true. Now my own company! I felt I would break out in a sweat at any moment. Suppose they still refused. They were nearly all new men, recently trained miners; they hated the army. They did not know us, their officers. If I had not been scared I would have laughed at an implication that had they known us—what fine chaps we were, comrades in arms and all that—they would *never* have mutinied. *If* they knew us it would be a ruddy miracle if they obeyed at all.

"Sir!" I wish to hell he wouldn't make me jump by being so hellish military. It was as bad as the clicking door in the Trappist monastery at Mont des Cats. Each time it clicked it made us all, every officer in the place, duck the bullet, curse and swear and do it again at once as the door clicked open again.

"Sir!" I knew it was Cannon. I was only pretending, to gain time, like "Is Captain Bion there? You're wanted up the line sir."

"Yes, Sergeant-Major?"

"They won't come out sir." I knew it. What do I do now? No idea. It was with surprise and relief that I heard myself say, "Tell the Lewis gun crews to fall in with their guns at once. Post them to cover the huts."

"Sir!" Blast him! Those clickings were getting on my nerves. He was back again in less than five minutes. "They are in position sir. Six guns facing the huts."

"With the hill behind the huts?"

"Yes sir."

"Go and tell the men again—'Don't be a lot of bloody fools'." He hesitated. I knew he was going to ask me what he was to do then. I still had no idea. "If they go on being idiotic, call me."

"Sir!" Those damned clicking heels of his. Anyway it might be his last chance of being military. I wished to God I didn't feel so scared! 'The war was over last July. It said so in GHQ orders'. Had anyone told the Boches?

Sergeant Cannon again. "They've come out sir. They are on parade." I could have wept with relief. "I'll be out in a minute Sergeant-Major. They can stand easy till I come." What *was* I talking about? Of course they could—there was nothing else for them to do.

Alone in the hut I wiped the sweat off my face and tried to stop my trembling. At last I couldn't stand it any more and walked onto the parade ground.

The guns were in position, glistening. The crews were looking at me intently; I could *feel* the penetrating curiosity. The company were fuming, angry. Wherever I let my eyes rest I fancied that the answering glance was angry, resentful, humiliated.

At last Sergeant-Major Cannon reported, "All present and correct sir." I told him to stand at ease.

"Sergeant-Major Cannon tells me you fellows didn't want to come on parade. You forget the war's not over—this is only an armistice. We'd have looked a bloody lot of fools if the Boches has come over there"—I pointed my stick at the hills behind—"and caught us while you were all stuck in there."

While the officers were preparing to move their men off to the various section exercises I watched and carefully paid attention to the Lewis guns ready for action behind. Then, before they moved off I went over to the guns and carried out a minute inspection as if it were an ordinary everyday routine. I chose not to remark that they were loaded with ball ammunition.

At last they had all moved off leaving Sergeant-Major Cannon and myself alone. "Tomorrow I want all the men to parade in sections. Give them some instruction on military law, King's

Regulations and a snappy bit about the Mutiny Act." He seemed to want to say something, but changed his mind, saluted and went off.

There was some kind of football league competition in which all companies in the brigade took part. In our company excitement reached fever heat because the miner reinforcements we had received included some first-rate footballers who were extremely serious about the game however much they hated the army and the war. Keeping, without in any way being aware of it, to my groove, I showed the conventional enthusiasm for the company to which I was now second in command. I watched the football; I knew the names of the stars of the team; I knew enough football to appreciate the matches which were often skilful displays, so this aspect of my duties was not at all unpleasant. But I was puzzled and slow to understand that whether I was interested or not was a matter of complete indifference to the men. The majority of the company were reinforcements but even those who were not shared the new spirit, a spirit which could be expressed by a civil but slightly incredulous, 'Who the hell are you to be asking about our boys, their matches and successes?' I was now twenty-one and had not experienced what it was to be an antiquity, a survival from a remote past.

Carter, Hauser and I were the only officers who had served with the battalion from the start in England. The Quartermaster, who of course did not go into action, was the only warrant officer; of the men there was none. Even of those who had seen more than six months fighting there was a mere handful. Though we did not realize it, we were men who had grown from insignificance to irrelevance in the passage of a few short years.

Christmas released a delayed, hectic, hysterical excitement of celebration. 'Everyone suddenly burst out singing', wrote Siegfried Sassoon. Our singing had alcoholic overtones; there were too many missing faces. The jubilation of the winning footballers was not greatly different from the jubilation of those who had survived fighting. Keep the men occupied; sport, trophies, homes 'fit for heroes to live in', anything to hold at bay the dark and sombre world of thought.

A mixed crowd of some two thousand troops toiled—it could hardly be called 'marched'—up the hill to Shoreham camp. I had been demobilized immediately after Christmas. An old woman stood at the door of a respectable but dreary house, waving a Union Jack. Anxiety about the reception she would be likely to receive from a lot of 'rough Tommies' made her voice tense. "Welcome home boys, welcome home", she squeaked. For a moment there was astonishment at the apparition. The impulse to jeer was suppressed. "Give the old fool a cheer", said someone and to this invitation the succeeding files somewhat embarrassedly responded. "They might have given us a band up this bloody hill."

At the station the train to take us to London had no lights. In the growing darkness a man clambered onto the roof of the train to protest.

"It was the same after the Boer War. It's the same now. Ruddy heroes when you're wanted; so much muck when it's finished. It'll be the same next time as this."

And as things have been they remain. Insignificance to Irrelevance in a few years. No one could explain that if the British Empire did not share the same fate it was because of a few poets. But what can poets do against nuclear fission or, even more potent, some germ being carefully tended and nurtured by biologists of marvellous skill and foresight—as is the way with that clever tool-making animal, man?